THIRD EDITION

Ongoing Crisis Communication

To all those who have managed or will manage crises

THIRD EDITION

Ongoing Crisis Communication

PLANNING, MANAGING, AND RESPONDING

W. Timothy Coombs
The University of Central Florida

◆SAGE

Los Angeles | London | New Delhi
Singapore | Washington DC

For information:

 SAGE Publications, Inc.
2455 Teller Road
Thousand Oaks,
    California 91320
E-mail: order@sagepub.com

SAGE Publications India Pvt. Ltd.
B 1/I 1 Mohan Cooperative
    Industrial Area
Mathura Road, New Delhi 110 044
India

SAGE Publications Ltd.
1 Oliver's Yard
55 City Road
London EC1Y 1SP
United Kingdom

SAGE Publications
    Asia-Pacific Pte. Ltd.
33 Pekin Street #02-01
Far East Square
Singapore 048763

Printed in the United States of America

Library of Congress Cataloging-in-Publication Data

Coombs, W. Timothy.
Ongoing crisis communication : planning, managing, and responding /
W. Timothy Coombs.—3rd ed.
    p. cm.
Includes bibliographical references and index.
ISBN 978-1-4129-8310-5 (pbk.)   26145812
    1. Crisis management. 2. Communication in management. I. Title.

HD49.C664 2012
658.4'056—dc22   2010047820

This book is printed on acid-free paper.

11   12   13   14   15   10   9   8   7   6   5   4   3   2

Executive Editor:	Diane McDaniel
Senior Acquisitions Editor:	Matthew Byrnie
Editorial Assistant:	Nathan Davidson
Production Editor:	Libby Larson
Copy Editor:	Sarah J. Duffy
Typesetter:	C&M Digitals (P) Ltd.
Proofreader:	Wendy Jo Dymond
Indexer:	Wendy Allex
Cover Designer:	Gail Buschman
Marketing Manager:	Liz Thornton
Permissions Editor:	Karen Ehrmann

Brief Contents

(handwritten annotations:) pre crisis; — signal detection; prevention; preparation; crisis; containment; containment; Postcrisis

Detailed Contents

Preface

■ PURPOSE OF THE TEXT

Crisis management is a challenge any organization can face, and many fail. When crisis management fails, stakeholders and organizations suffer. All organizations must become prepared for crises. Merck, Cadbury, and Bausch & Lomb are prominent and respected companies, but each one mishandled a very public product harm crisis that affected millions of consumers. Crisis communication is the lifeblood of crisis management. When crisis communication is ineffective, so is the crisis management effort.

There is a lot of research and many cases about crisis communication and management. These vast writings remain a blessing and a curse. It is great to have so much information, but it is hard to find and organize it all. The writings about crisis communication and management are fragmented, as people write about crises from very different perspectives. This situation can leave managers struggling to organize bits of information or missing critical resources entirely. Writers often focus on their specialties and fail to make connections to ideas and concepts developed in other specialties. In turn, this fragmentation precludes a fuller understanding of crisis communication and management that is gained by integrating the various perspectives. Add to this the fact that a number of related communication concepts have applications to crisis management but have yet to be integrated into the literature, and the situation becomes even more complicated. Practitioners, researchers, and educators are limited by this fractured approach. The primary purpose of this book is to provide a resource that integrates and organizes a wide array of practitioner and research writings about crisis management.

Management in general must recognize the value of strategic crisis communication and the value of crisis management. This book emphasizes the role of communication throughout the crisis management process and is designed to be a body of knowledge that aids managers, researchers, and educators. *Process* is an important word here. Too many people think that crisis management means having a crisis management plan or responding when a crisis hits. This is a very reactive and rather limited approach to crisis management. A richer, more proactive approach to crisis management explores the entire process. Managers should think of crisis management as akin to SWOT analysis. *SWOT* stands for strengths, weaknesses, opportunities, and threats. Through crisis management, an organization can identify its weaknesses, what it is failing to do to address threats and prepare for crises. Strengths are the elements of crisis management that the organization does well. Opportunities are the resources the organization can access before, during, and after a crisis. Threats are those factors that can evolve into crises. A quick crisis SWOT analysis will awaken management to the need to take crisis management and crisis communication very seriously.

■ AUDIENCE FOR THE TEXT

This book is written for both students and practitioners. Students, primarily undergraduate, are given an applied approach to crisis communication that is rooted in theory. Ideally, theory should inform practice, and I have selected the best of the crisis communication and management research for gaining insight into the process. Practitioners can use the book to enhance their understanding and execution of crisis communication. This book is designed to be used to help those who are or may become crisis managers. Any individuals with a background in corporate communication, organizational communication, public relations, or management may find themselves on a crisis team. The information in this book should help to make them more effective crisis team members.

■ ORGANIZATION OF THE TEXT

Throughout this preface I have noted the crisis management process. Crisis management can be viewed as having three stages: precrisis, crisis event, and postcrisis. The book follows this three-part structure. Chapter 1 provides a discussion of the three-stage approach to crisis management. Chapter 2 highlights the increased importance of social media to crisis management. Chapters 3 and 4 focus on the prevention aspect of precrisis, while Chapters 5 and 6 develop the preparation aspect of precrisis. Chapters 7 and 8 concentrate on the crisis event stage, and Chapter 9 explains the postcrisis stage. The Epilogue provides a summary of the lessons crisis managers can learn from the various research and writings on crisis communication.

Pedagogical Features

Throughout the book are **"What Would You Do?"** cases. Each case fits the key points found in a particular chapter. Information from a real crisis event is presented along with a series of questions designed to enable readers to apply text concepts to the case.

Each chapter ends with a **Conclusion** that sums up the main points of the chapter, as well as **Discussion Questions** that help readers extend their understanding of the material.

■ NEW TO THE THIRD EDITION

Writing a third edition of this book was in many ways a necessity. Crisis communication and management is so dynamic that the field has changed significantly in the few years since the second edition. Research continues to yield additional insights into the crisis management process. The Internet, especially social media, has added to the complexity of crises. Researchers are systematically examining the effects of crisis response strategies on stakeholders, and we are moving away from speculation to real knowledge about these strategies. Situational Crisis Communication Theory and Contingency Theory are two examples of the systematic and social scientific study of crisis communication. The Internet, including social media, has become an indispensable tool for collecting information about warning signs and crisis as well as an option for communicating with stakeholders during a crisis. Oddly, the Internet has also increased the crisis risks that organizations face through computer hacking, denial of service, and amplifying challenges from stakeholders that management might be operating an organization in an inappropriate manner.

The main changes to the third edition are outlined here:

- It includes a new **Chapter 2** exploring the effect that the Internet, especially social media, has on crisis communication and management.

- **Chapter 3** is a refined integration of crisis management with three other proactive management functions: issues management, reputation management, and risk management. The interrelationships are explored in more depth in this edition.

- **Chapters 4, 6, 8, and 9** include extensive updates related to the Internet. **Chapter 4** introduces the concept of the paracrisis, a threat that is managed publicly much like a crisis but is itself not a crisis. The Internet plays a key role in the emergence of paracrises. **Chapter 6** considers what Internet-related preparation is needed prior to a crisis. **Chapter 8** discusses the effects of social media on the crisis response, while **Chapter 9** explores the emergence of online memorials.

- Finally, the **Epilogue** is designed to summarize the key lessons the vast crisis communication research literature provides for crisis managers.

Acknowledgments

B ooks are driven by many sources, so no book is really sole-authored. I would like to acknowledge those who have helped with this revision. I appreciate the faith that the people at Sage, especially Todd Armstrong and Nathan Davidson, have shown in updating this book and increasing its value as a reference for crisis communication and crisis management. The quick adoption of social media is a key factor in creating the need for updating. Thanks also to Joe R. Downing, Penn State York; Tomasz A. Fediuk, Illinois State University; Sora Kim, DePaul University in Chicago; Linda Lopez, Baruch College, City University of New York; Michael J. Palenchar, University of Tennessee; and Shari R. Veil, University of Kentucky. Finally, many thanks to Sherry for reading and commenting on the various drafts of this book.

A Need for More Crisis Management Knowledge

Merck, BP, Enron, Bausch & Lomb, Hurricane Katrina, and the 9/11 attacks are all reminders that no organization is immune to crises. If no organization is immune, then all organizations should be prepared. Pick any day of the week and you will find stories about train derailments, plane crashes, funds used inappropriately at nonprofit organizations, explosions in manufacturing facilities, workers shot or injured on the job, or *E. coli*–tainted beef, turkey, chicken, or even bean sprouts. The bottom line is that all organizations should learn as much as they can about crisis management.

Developing a comprehensive crisis management program (CCMP) that captures the ongoing nature of crisis management is not an easy task. The crisis management process is varied and requires the integration of knowledge from such diverse areas as small-group decision making, media relations, environmental scanning, risk assessment, crisis communication, crisis plan development, evaluation methods, and reputation management. A diverse set of crisis management writings must be navigated in order to develop a complete CCMP that covers every stage and substage of the crisis management process. It is a daunting but necessary task to sort through the plethora of crisis management information. How else can a CCMP be developed?

The primary goal of this book is to offer an integrative framework that simplifies the task of organizing crisis management knowledge. An ongoing approach based upon a three-stage model of crisis management provides the foundation. The three stages are precrisis, crisis event, and postcrisis, each of which is composed of three substages.

The stages are used to summarize and organize various insights into the crisis management process. Myriad ideas from different areas are synthesized into one continuous process. The end product is a guide for developing each stage in the ongoing crisis management process. This book is a living guide because future developments in crisis management can be easily assimilated into the comprehensive framework of the three-stage approach.

The three-stage model articulated here provides a variety of suggestions about how to "do" crisis management. This book is designed to aid those interested in practicing, researching, or teaching crisis management. To those interested in practice, the book offers a comprehensive approach for structuring a crisis management program. For those interested in research, the book provides an analytic framework for the study of crisis management efforts. Those involved in teaching are offered an additional resource for educating future crisis managers. The book ends with a summary of key ideas and highlights some of the insights offered to practitioners, researchers, and educators. In addition, an appendix suggests a number of crises that can be used for study and research.

■ CRISIS MANAGEMENT DEFINED

There are a lot of books written about crisis management, but there is no one accepted definition of a crisis. Having a specific definition is important because how a subject is defined indicates how it is approached. I choose to start with a definition so that readers will understand how this book approaches the subject.

Crisis Defined

A crisis is the perception of an unpredictable event that threatens important expectancies of stakeholders and can seriously impact an organization's performance and generate negative outcomes. This definition is a synthesis of various perspectives on crisis. It tries to capture the common traits other writers have used when describing crises.

A crisis is perceptual. What we typically think of as crises are events that are easy to perceive as such. That is why few people would dispute industrial accidents or hurricanes being crises. However, it is the perceptions of stakeholders that help to define an event as a crisis. A stakeholder is a person or group that is affected by or can affect an organization (Bryson, 2004). If stakeholders believe an organization is in crisis, a crisis does exist, and stakeholders will react to the organization as if it is in crisis. For nearly a decade, Audi told its customers there was nothing wrong with its transmissions. However, customers did perceive a crisis. Cars were jumping into gear from neutral—with sudden acceleration—resulting in injuries and deaths. We fast-forward to 2009 and Toyota is wrestling with gas pedals that stick, causing cars to accelerate uncontrollably and at times fatally. Toyota was criticized for a slow response to the crisis. Toyota management had a difficult time seeing the problem and realizing the organization was in a crisis. Management must be able to see the event from the stakeholders' perspective to properly assess whether a crisis has occurred.

A crisis is unpredictable but not unexpected. Wise organizations know that crises will befall them; they just do not know when. Crises can be anticipated. Crises strike suddenly, giving them an element of surprise or unpredictability (Barton, 2001; National Research Council, 1996). But some crises offer a great deal of warning (Irvine & Millar, 1996). For instance, if a major television news magazine is planning to run a negative story about an organization, management will know the event months in advance. Metabolife, a diet supplement company, faced just such a crisis in 1999. It used the lead time to create an aggressive multimedia campaign to defend itself from charges linking its product to harmful side effects. Radio and newspaper advertisements were used to drive people to a specially created Web site where people could watch an unedited video of the interview and learn how news shows can distort the truth.

Crises can violate expectations that stakeholders hold about how organizations should act. Planes should land safely, products should not harm us, management should not steal money, and organizations should reflect societal values. Crises disturb some stakeholder expectations, resulting in people becoming upset and angry, which threatens the relationship between the organization and its stakeholders. That is why crises are considered dangerous to organizations' reputations (Barton, 2001; Dilenschneider, 2000). A reputation is how stakeholders perceive the organization. When expectations are breached, stakeholders perceive the organization less positively: the reputation is harmed.

The difference between incidents and crises illustrates the meaning of *serious impact*. An *incident* is a minor, localized disruption. Say a water valve breaks and sprays water in the vending and meeting areas of a plant. The valve is repaired, some meetings are rescheduled, and vending machines are down for a day. The valve is replaced without harming the larger organizational routine, making it an incident not a crisis. If the broken water valve leads to the plant being shut down, then it becomes a crisis as it disrupts the entire organization (Coombs, 2006b; Pauchant & Mitroff, 1992). A crisis disrupts or affects the entire organization or has the potential to do so.

Crises also have the potential to create negative or undesirable outcomes. If business is disrupted, an organization will usually suffer financial losses (e.g., lost productivity, a drop in earnings). Crisis damage extends beyond financial loss, however, to include injuries or deaths to stakeholders, structural or property damage (on- and off-site), tarnishing of a reputation, and environmental harm (Loewendick, 1993). The damage can affect a variety of stakeholders. An entire industry can be affected by a crisis in one of its member organizations. An industry can suffer financial loss (e.g., new, costly regulations) or reputational damage as people project a localized crisis onto an entire industry. In 2006, the cruise ship industry became involved in the Carnival Cruise Lines fire because the crisis was an industry-wide threat, not just a company-specific one. Fires were a risk on every cruise ship, and people needed to feel safe. Employees, customers, or community members can be injured or killed by industrial or transportation accidents. A plane crash can kill crew members, passengers, and people on the ground.

Environmental damage is another outcome of accidents. Community members can suffer structural or property damage from accidents as well. Explosions can shatter windows, and evacuations can cost community members in terms of money, time, and disruption. Careless handling of an accident can add to the damage. Investors can lose money from the costs of the crisis. For example, an organization can incur repair expenses from an accident, while a faulty product can result in product liability lawsuits and recall costs. A crisis presents real or potential negative outcomes for organizations, their stakeholders, and their industries. Crisis management is designed to ward off or reduce the threats by providing recommendations for properly handling crises.

WHAT WOULD YOU DO? BP AND TEXAS CITY: ACT 1

It's 1:20 p.m. on March 23, 2005, in Texas City, Texas. You work at the BP refinery in the town. Suddenly an explosion rocks the ground. You go outside and see large flames and smoke coming from the direction of the isomerization unit. You know that workers were performing a startup at the isomerization unit today, and startups are one of the most dangerous procedures at refineries. Alarms are going off, people are running and shouting, and some personnel are heading over to help. You are the public relations person on the BP Texas City crisis team.

- What do you do now?

- What does the organization need to do to respond to this event?

Crisis Management

Crisis management represents a set of factors designed to combat crises and to lessen the actual damage inflicted. Put another way, it seeks to prevent or lessen the negative outcomes of a crisis and thereby protect the organization, stakeholders, and industry from harm. Crisis management has evolved from emergency preparedness, and drawing from that base, comprises a set of four interrelated factors: prevention, preparation, response, and revision.

1 *Prevention,* also known as mitigation, represents the steps taken to avoid crises. Crisis managers often detect warning signs and then take actions designed to prevent the crisis. For instance, a faulty toaster is recalled before its overheating problem causes any fires or injuries to customers. Prevention is largely unseen by the public. News stories about crises that did not happen are rare.

2 *Preparation* is the best-known factor in crisis management because it includes the crisis management plan (CMP). If people know nothing else about crisis management, they know an organization should have a CMP. The CMP is the tip of the crisis management iceberg. Although people think the CMP is the crisis management process, in actuality most of the process is unseen. Preparation also involves diagnosing crisis vulnerabilities, selecting and training a crisis management team and spokespersons, creating a crisis portfolio, and refining a crisis communication system.

3 *Response* is the application of the preparation components to a crisis. A crisis can be simulated (as in an exercise) or real. The preparation components must be tested regularly. The testing involves running simulated crises and drills that determine the fitness of the CMP, crisis team members, spokespersons, and the communication system. A real crisis involves the execution of the same crisis management resources, only the outcomes are real rather than hypothetical. Response is very public during an actual crisis. An organization's crisis management response is frequently reported and critiqued in the news media (Pearson & Clair, 1998). Many publications critiqued Bausch & Lomb's failure to recall ReNu with MoistureLoc when it was linked to a 2006 outbreak of Fusarium keratitis, a form of fungal eye infection that can produce blindness (e.g., Dobbin, 2006; Mintz & Di Meglio, 2006). Bausch & Lomb did stop shipping the product and eventually asked retailers to remove the product from shelves. However, it was not until May 15, a month after the crisis began, that an official recall was issued (Mintz & Di Meglio, 2006). Remember, crises make for good news stories, and news of ReNu with MoistureLoc was everywhere.

Part of the response is *recovery,* which denotes the organization's attempts to return to normal operations as soon as possible following a crisis. *Business continuity* is the name used to cover the efforts to restore operations to normal. As noted earlier, downtime from a crisis is a financial drain. The quicker an organization can return to normal operations, the fewer financial losses it will incur.

Revision is the fourth crisis factor. It involves evaluation of the organization's response in simulated and real crises, determining what it did right and what it did wrong during its crisis management performance. The organization uses this insight to revise its prevention, preparation, and response efforts. Ideally, in the future the right moves are replayed while the mistakes are avoided and replaced by more appropriate actions. Revision is the development of an institutional or organizational memory, which can improve the effectiveness of crisis management by expanding the organization's perception of crises and its response capacity (Li, YeZhuang, & Ying, 2004; Weick, 1988). The more and varied the crises an organization experiences through practice sessions, the better it can handle similar situations in reality. The factors are linked in a spiral. If prevention fails, preparation is required for optimal performance. Revision is derived from performance and informs both the prevention of and preparation for future crises. In turn, improving preparation should improve response.

Understanding the crisis management process is a necessity for effective crisis communication. We can extend the notion of process by creating a framework for crisis management that involves distinct stages that influence one another.

■ THE INITIAL CRISIS MANAGEMENT FRAMEWORK

The idea that crises have an identifiable life cycle is a consistent theme that permeates the crisis management literature. The crisis manager needs to understand this life cycle because its different phases require different actions (Gonzalez-Herrero & Pratt, 1995; Sturges, 1994). The crisis life cycle has been translated into what I term *staged approaches* to crisis management. A staged approach means that the crisis management function is divided into discrete segments that are executed in a specific order. Moreover, the life cycle perspective reveals that effective crisis management must be integrated into the normal operations of an organization. Crisis management is not merely developing a plan and executing it during a crisis. Instead, it is appropriately viewed as an ongoing process. Every day, organization members can be scanning for potential crises, taking actions to prevent them, or considering any number of the aspects of the crisis management process detailed in this book.

Crisis management should be a part of many people's full-time jobs in an organization, not a part-time fancy. Each working day, crisis managers can be doing something to improve crisis prevention and response (Coombs, 2006a).

The life cycle perspective has yielded a variety of staged approaches to crisis management. These provide a mechanism for constructing a framework for organizing the vast and varied crisis management writings and for creating a unified set of crisis management guidelines. Regardless of discipline, the various topics addressed can be placed within a comprehensive, incremental approach to crisis management. An overarching framework organizes the scattered crisis management insights and permits crisis managers to easily envision their best options during any stage of the process. Crisis managers can find it easier to access and apply available resources, thereby improving the crisis management process. The framework I use in this book is influenced by existing models of the process. Reviewing these models will reinforce the importance of process in crisis management.

Past Staged Approaches to Crisis Management

Three influential approaches emerge from a study of the various crisis management models. Influence was gauged by the number of people citing the approach in the development of their crisis models. These three are Fink's (1986) four-stage model, Mitroff's (1994) five-stage model, and a basic three-stage model. Fink's is the earliest and can be found in his seminal book, *Crisis Management: Planning for the Inevitable.* His cycle is well represented in writings that have appeared since the 1990s. He uses a medical illness metaphor to identify four stages in the crisis life cycle: (1) prodromal: clues or hints of a potential crisis begin to emerge, (2) crisis breakout or acute: a triggering event occurs along with the attendant damage, (3) chronic: the effects of the crisis linger as efforts to clean up the crisis progress, and (4) resolution: there is some clear signal that the crisis is no longer a concern to stakeholders—it is over.

Fink's (1986) approach is one of the first to treat a crisis as an extended event. Of particular note is his belief that warning signs precede the trigger event. The job of crisis managers expands and becomes more proactive when they know and read the warning signs. Well-prepared crisis managers do not just enact the CMP when a crisis hits (being reactive); they are also involved in identifying and resolving situations that could become or lead to a crisis (being proactive). In addition, Fink divides the crisis event into three stages. A crisis does not just happen, it evolves. It begins with a trigger event (acute phase), moves to extended efforts to deal with the crisis (chronic phase), and concludes with a clear ending (resolution). The different stages of the life cycle require different actions from the crisis manager. As a result, crisis management is enacted in stages and is not one simple action.

Sturges's (1994) elaborations on Fink's (1986) model illustrate how different actions are required during various crisis phases. Sturges proposes that different types of communication are emphasized during the various phases of the crisis life cycle. The acute phase is dominated by the eruption of the crisis. Stakeholders do not know what is happening; therefore, they require information about how the crisis affects them and what they should do to protect themselves. For example, information such as whether community members should evacuate an area or whether employees should report for the next shift is highly relevant. In contrast, the resolution stage sees the end of the crisis. At that point, stakeholders would be receptive to messages designed to bolster the organization's reputation. Stakeholders need to know how a crisis affects them when it breaks but are open to reputation-building messages once it ends (Sturges, 1994). The demands of the crisis stage dictate what crisis managers can and should be doing at any particular time. The later chapters of this book detail the different actions required during the various stages.

The second influential approach is from prolific crisis writer and expert Ian Mitroff (1994). He divides crisis management into five phases: (1) signal detection: new crisis warning signs should be identified and acted upon to prevent a crisis, (2) probing and prevention: organization members search known crisis risk factors and work to reduce their potential for harm, (3) damage containment: a crisis hits and organization members try to prevent the damage from spreading into uncontaminated parts of the organization or its environment, (4) recovery: organization members work to return to normal business operations as soon as possible, and (5) learning: organization members review and critique their crisis management efforts, thereby adding to the organization's memory.

While subtle differences are apparent, the similarities between the Fink (1986) and Mitroff (1994) approaches are strong. Mitroff's stages reflect Fink's crisis life cycle to a large degree. Signal detection and probing can be seen as part of the prodromal phase. The difference is the degree to which Mitroff's model emphasizes detection and prevention. While Fink's model implies that crises can be prevented, Mitroff's model actively identifies them, seeking to prevent them.

There is a strong correspondence between the damage containment and crisis breakout stages and the recovery and chronic stages. Both damage containment and crisis breakout focus on the trigger event—when the crisis hits. However, Mitroff's (1994) model places greater emphasis on limiting the effects of the crisis. Augustine (1995) and Ammerman (1995) both highlight the need to limit the spread of a crisis to healthy parts of the organization. The recovery and chronic stages reflect the natural need to restore normal operations. In fact, one measure of success for crisis management is the speed with which normal operations are restored (Mitroff, 1994). Mitroff's model emphasizes how the crisis management team can facilitate the recovery, while Fink's (1986) model simply documents that organizations can recover at varying speeds.

Both the learning and resolution stages signal the end of the crisis. The additional review and critique of the learning stage is a function of Mitroff's (1994) focus on crisis management rather than just crisis description. Fink's (1986) model simply notes that the resolution stage occurs when a crisis is no longer a concern. For Fink, termination marks the end of the crisis management function. In contrast, Mitroff's model is cyclical because the end also represents a new beginning. The crisis management effort is reviewed and critiqued in order to find ways to improve the system. The last stage signals the start of implementing improvements in the crisis management system. Hence, the learning phase can feed back to either the signal detection phase or the probing and prevention phase. Gonzalez-Herrero and Pratt (1995, 1996) extend Mitroff's (1994) thinking by treating the final stage as a continuation of the recovery phase. In addition to evaluation and retooling, the final stage involves maintaining contact with key stakeholders, monitoring the issues tied to the crisis, and providing updates to the media (Gonzalez-Herrero & Pratt, 1995, 1996). Communication and follow-up with stakeholders from the recovery phase are carried over to the learning phase.

The essential difference between the Fink (1986) and Mitroff (1994) models is revealed by comparing the last phases. Mitroff's is active and stresses what crisis managers should do at each phase. Fink's is more descriptive and stresses the characteristics of each phase. This is not to say that Fink is not offering recommendations to crisis managers. Rather, the Mitroff model is more prescriptive than Fink's. Fink is concerned with mapping how crises progress while Mitroff is concerned with how crisis management efforts progress. Early models tended to be descriptive, so this essential difference is not unexpected.

The three-stage model has no clearly identifiable creator but has been recommended by a variety of crisis management experts (e.g., Birch, 1994; Guth, 1995; T. H. Mitchell, 1986; Seeger, Sellnow, & Ulmer, 2003). However, Richardson (1994) provides the first detailed discussion of its components: (1) precrisis or predisaster phase: warning signs appear and people try to eliminate the risk, (2) crisis impact or rescue phase: the crisis hits and support is provided for those involved in it, and (3) recovery or demise phase: stakeholder confidence is restored.

Following from this three-stage approach, I divide the crisis management process into three macrostages: precrisis, crisis, and postcrisis. The term *macro* indicates that the stages are general and that each contains a number of more specific substages: the micro level. This is similar to economics, where macroeconomics deals with all the forces at work on the economy while microeconomics deals with specific factors. Both the Fink (1986) and Mitroff (1994) models fit naturally within this general three-stage approach. The precrisis stage encompasses all of the aspects of crisis preparation. Prodromal signs, signal detection, and probing would be included in the precrisis stage. The crisis stage includes the actions taken to cope with the trigger event—the time span when the crisis is being actively dealt with. Damage containment, crisis breakout, and recovery or the chronic phase all fall within the crisis stage. The postcrisis stage reflects the period after the crisis is considered to be over or resolved. Learning and resolution are each a part of this stage. Table 1.1 summarizes the comparisons of the three different staged approaches to crisis management.

Table 1.1   Comparison of Staged Approached to Crisis Management

Fink	Mitroff	Three-Stage
Prodromal	Signal Detection	Precrisis
	Probing and Prevention	
Crisis Breakout	Damage Containment	Crisis
Chronic	Recovery	
Resolution	Learning	Postcrisis

■ OUTLINE OF THE THREE-STAGE APPROACH

The three-stage approach was selected as the organizing framework for this book because of its ability to subsume the other staged approaches used in crisis management. The ideal crisis management model would accommodate all of the various models plus additional insights provided by other crisis management experts. Not all crisis managers have placed their ideas within a phased model. Therefore, a comprehensive model must be able to place random insights into the crisis management process.

The three-stage approach has the appropriate macro-level generality for constructing the comprehensive framework necessary for analyzing the crisis management literature. The three stages are general enough to accommodate the other two dominant crisis management models and to allow for the integration of ideas from other crisis management experts.

Within each stage there are separate substages or sets of actions that should be covered during that stage. Each substage integrates a cluster of writings about that particular crisis management topic. Each cluster of writings has been carefully examined to distill the essential recommendations they could offer to crisis managers. For each substage, the crisis wisdom and any tests of that wisdom are reported along with a discussion of its utility to crisis managers. Moreover, this three-stage approach provides a unified system for organizing and utilizing the varied insights crisis managers offer.

Precrisis

The precrisis stage involves three substages: (1) signal detection, (2) prevention, and (3) crisis preparation. Chapters 3, 4, 5, and 6 are devoted to the development of this stage. Organization members should be proactive and take all possible actions to prevent crises. The precrisis stage entails actions to be performed before a crisis is encountered. However, not all crises can be prevented, so organization members must prepare for crises as well.

Chapter 3 deals with signal detection. Most crises do emit early warning signs. If early action is taken, these crises can be avoided (Gonzalez-Herrero & Pratt, 1995). Crisis managers must identify sources for warning signs, collect information related to them, and analyze the information. For example, a pattern in customer complaints could identify a product defect. Reporting the complaints to the appropriate manufacturing sector of the organization could result in corrective action being taken. In turn, the corrective action could prevent further complaints and the potential of a highly visible recall, battle with customers, or both. Crisis managers must develop a system for detecting potential crises and responding to them.

Chapter 4 is devoted to crisis prevention. Once the potential is detected, actions must be taken to prevent the crisis. Preventative measures fall into three categories: issues management, risk management, reputation management. Issues management means taking steps to prevent a problem from maturing into a crisis. Risk management eliminates or lowers risk levels. Reputation management seeks to resolve problems in the stakeholder–organization relationship that could escalate and damage the company's reputation. Chapters 5 and 6 develop the idea of crisis preparation. Crisis managers must be prepared for a crisis happening. Preparation typically involves identifying crisis vulnerabilities, creating crisis teams, selecting spokespersons, drafting CMPs, developing crisis portfolios (a list of the most likely crises to befall an organization), and structuring the crisis communication system.

Crisis Event

This stage begins with a trigger event that marks the beginning of the crisis. The crisis stage ends when the crisis is considered to be resolved. During the crisis event, crisis managers must realize that the organization is in crisis and take appropriate actions. This phase has two substages: (1) crisis recognition and (2) crisis containment. Communication with stakeholders is a critical facet of this phase. An organization communicates to stakeholders through its words and actions.

Chapter 7 is devoted to crisis recognition. People in an organization must realize that a crisis exists and respond to the event as a crisis. Crisis recognition includes an understanding of how events get labeled and accepted as crises—how to sell a crisis to management—and the means for collecting crisis-related information. Chapter 8 covers the crisis response and includes topics related to crisis containment and recovery. Crisis containment focuses on the organization's crisis response, including the importance and content of the initial response, communication's relationship to reputational management, contingency plans, and follow-up concerns.

Postcrisis

When a crisis is resolved and deemed to be over, an organization must consider what to do next. Postcrisis actions help to (a) make the organization better prepared for the next crisis, (b) make sure stakeholders are left with a positive impression of the organization's crisis management efforts, and (c) check to make sure that the crisis is truly over. Chapter 9 addresses evaluating crisis management, learning from the crisis, and other postcrisis actions, such as follow-up communication with stakeholders and continued monitoring of issues related to the crisis.

WHAT WOULD YOU DO?	BAUSCH & LOMB AND RENU WITH MOISTURELOC: ACT 1

It is early April 2006, and you work for Bausch & Lomb, an eye health company. You have just received a call from the Food and Drug Administration (FDA) and the Centers for Disease Control and Prevention (CDC). These two agencies are tracking an unusually large outbreak of an eye fungus known as Fusarium keratitis, which can cause blindness. There have been over 100 reported cases. So far, the only link the government has found is that a high percentage of those infected had used Bausch & Lomb's ReNu with MoistureLoc contact lens solution. The FDA and CDC are not saying your product is the cause, but it is the only product that stands out in their investigation. This is your newest product line, and the company is hoping it will help to increase profits. The FDA and CDC tell you that they will be issuing a warning about Fusarium keratitis to the media and on their Web sites. These warnings will mention ReNu with MoistureLoc but not state it as the source of the problem.

- Who are the key stakeholders in this situation?
- What actions should your organization take?
- How should the organization communicate those actions to key stakeholders?

■ IMPORTANCE OF CRISIS MANAGEMENT

The first paragraph of this chapter offers a reminder that crises are ubiquitous. In fact, today's environment seems to be placing higher premiums on crisis management; unprepared organizations have more to lose today than ever before. A variety of developments has made all types of organizations more susceptible to crises. In turn, a higher premium is placed on crisis management, as mismanagement costs seem to escalate. To recap, the developments that increase the need for effective crisis management are an increased value of reputation, stakeholder activism through communication technologies, negligent failure to plan, and broader views of crises.

Value of Reputations

As late as the 1990s, writers were still debating the value of reputation. A reputation is evaluative, with organizations being seen as having favorable or unfavorable reputations (Coombs & Holladay, 2005). There is a strong consensus in the practitioner and academic writings that a reputation is an extremely valuable intangible organizational resource. Favorable reputations have been linked to attracting customers, generating investment interest, attracting top employee talent, motivating workers, increasing job satisfaction, generating more positive media coverage, and garnering positive comments from financial analysts (Alsop, 2004; Davies, Chun, da Silva, & Roper, 2003; Dowling, 2002; Fombrun & van Riel, 2004). An impressive list of key stakeholders that control resources vital to an organization's success is represented here (Agle, Mitchell, & Sonnenfeld, 1999). A reputation is built through the direct and indirect experiences stakeholders have with the organization (Fombrun & van Riel, 2004). Positive interactions and information about the organization build favorable reputations, while unpleasant interactions and negative information lead to unfavorable reputations. A crisis poses a threat to reputational assets (Barton, 2001; Davies et al., 2003; Dilenschneider, 2000). As greater emphasis is placed on reputation, a corresponding emphasis must be placed on crisis management as a means of protecting reputational assets (Coombs & Holladay, 2002).

Stakeholder Activism

Today, angry stakeholders are more likely to generate crises (*The Changing Landscape of Liability*, 2004). Consumers, shareholders, employees, community groups, and activists are becoming increasingly vocal when dealing with organizations and are using the Internet to voice those concerns (Coombs, 2002; Heath, 1998). The Internet provides various means of stakeholder expression, including Web pages, discussion boards, blogs (weblogs), microblogs, social networks, and content-sharing sites. The key feature of these Internet channels is the ability of users, rather than just the organizations, to create the content. Collectively, the Internet channels where stakeholders create the content are called social media, a concept Chapter 2 explores in more detail. The vast majority of social media messages never find an audience. However, when disgruntled stakeholders strike a responsive chord and connect with other stakeholders online, a crisis can occur. These crises evolve from the value of the organizational reputation. Legitimate criticism that spreads among stakeholders poses a direct threat to the organization's reputation. Here's an example: Kryptonite manufactures one of the most popular and expense bicycle locks available. When the company did not respond quickly to consumer concerns about a certain type of lock being easy to pick, the complaints appeared in social media and created a crisis for Kryptonite. The company appeared to be forced to recall the product by consumer pressure rather than concern for the consumers. Kryptonite looked unresponsive and uncaring. Social media has the potential, even if remote, to create a crisis.

Activist groups are using the Internet to organize and to pressure organizations to change their behaviors. Social media, online communication channels where content is controlled by the users, is part of a mix of pressure tactics, along with negative publicity campaigns and boycotts. The Internet has the potential to increase the power of activist groups, thereby making them audible to managers and on an organization's agenda for consideration (Coombs, 1998, 2002; Heath, 1998; T. Putnam, 1993). Consider how People for the Ethical Treatment of Animals was able to pressure Burger King and Wendy's to change their purchasing practices for beef and poultry through integrated pressure campaigns orchestrated on the Internet. The campaigns had the not-so-subtle titles "Murder King" and "Wicked Wendy's." Stakeholder activism is now global. Concerns over environmental issues in Europe encouraged Chiquita to change how it grows bananas in Central and South America. Partnering with the Rainforest Alliance, Chiquita has had 100% of its banana farms certified as Better Banana Grower ("*Corporate Conscience Award,*" 2003).

Communication Technologies

The discussion of stakeholder activism demonstrates one of the ways advances in communication technologies has begun to shape crisis management. These advances make the transmission of communication easier and faster. Another way to think about communication technologies is that they make the world more visible. Events that would have gone unnoticed a decade ago are now highly visible. There are no remote areas of the world anymore. The 24-hour news networks, or even just concerned individuals, have the opportunity to reveal crises, complete with video clips. Moreover, crises are now global thanks to communication technologies. Because news is global, news of an event in an isolated area of Africa appears rapidly around the world. Organizations no longer have isolated crises because the once-remote or far-flung areas of the world are accessible to the media and to other stakeholders. A crisis may appear on CNN or some other international news service or be the subject of a Web site. Coca-Cola's issues with worker abuses in South America became known globally in 2005 and 2006, due in large part to the Killer Coke Web site. PepsiCo was forced to sell operations in Myanmar due to a consumer pressure campaign emanating from social media (Coombs, 1998). Crises are now more likely to be seen, and to be seen by the world, thanks to advances in communication technologies.

Broader View of Crises

Prior to the horrific events of September 11, 2001, most organizations were focused on their own little world. Crisis management was driven by what might happen to them on their sites.

However, 9/11 showed that attacks or events at other locations can affect your organization. An event does not have to be a major terrorist event to create collateral damage. An explosion at a nearby chemical facility can create a need to evacuate and close your facility. An airplane crash may prevent vehicles from reaching your offices or plant.

Consequently, organizations are now broadening their view of crises to include nearby facilities that could create crises for them. A second way that the 9/11 attacks have broadened the view of crisis management is the increased emphasis on security and emergency preparedness. Security is one element of prevention and mitigation. Spending and managerial focus on security spiked dramatically after 9/11 and continue to stay high on the list of managerial priorities. While driven by terrorism concerns, security can help with other crises, such as workplace violence. In addition, the security focus has been coupled with the recognition of the need for emergency preparedness. Organizations should be prepared for an evacuation or to provide shelter in place, the two basic emergency responses. Emergency preparedness will help organizations with any crisis they face, not just with terrorism (Coombs, 2006b). The tragic events of 9/11 have been a wakeup call to crisis managers to expand their view of crisis management. The expectation is that this broader view will serve organizations well by saving lives in future crises.

Negligent Failure to Plan

Organizations have long been considered negligent if they did not take reasonable action to reduce or eliminate known or reasonably foreseeable risks that could result in harm. This liability is based on the 1970

Occupational Safety and Health Act (Headley, 2005). The scope of fore-seeable risks is expanding to include workplace violence, industrial accidents, product tampering, and terrorist attacks (Abrams, n.d.). This new area of liability is known as negligent failure to plan and is closely tied to crisis management. Organizations can be found legally liable if they did not take precautions to prevent potential crises and were not prepared to respond. Both crisis prevention and crisis preparation serve as defenses against negligent failure to plan. Juries are already punishing organizations that are not engaging in proper crisis man-agement (Blythe & Stivariou, 2003; Headley, 2005). Crisis management is becoming firmly established as a form of due diligence (efforts to avoid harm to others or the organization) that will protect an organi-zation not only from the immediate harm of a crisis but also from sec-ondary harm resulting from lawsuits.

■ CONCLUSION

As the potential for crises increases, so does the potential for negative outcomes. Organizations are playing for high stakes when confronting crises. The developments just reviewed demonstrate that the need for crisis management is increasing, not decreasing. The value of crisis management is greater now than when experts first began preaching about the need for crisis preparedness in the late 1970s. The end result is a higher premium on effective crisis management. Organizations must continue to improve their crisis management processes. Crisis management acts as a hedge against the negative outcomes of crises. Effective crisis management can protect lives, health, and the environ-ment; reduce the time it takes to complete the crisis life cycle; prevent loss of sales; limit reputation damage; preclude the development of public policy issues (i.e., laws and regulations); and save money. Today's operating environment demands that organization be prepared to manage crises.

Generally we experience crises through the news media and the Internet. As a result, it is easy to view crisis management as a short-term process and crisis managers as having few demands on their time. However, what the public sees of the response to a crisis is a small part of crisis management. Effective crisis management is ongoing. Crisis managers continually work to reduce the likelihood of a crisis occur-ring and to prepare the organization for the day when a crisis does occur. Moreover, crisis managers carefully dissect each crisis in order to improve prevention, preparation, and response. An appreciation of the phases of crisis management helps people better appreciate the complexity and ongoing nature of crisis management and communication.

DISCUSSION QUESTIONS

1. What would be some arguments managers would use against implementing a crisis management system?

2. Do you agree or disagree with the idea that a crisis is perceptual?

3. What do you think makes an event a crisis?

4. What alternatives are there to a staged approach to crisis management?

5. Some people question the value of precrisis activities. What reasons do you see that argue for and against precrisis activities?

2

Effects of the Online World on Crisis Communication and Crisis Management

T he word *revolution* is often used in reference to the Internet and crisis communication. Revolution does capture your attention and sells people on seminars for improving crisis communication, but it is an overstatement. It is more appropriate to think of the Internet as hastening the evolution of crisis communication. Let's start by refining what we mean by the Internet. The Internet is many communication channels, not just one. These channels include Web sites, discussion boards, blogs, microblogs, chat rooms, Listservs, image sharing, and social networking sites, to name but a few. Internet communication channels emphasize the interactive and interconnected nature of the Internet. Users can find information, connect with other users, and express their concerns more easily with the Internet than with traditional communication channels. We should remember that people did essentially the same communication tasks prior to the Internet. However, it took more time, effort, and resources to accomplish them.

The Internet is an important evolutionary step in crisis communication, rather than a revolution. Crisis managers still face the same needs to identify warning signs, confront the same basic communication demands, utilize the same concepts, and must enact effective strategic responses. Crisis managers need to identify warning signs in order to prevent crises and/or limit the damage from an emerging crisis. What has changed is how the information is collected and, in some cases, how that information is processed. Crisis managers are faced with the demand to create a quick and accurate response. What has changed is what constitutes "quick" and how that initial response is delivered. Crisis management plans (CMPs) and crisis teams still compose the heart of the crisis management effort. What has changed is how CMPs are stored and accessed and how team members interact with one another (see Chapters 5 and 6). Crisis managers must weight key crisis factors and devise an appropriate and effective crisis response. What has changed are the ways of identifying critical crisis information and how their messages are delivered. This chapter highlights key ways in which the Internet is affecting crisis communication and crisis management. Many of these are developed further in later chapters.

Let's begin with a short discussion of the online environment, which provides the context for appreciating this environment's effects on crisis communication. I'll then highlight the effects of social media on crisis communication organized by the three phases of crisis management.

■ THE ONLINE ENVIRONMENT:
MULTIPLE COMMUNICATION CHANNELS

We cannot have a discussion about the Internet's effects on crisis communication and management without first discussing the online environment itself. This will be a very basic discussion given that crisis, not the online environment, is the focus of this book. Organizations entered the online world, and thus created an online presence, with the use of Web pages. Taylor and Kent (2007) led the initial research investigating whether and how Web sites were used in a crisis. They observed how important it was to incorporate Web sites into crisis communication efforts as more and more stakeholders were utilizing this channel during a crisis (Taylor & Perry, 2005). Practitioners have embraced this advice, though many organizations still make no mention of a crisis on their Web sites. Web sites, however, were just the beginning of the online communication tools that would shape current crisis communication and management thinking.

Web sites generally reflect Web 1.0 rather than Web 2.0. Web 2.0 refers to applications that promote user-generated content, sharing of that content, and collaboration to create content. Web 2.0 promotes interaction and allows users to create Web content (O'Reilly, 2005). Corporate Web sites primarily distribute content (Web 1.0) rather than promote the creation and sharing of content. Web 2.0 was the foundation for social media. Social media is a collection of online technologies that allow users to share insights, experiences, and opinions with one another. The sharing can be in the form of text, audio, video, or multimedia (Safko & Brake, 2009). Social media is responsible for the growing link between crisis communication/management and the online world. Social media is an evolutionary stimulus because users, not organizations or the traditional news media, now control the creation and distribution of information. Users bypass the traditional information gatekeepers. It is important to refine our understanding of social media before exploring its effects on crisis communication/management.

Social media is a collection of online communication channels/ tools that share five common characteristics: (1) participation: anyone can create and give feedback on content, (2) openness: most social media permits people to post content and feedback, (3) conversation: it facilitates two-way interaction, (4) communities: groups with similar interests can form quickly, and (5) connectedness: there is heavy utilization of links to other content (Voit, 2008). Note how interactivity is the key factor connecting the five characteristics. These characteristics are self-explanatory, but community warrants further attention. One of the original qualities of the Internet that attracted public relations people was the way online communities formed. *Online communities* can be defined as groups of people with similar goals or interests that connect with one another and exchange information using Web tools (Owyang, 2007). Social media has increased the speed and ease with which online communities form. Online communities can be collections of important stakeholders for an organization. The comments and actions of these communities, in turn, can have a significant effect on an organization. Negative online comments can threaten valuable reputational assets (dna13, 2010; Oneupweb, 2007). That potential to affect organizations is what makes online communities and social media so important to crisis communication/ management. An example will help to illustrate the point.

On May 6, 2010, Pampers, a product of Procter & Gamble, issued a news release with the title *Pampers Calls Rumors Completely False*. Here is an excerpt from the news release that summarizes the situation:

> Jodi Allen, Vice President for Pampers, said, "For a number of weeks, Pampers has been a subject of growing but completely false rumors fueled by social media that its new Dry Max diaper causes rashes and other skin irritations. These rumors are being perpetuated by a small number of parents, some of whom are unhappy that we replaced our older Cruisers and Swaddlers products while others support competitive products and the use of cloth diapers. Some have specifically sought to

promote the myth that our product causes 'chemical burns.' We have comprehensively and thoroughly investigated these and other claims and have found no evidence whatsoever that the reported conditions were in any way caused by materials in our product. Independent physicians, highly respected in the field, have analyzed our data and have confirmed our conclusions." (para. 1)

Parents were making online comments that Pampers's new version of its product was harming infants. That is a serious charge for a company trying to sell diapers to parents. Parents do not want to buy a product that will hurt their children. Social media (e.g., blogs, microblogs, social networking sites) was the route for spreading the "rumor." The popular social networking site Facebook is a prime example of social media fanning the rumor. A discussion thread on a Pampers page appeared, claiming that Pampers created severe diaper rash, which even included blistering. The Facebook page had over 10,000 members, many of whom were parents who posted their concerns and experiences on the page. Pampers has its own Facebook page with over 100,000 fans, and even that page had parents posting stories of bad reactions to new Pampers under the discussion heading "New Pampers are HORRIBLE!" (the discussion thread is no longer available online). Pampers did respond to those concerns. Here is an exchange:

Sherrie Lejeune: I know I'm going to get a lot of flak for this, but oh well. I want to let people know my experience.

I've been using Pampers on my daughter since she was born in Oct. 08. I never had a problem with them and LOVED them. The softness of them was what made me use them at first. Then it was the absorbancy. My daughter has sensitive skin and everything else made her breakout besides Pampers and Huggies. And I didn't like Huggies because of the stiffness.

When the new Pampers came out Avagail was wearing the Cruisers and I had no clue they changed. I bought a box and it looked EXACTLY the same as the ones I was buying before. When we opened the box to start using them we noticed right away that they were different. They were REALLY thin and didn't feel as soft, but I tried them anyway.

Avagail started getting rashes RIGHT away. And when I say rashes, I mean REALLY BAD rashes. I change her right when I notice she's gone. Usually a minute or two after she's gone because I know her cues. Her rashes were blistering and bleeding. And when I'd get them to clear up they'd come right back. I started asking around and found out a LOT of people were having the same problem with their children.

We switched over to Huggies Little Movers and Huggies Overnight and we haven't had rashes like that since.

To the pampers people: You REALLY need to look into this. This is NOT an isolated problem. It's happening to a LOT of parents.

Pampers: Hi Sherrie. You definitely won't get flak from us for sharing your experience. We appreciate it, but I'm just so sorry to hear about Avagail's rashes, as well as Colleen's children and Kat's baby.

Please do understand that we thoroughly evaluate our diapers to ensure they are safe and gentle on your little one's skin. Although I'll be passing this information along to our Health & Safety Division, I really hope that you, Kat, and Colleen get in touch with us directly at 1-866-586-5654. We're available M–F, 9–6, EST.

Anne—I'll be sure to share your feedback with our Quality Control Team. We'd love you to give them another try since you had trouble with the tabs. Just get in touch with us at the same number and we can offer some help.

Pampers was reaching out to people expressing their concerns via social media. Pampers even held a summit with four influential "mommy bloggers," women who blog about consumer products intended for family use: Renee Bigner, Kate Marsh Lord, Tiffany Snedaker, and Stephanie Manner Wagner. The summit was a chance for Pampers and independent experts to provide information about the situation and to dispel the rumor. The four bloggers agreed that after the meeting they had greater confidence in the diapers (Sewell, 2010). Managers do consider negative information appearing in social media as legitimate threats to the reputations of the organizations, the reputation of products, and the sales of those products. In other words, social media can be a warning sign for a problem that has the opportunity to grow into a full-scale crisis.

Social media is a broad term that covers a variety of different online communication tools. Developing a comprehensive list of social media is like trying to count sand on the beach. New tools keep emerging, so you cannot have a complete and comprehensive list. But we can construct a system for categorizing the various types of social media. A category system is functional for crisis communication. By understanding how the different categories can be used in crisis communication, crisis managers can understand how to use any of the individual tools within the category. There are many different ways to categorize social media. Table 2.1 presents a synthesis of various lists along with definitions of the categories. True to the interconnected nature of the Internet, the categories are often used in combination with one another, making it appear as though they overlap. However, each category does have distinctive features that separate it from the others. They all possess the basic ability to share information and opinions with other users.

Table 2.1   Social Media Categories

Social networks	Individual Web pages from which people share content and communicate with friends (Examples: Facebook, MySpace, Bebo)
Blogs	Online journals where people post content and others can comment on it
Wikis	Web pages where people work together to create and edit content (Example: Wikipedia)
Podcast	Audio and video content created and distributed through a subscription based service (Example: The Executive Lounge With Andrew Coffey)
Forums	Online discussions revolving around specific interests and topics
Content communities	Places where people organize themselves around specific content that they create and comment on (Examples: YouTube, Flickr)
Microblogs	Sites on which people share small amounts of information through posts (Example: Twitter)
Aggregators	Tools that collect content (e.g., news stories, blogs) from different sites in one site; content is frequently ranked by popularity and can include comments from users (Example: Google Reader)
Social bookmarking	Tool with which people share and rate content they have found online (Example: Delicious)

It is important to realize that social media is dominated by user-created content. This means stakeholders are accustomed to being in control. It follows that basic ideas from traditional media relations do not and should not be applied. It is easy to find online rants about how public relations people pitch bloggers just like they pitch the traditional news media. Social media is about interaction and control, not being fed information. I make this point because crisis communicators must be savvy if they are to use social media strategically. Keep in mind that the primary values of social media are listening to what stakeholders are saying, not in sending them information, and providing access to information when stakeholders might need it. Listening and access will be used to illustrate the potential value of social media to crisis managers by coupling it with the steps of crisis management.

■ EFFECTS ON CRISIS COMMUNICATION

Social media has a variety of effects on crisis communication. The three stages of crisis management provide a useful framework for organizing the discussion of these effects. This section reviews key effects that are discussed in later chapters.

Precrisis

Listening is what scanning for crisis warning signs is all about. Social media provides an opportunity for finding warning signs generated by stakeholders. Blogs, microblogs, content communities, social networks, forums, aggregators, and social bookmarking are all excellent scanning tools for crisis managers. The challenge is wading through the vast amounts of information to locate emerging trends that appear ready to develop into crises, a point we will return to in Chapter 4. Not every online statement or video is really a potential crisis. However, the nature of the Internet is that ideas from seemingly unimportant sources can spread rapidly, thereby creating the potential for a crisis. This concern is rooted in the big-seed approach to viral messages.

The big seed is used in contrast to the small-seed notion of how ideas spread on the Internet—how a message becomes viral. The small-seed concept argues that only a few influential people need to spread the message for an idea to emerge online (Thompson, 2008). Duncan Watts, a network researcher at Yahoo!, has used computer modeling to show that average people are the most likely source for a successful viral message. In the big-seed approach, a large number of people (seeds) are targeted with the initial message. There is a mass effort to reach a broad spectrum of the target audience rather than identifying a few influentials. Watts and Peretti (2007) argue that any individual from the mass audience can create the viral spread of a message. Hence, crisis managers cannot just monitor what influential stakeholders are saying but must be attuned to a wide array of stakeholders. It is helpful at this point to introduce the idea of a paracrisis.

The term *para* means resembling or protection from something. A paracrisis resembles a crisis because it threatens the organization's reputation and related assets. However, a paracrisis would not require the activation of the crisis team and does not disrupt the organization. Still, a paracrisis warrants attention because neglect or mismanagement could create an actual crisis. A paracrisis is a specific type of crisis warning sign. It mimics a crisis itself. Motrin's offensive ad to mothers is an example of a paracrisis. In 2008, Motrin created an edgy ad that noted how mothers have back pain from using sling-type baby carriers. The ad was in print and online in video form. Many mothers were offended by it and took to social media to express their outrage. Twitter was a popular location for mothers to attack Motrin. There was even a nine-minute YouTube video featuring the Twitter complaints. The ad appeared online on a Saturday morning. The social media criticism stormed Twitter by Saturday evening. On the following Monday, McNeil Consumer Healthcare, the makers of Motrin, removed the ad from the Internet and replaced it with an apology (Tsouderos, 2008). McNeil Consumer Healthcare did not see any disruption in the production or sale of Motrin. There was minor damage to the corporate and product reputation that had the potential to escalate if the paracrisis was not handled swiftly and effectively. By removing the ad and apologizing, McNeil Consumer Healthcare managed the paracrisis, thereby defusing a potential crisis.

Paracrises that emerge in social media are unique crisis warning signs because they appear in full view of stakeholders. Typically, crisis prevention efforts are invisible to stakeholders. For instance, organizations revise safety procedures or replace a dangerous chemical to reduce the threat of hazardous chemical releases. Visibility is what gives a paracrisis its impact. The public appearance of the paracrisis demands public management. Managers must explain to all stakeholders what is being done to address the concern or why they are choosing to ignore it. The paracrisis blurs the line between precrisis and crisis response because addressing the paracrisis can appear to be a crisis response rather than preventative action. The key point here is that social media increases the visibility and number of paracrises because the Internet can highlight the stakeholder concerns that drive paracrises.

Crisis Response

It is very easy to find an online webinar or physical seminar where "experts" will tell you how to use the online environment to manage a crisis. The "selling" of online crisis communication creates the illusion that traditional media no longer matter. In fact, overusing online crisis communication is a dangerous delusion. Media selection must be driven by your target audience. Crisis managers select communication channels that effectively and efficiently reach the desired target audience. If online channels are relevant to your stakeholders during a crisis, then add online channels to the mix. However, crisis managers must integrate the online and traditional communication channels into a seamless and consistent crisis response (Wehr, 2007). Above all, crisis managers must use online channels strategically rather than just because someone said they should (Oneupweb, 2007).

I argue there are three basic rules when using online crisis communication channels (1) be present, (2) be where the action is, and (3) be there before the crisis. *Be present* means that crisis managers should not hide from the online world. Stakeholders, including the news media, will look to the corporate Web site and existing social media activities of an organization for information. If the crisis is never mentioned in the organization's online communication, the absence will be noticeable. The organization will be criticized for being silent and miss the opportunity to present its interpretation of the crisis. Chapter 8 returns to the importance of presenting the organization's side of the crisis.

Be where the action is refers to using the online origins of the crisis as one location for the crisis response messages (dna13, 2010). If the crisis began as a YouTube video, then YouTube should be one of the places where the crisis response appears. Domino's Pizza followed that advice when its CEO posted an apology on YouTube after a disgusting video of Domino's employees supposedly tampering with food was posted on YouTube. If the crisis breaks on Facebook, then the organization's Facebook page should address the crisis. Will the CEO's message about the crisis be popular or viewed as much as the crisis-inducing video? Will the organization have as many favorable comments as its critics do? The answer is clearly no, but placing the message in the source channel increases the likelihood of people encountering your message along with the crisis-inducing message.

Be there before the crisis means that implementing a social media push after a crisis is less effective than if the organization was already utilizing social media. Social networking sites, blogs, and microblogs are most effective when there are followers—people viewing the content regularly. Having an existing presence builds credibility and authenticity for your crisis messages. When American Airlines and Southwest Airlines had to ground planes for safety inspections, both used blogs to discuss the problem. Prior to the crisis, Southwest had a popular blog called *Nuts About Southwest*. American had no blog. Southwest used its blog to help inform passengers and answer their questions. There were quickly over 140 responses after the first crisis post by Southwest. When American started a blog after the crisis, stakeholders did not know about it and virtually no one accessed it. American did nothing to promote the blog, including no link from its corporate Web site. Eventually American dropped the blog. American's experience demonstrates that arriving late to the social media game is problematic (Holtz, 2007). However, there is still value in starting to use social media after a crisis because of the need to be where the action is. Crisis managers must never forget the strategic aspect of the crisis response (Martine, 2007). The nature of the crisis plays a critical role in strategic choices about the selection of social media options to deliver a crisis response, a point developed in Chapter 8.

Postcrisis

Stakeholders may still require follow-up information and updates after the crisis is officially over. Social media provides another channel for delivering the updates and addressing specific follow-up questions stakeholders may have. Crisis managers will need to determine how long to keep special crisis Web pages or blogs operational. One criterion would be to decommission such sites when interest wanes. Managers may want to move past the special crisis pages and blogs as another sign that the crisis is over. That is when social media can be valuable. Microblogs, such as Twitter, provide excellent outlets for updates and to answer lingering questions (dna13, 2010). If people begin following the organization during the crisis, the microblog can post updates that will reach interested stakeholders. Moreover, microblogs have the capacity to answer question if the answer is, in the case of Twitter, 140 characters or less. Regular corporate blogs and social network pages provide opportunities for posting updates and responding to questions, too. Social media provides channels for reaching stakeholders who are still looking to engage the organization about crisis issues in the postcrisis phase, a point covered in Chapter 9.

■ CONCLUSION

This chapter began by noting that the Internet is speeding, rather than revolutionizing, the evolution of crisis communication. I argue for evolution because the Internet, especially social media, is helping crisis managers execute existing communication-related tasks rather than creating the need for entirely new ones. But crisis managers would be engaging in malpractice if they did not integrate social media into their activities. For instance, social media places a greater demand on scanning while providing more tools for accomplishing the task. Social media is important enough to crisis communication to warrant a separate chapter to highlight its impact. As noted earlier, later chapters extend the ways that social media is insinuating itself into crisis communication throughout the entire crisis management process.

DISCUSSION QUESTIONS

1. Why is it important to understand that online and social media are really multiple channels and not one communication channel?

2. Which do you find more appealing and why, the small-seed or big-seed approach?

3. What do you think makes word of mouth so powerful?

4. What are the dangers associated with using any social media?

5. What, if any, value is there in differentiating between crises and paracrises?

6. Besides the cases listed in this chapter, what other evidence can you find that social media is affecting crisis communication?

7. Which social media do you use? Do you think organizations could use it to reach you during a crisis? Why or why not?

3

Proactive Management Functions and Crisis Management

The best way to manage a crisis is to prevent one. If the crisis does not occur, no stakeholders are harmed and the organization suffers no damage. Generally, people think of crisis management as reactive because they focus on what an organization does in response to a crisis, which is the topic of Chapter 8. However, clever crisis managers are proactive as well by seeking crisis warning signs and taking measures designed to reduce or eliminate the possibility of the warning sign evolving into a crisis. In fact, crisis managers must develop a system designed to scan and monitor for crisis warning signals—what I term the *crisis-sensing mechanism*—and to act on those signals when necessary.

Crisis management should draw upon existing resources in organizations to prevent wasted time, effort, and money. Crisis prevention is facilitated by tapping into the three management functions that actively scan the environment for threats: issues management, reputation management, and risk management. This chapter integrates these three proactive functions into crisis management to develop the concept of crisis prevention. Each of the three functions is defined, and their relationships to crisis management explored, followed by a discussion of why the functions are so strongly interrelated.

■ THE PROACTIVE MANAGEMENT FUNCTIONS

Crisis prevention seeks crisis warning signs with the hopes of reducing the likelihood of a crisis developing. The search for warning signs is known as signal detection. Signal detection begins with scanning, a systematic search for and analysis of events. Crisis managers scan both outside of the organization (the environment) and inside of the organization for crisis warning signs. Neglecting either area could result in overlooking important warning signs of an impending crisis. As part of this process, crisis managers must evaluate the information they have collected for warning signs. Those warning signs with the greatest potential for signaling danger are then monitored for further developments. Scanning is a form of radar; it identifies as many warning signs as possible. Monitoring is a form of focused tracking; it keeps a close watch on the warning signs that have the greatest potential to become crises. Therefore, the signal detection stage must include collecting and analyzing information that may contain warning signs.

Issues Management

An issue is "a trend or condition . . . that, if continued, would have a significant effect on how a company is operated" (Moore, 1979, p. 43). In essence, an issue is a type of problem whose resolution can impact the organization. Issues management includes the identification of issues and actions taken to affect them (Heath, 1990). It tries to lessen the negative impact of an issue and is a systematic approach intended to shape how an issue develops and is resolved. Issues management is a proactive attempt to have an issue decided in a way that is favorable to an organization. While issues management can address internal concerns (Dutton & Jackson, 1987; Dutton & Ottensmeyer, 1987), the emphasis is on societal and political issues that populate the organization's environment—external issues (Heath, 2005).

Managing an issue involves attempts to shape how the issue is resolved. The idea is to have the issue resolved in a manner that avoids a crisis. For instance, say that legislation is proposed that would threaten the financial viability of the railroad by making trucking companies more competitive with rail transportation. The issues management effort prevents a crisis by persuading Congress to reject the legislative proposal. Communication is used to influence an issue's resolution.

The Jones and Chase (1979) model (issue identification, analysis, change strategy option, action program, and evaluation) is the classic model familiar to most people involved in issues management. The action step centers on communicating the organization's position on the issue to stakeholders involved with the issue. Goals and objectives for the communication program are developed, followed by the selection of the means and resources needed to achieve them. Decisions are made about the specific messages to be communicated, when to communicate them, and the channels of communication to be used (Jones & Chase, 1979). The exact mix of communication strategies depends upon the stakeholders involved in the issues management effort and the current stage of the issue's progression (Crable & Vibbert, 1985). Developing the previous transportation example can clarify the issue action program. The railroad company decides the goal is to prevent passage of the pro-trucking legislative proposal. Legislators, the media, and voters are the stakeholders to be targeted. The message centers on the danger to automobile drivers created by the pro-trucking legislation, and the message must be sent immediately because a vote will be held in a few months. Advertisements, publicity, and lobbying are the communication channels used. The focus in this example is on how organizations use issues management to shape their environments. Figure 3.1 is visual depiction of the Jones and Chase model.

Issues management can also involve changing the organization. Issue managers may decide that the best way to resolve an issue would be to correct or improve operating standards and plans. McDonald's illustrated this point when it abandoned the polystyrene "clamshell" burger boxes. Environmentalists had been complaining about the environmentally unfriendly clamshell packaging for years. The company's original plan was to win acceptance of the clamshell by emphasizing recycling. By recycling, McDonald's would eliminate the complaint that its packaging would clog landfills for hundreds of years. McDonald's was trying to change stakeholder attitudes. However, consumers did not respond well to the early recycling tests, so McDonald's abandoned the clamshell recycling campaign and simply ended use of that packaging (A. Snyder, 1991). McDonald's changed its procedures rather than trying to change its stakeholders' opinions.

As Gonzalez-Herrero and Pratt (1996) note, some issues can develop into crises, making issues management relevant to crisis scanning. Issues management can be a form of crisis prevention when the issues management effort prevents an issue from developing its crisis potential (Grunig & Repper, 1992). An example of this is pharmaceutical companies' use of direct-to-consumer (DTC) advertising. You have no doubt seen many DTC messages. Have you seen television

Figure 3.1   Jones and Chase Issues Management Model

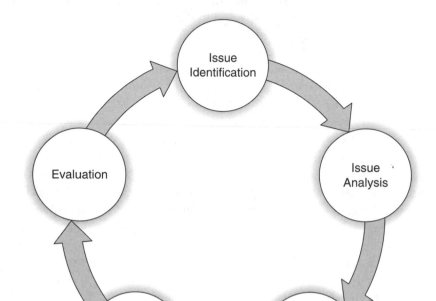

advertisements for drugs to address cholesterol, high blood pressure, social anxiety, acid reflux, or sexual dysfunction? Then you have been exposed to DTC. The United States and New Zealand are the only major countries to allow DTC efforts.

In 2005, the U.S. Senate and the Food and Drug Administration (FDA) began deliberating on the need to regulate DTC. To prevent government regulation, the pharmaceutical industry decided to self-regulate. In August 2005, PhRMA, the industry association for major pharmaceutical manufacturers, announced a new 15-point Guiding Principles document for DTC. Most of the principles repeated existing FDA regulations, such as that DTC information should be accurate and not misleading. New measures included educating physicians prior to a DTC campaign and allowing no DTC messages in media targeted to age-inappropriate audiences (PhRMA, 2005). Most of the major pharmaceutical companies publicly endorsed the plan. Talk about regulating DTC all but disappeared. PhRMA used the complete spectrum of issues management communication tools: advocacy advertising, direct lobbying, grassroots lobbying, letter writing, e-mail, Web pages, and publicity.

A crisis or ineffective crisis management can spawn an issue, creating the need for issues management. When three students were killed in the 2000 Seton Hall dormitory fire, new legislation was passed in New Jersey requiring all dormitories to have sprinkler systems. Ineffective management of the *Exxon Valdez* crisis helped to block oil exploration in the Arctic National Wildlife Refuge for decades. The laxative market offers an example of how issues management can both avert and create a crisis. Until the 1990s, the main ingredient in the two leading laxatives, Correctol and ex-lax, was phenolphthalein. In the early 1990s, the FDA began investigating a link between phenolphthalein and cancer. In 1995, the preliminary study with rats indicated that phenolphthalein could be a carcinogen. The FDA now thought about banning phenolphthalein. Novartis, the manufacturer of ex-lax, did not see a problem and defended the use of phenolphthalein. Schering-Plough, the maker of Correctol, decided to switch from phenolphthalein to bisacodyl and supported the FDA move to ban phenolphthalein.

Additional evidence was collected by the FDA that supported the phenolphthalein–cancer link. In April 1997, the FDA went public with its cancer concern over phenolphthalein. Schering-Plough supported the decision and informed customers that it had removed phenolphthalein from Correctol over a year earlier, while ex-lax still used it. Novartis kept fighting the phenolphthalein ban issue. The company advocated a public education campaign to curb laxative abuse. The idea was that proper, limited use would not place people at risk, that only those who abuse laxatives were at risk for cancer. In August 1997, the FDA proposed a ban on phenolphthalein. At that time, Novartis recalled ex-lax and introduced a new formula shortly thereafter. However, Correctol had already established its competitive advantage by demonstrating greater concern for customers because Schering-Plough had acted much faster to protect customers from the phenolphthalein threat (McGinley, 1997).

Reputation Management

A reputation is an evaluation stakeholders make about an organization. Hence, we can talk about favorable and unfavorable reputations. Stakeholders are any group that can affect or be affected by the behavior of an organization (Bryson, 2004), a point developed in more detail shortly. As noted in Chapter 1, reputations are widely recognized as a valuable if intangible asset.

Reputation management involves efforts designed to influence stakeholder evaluations of an organization. Reputations are formed as stakeholders evaluate organizations based upon direct and indirect interactions. Direct interactions form the basics of the organization-stakeholder relationship (Fombrun & van Riel, 2004). Positive interactions build favorable reputations, while unpleasant interactions lead to unfavorable ones. Favorable stakeholder relationships can be taken as a marker of a positive reputation. The relationship history—how the organization has treated stakeholders in the past—is a function of an organization meeting or failing to meet stakeholder expectations (Finet, 1994). Organizations build favorable relationship histories that create positive reputations by meeting and exceeding stakeholder expectations (Coombs, 2004a).

Indirect interactions are mediated reports of how the organization treats its stakeholders. News reports, comments from friends or family, online comments, and messages sent by an organization are important sources of information for evaluating organizations. Do you dislike Enron? Did you meet anyone from Enron, buy Enron stock, or purchase products from Enron? The odds are that you built your opinion of Enron based on media reports. In fact, stakeholders are more likely to draw upon indirect than direct experiences when crafting their personal views of an organization's reputation (Carroll & McCombs, 2003; Stephenson & Blackshaw, 2006). Being evaluative, reputations are based in large part on how stakeholders assess an organization's ability to meet their expectations. How well an organization does this is a rough guide for determining whether a reputation will be positive or negative. In some respects, a reputation is a reflection of the organization-stakeholder relationship. A threat to the relationship is a threat to the reputation. It is important to dig deeper into the relationship to appreciate its connection to reputations.

But what does the term *relationship* mean? Talking about organizational relationships with stakeholders assumes that we all understand and agree on what is meant by *relationship* and *stakeholder*. For crisis management, a useful definition of relationship is the interdependence of two or more people or groups. This definition is a modification of one developed by O'Hair, Friedrich, Wiemann, and Wiemann (1995) and centers on interdependence, some factor that binds the two people or groups together. The interdependence definition of relationship is useful because it is consistent with the stakeholder theory that guides most business thinking (Rowley, 1997).

Stakeholder theory posits that an organization's environment is populated with various stakeholders. An organization survives or thrives by effectively managing these stakeholders (Bryson, 2004; Clarkson, 1991; Wood, 1991). Stakeholders are generally defined as any persons or groups that have an interest, right, claim, or ownership in an organization. Stakeholders are separated into two distinct groups: primary and secondary. Primary stakeholders are those people or groups whose actions can be harmful or beneficial to an organization. Failure to maintain a continuing interaction with a primary stakeholder could result in the failure of the organization. Typical primary stakeholders include employees, investors, customers, suppliers, and the government. For instance, organizations cannot operate without employees, and government officials may close a facility for a variety of legal or regulatory reasons. Secondary stakeholders or influencers are those people or groups who can affect or be affected by the actions of an organization. Typical influencers include the media, activist groups, and competitors. Influencers cannot stop an organization from functioning, but they can damage it (Clarkson, 1995; Donaldson & Preston, 1995).

Primary and secondary stakeholders are interdependent with an organization, thus the relevance of the earlier definition of *relationship*. Each of the stakeholders has a connection with the organization that links them in some way. The links include economic, social, and political concerns. Reputation management is the management of the relationships between the organization and its various stakeholders, and organizational success is predicated on maintaining an effective balance in these relationships (Donaldson & Preston, 1995; Rowley, 1997; Savage, Nix, Whitehead, & Blair, 1991). It follows that stakeholders can play an important role in crisis management.

Primary stakeholders can stop organizational operations and trigger a crisis. Conflict with an organization can lead primary stakeholders to withhold their contributions. As a result, an organization may stop operating if those contributions cannot be replaced. For instance, unhappy workers can strike, and discontented customers can boycott. In 1997, the Teamsters' 15-day strike against UPS cost the company $600 million in revenues. A total of 185,000 Teamsters, nearly two-thirds of the UPS American workforce, joined the strike. At best, UPS was able to operate at only 10% capacity, using management personnel and drivers who did not strike. UPS found it could not function without the drivers, so it conceded to their demands (Sewell, 1997).

In 2004, Kryptonite announced it would recall some of its popular and high-priced bicycle locks. The problem was that many locks could be picked using just the outside casing of a Bic pen. The impetus for the recall was a complaint from a group of angry bikers taking their case to the Internet via discussion group postings and blogs. Some people even posted videos showing how to pick the lock to prove the claim was true. The bikers were angry that their very expensive bikes were being stolen or were at risk from the faulty locks. It took Kryptonite a week to respond to customer concerns, a long time in the Internet world (Wagstaff, 2006). Primary stakeholders are powerful because it is difficult and often impossible to replace the contributions they provide the organization (R. K. Mitchell, Agle, & Wood, 1997).

For crisis management, it would be a mistake to focus solely on primary stakeholders. Problems in relationships with secondary stakeholders can also harm reputations and trigger crises. The media can expose organizational misdeeds or generate other negative publicity, competitors can instigate lawsuits that bind an organization's operations, and activists can launch boycotts or protests against an organization. A few examples illustrate the role of secondary stakeholders in creating crises.

In February 2006, Airborne was brought down to earth by a *Good Morning America* (GMA) special report. On its packaging, Airborne claimed to fight colds. In fact, it claimed to be a miracle cold buster that could cure colds in an hour. The GMA investigation reported that the product was no more effective than hand washing during cold and flu season—it was not a cure. The key finding was that the clinical study Airborne used to support its claim was highly questionable. GMA found that the research firm was created just to study Airborne and that the main researcher had false credentials. Airborne promised to remove any mention of the study from its Web site and promotional materials (*Does Airborne Really Stave Off Colds?*, 2006). The company had to publicly address the concerns about its claims and documentation. A media story had precipitated a crisis.

Also in February 2006, Procter & Gamble (P&G) filed a lawsuit against Vi-Jon Laboratories, a manufacturer of health and beauty products. P&G alleged that Vi-Jon had infringed and diluted the unique trade dress of its Crest Pro-Health Rinse, saying that the Vi-Jon packing looked too much like Crest's and that consumers could be confused and buy the wrong product. P&G also alleged that Vi-Jon's advertising for its Vi-Jon Rinse was false and misleading (*Procter & Gamble Files Lawsuit*, 2006). In April 2006, a settlement was reached between P&G and Vi-Jon. Vi-Jon agreed to remove its product from the market, to stop using a bottle design similar to Crest Pro-Health Rinse, and to stop making gingivitis efficacy claims in its advertising (*P&G Reaches Settlement Agreement*, 2006)

In both cases, a secondary stakeholder had influenced organizational actions. Secondary, as well as primary, stakeholders can create a crisis for an organization. Mismanaging the organization–stakeholder relations can damage an organization's reputation and evolve into a crisis (Grunig, 1992; Heath, 1988). Therefore, watching organization-stakeholder relationships contributes to crisis scanning as a part of reputation management. Early problems related to reputations are signs that a crisis could erupt.

The broadening array of stakeholders that are important to organizations has promoted the integration of corporate social responsibility (CSR) into the conceptualization and management of reputations. CSR can be defined as "the management of actions designed to affect an organization's impacts on society" (Coombs & Holladay, 2010, p. 262). The societal impacts of CSR are quite diverse, including worker rights, sustainability, human rights, and eradication of disease. Traditionally, financial factors have dominated corporate reputation management. The financial factors became the criteria used to evaluate corporate reputations. The dominant reputation measures such as *Fortune* magazine's Most Admired list and the Reputation Institute's RepTrak (originally the Reputation Quotient) reflect a financial orientation. Social responsibility has been a more minor element within these measures. For instance, the RepTrak has seven dimensions: leadership, performance, products and services, innovation, citizenship, workplace, and governance. CSR is a part of citizenship (e.g., contributes to society), workplace (cares about employee well-being), and governance (e.g., responsible use of power) dimensions. The Most Admired list has eight dimensions, with only one, community and environmental responsibility, relevant to CSR.

CSR increasingly is playing a more important role in reputation discussions. Charles Fombrun (2005), a leader in reputation management thinking, now refers to CSR as an integral aspect of reputation. CSR is quickly becoming a key driver and integral part of reputation management. Reputations are evaluations and can range from favorable to unfavorable. Both CSR and reputation are dependent upon stakeholder expectations. In fact, the current thinking in CSR is that stakeholder expectations is the foundation for the process. Stakeholders define the constituents by determining what social concerns are appropriate for CSR efforts (e.g., Bhattacharya & Sen, 2003; Coombs & Holladay, 2010). Reputation managers can no longer concentrate exclusively on investors and their financial interests. CSR now is part of the key evaluation criteria for reputations.

As noted earlier in this book, crises have a negative effect on reputations. Reputations also have an effect on crisis management. A negative reputation prior to a crisis makes the crisis more difficult to manage. A prior negative reputation, for instance, increases stakeholder perceptions that the organization is responsible for the crisis and increases reputation damage (Coombs & Holladay, 2002, 2006). A positive reputation prior to a crisis acts as a resource that can make crisis management easier. Crisis experts agree that favorable organization–stakeholder relationships are a benefit during crisis management (e.g., Ulmer, 2001). As Alsop (2004) states, organizations "build up 'reputation capital' to tide them over in turbulent times. It's like opening a savings account for a rainy day. If a crisis strikes . . . reputation suffers less and rebounds more quickly" (p. 17). A crisis will inflict some reputation damage. "A crisis or other negative development will certainly tax any reputation and rob a company of some of its stored-up reputation capital" (Alsop, 2004, p. 17).

Risk Management

Risk management represents attempts to reduce the vulnerabilities faced by an organization (Smallwood, 1995). Vulnerabilities are weaknesses that could develop into crises. Basically, vulnerabilities are risks. Like crises, not all risks can be avoided or completely eliminated. Hence, risk management involves a number of strategies that vary in their crisis-prevention potential. The base for risk management is risk assessment.

Risk assessment attempts to identify risk factors or weaknesses and to assess the probability that a weakness will be exploited or developed into a crisis (Levitt, 1997; Pauchant & Mitroff, 1992). Every organization faces a variety of risk factors. Typically, they include personnel, products, the production process, facilities, competition, regulations, and customers (Barton, 2001). Risk factors exist as a normal part of an organization's operation. The following incidents illustrate their crisis potential. In May 2010, an employee of Boulder Stove & Flooring entered the building with a 9mm Smith & Wesson. He shot and killed the two co-owners and then himself—personnel risk. In January 2009, an explosion ripped through the Silver Eagle oil refinery near Salt Lake City, Utah. The blast sent four workers to the hospital with burns and caused the evacuation of local homes—production process risk. In January 2010, Johnson & Johnson expanded a recall of over-the-counter drugs due to a moldy smell. About 70 customers were made nauseous by the smell. The recall included regular and extra-strength Tylenol, children's Tylenol, eight-hour Tylenol, Tylenol arthritis, Tylenol PM, children's Motrin, Motrin IB, Benadryl Rolaids, Simply Sleep, and St. Joseph's aspirin—product and customer risk.

Risk assessment has more of an internal rather than external focus. The internal weaknesses identified through risk assessment provide vital information for crisis management scanning. For instance, Occupational Safety and Health Administration records might reveal a pattern of mishandling acids. The crisis team concerned would look for ways to break the pattern, thereby preventing injuries and reducing a crisis-inducing risk factor.

Once a risk is identified, decisions are made about risk aversion, the elimination or reduction of a risk. Two factors drive the use of risk-aversion decisions. The first factor is cost. Risk managers use procedures such as risk balancing to compare the costs of the risk (e.g., costs of deaths, injuries, litigation, and property damage) to the costs of risks reduction (e.g., equipment and actual work needed to prevent or reduce the risk). Organizations may take no action when the costs of risk reduction outweigh the costs estimated from the risk. However, ignoring risk can be a more costly move than anticipated. If stakeholders discover their safety was sacrificed for profit, a different and much worse type of crisis erupts. In May 2010, documents were released that shed new light on BP's deadly 2005 Texas City refinery explosion. Lawyer Brent Coon released a two-page BP document that showed the company favored profit over human safety and lives. The memo was a cost-benefit analysis of trailers to be used at Texas City. Most of the 15 fatalities from the Texas City explosion were workers in just such trailers. The memo showed a value of $10 million for a human life in the calculation to determine which type of trailer to buy. BP concluded that blast-resistant trailers were too expensive, costing 10 times more than the less protective trailers BP did buy for Texas City. The most disturbing aspect of the memo was that it used the analogy of the three little pigs, with the pigs being the workers and an accident being the big bad wolf. The final conclusion from the memo was that human life had a price and BP was not willing to overpay to protect workers—finance trumped human safety (Outzen, 2010).

When managers choose to engage in risk aversion, risk management becomes crisis prevention. Actions are taken to completely eliminate the risk or to reduce it to as low a level as reasonably possible (Levitt, 1997). The use of dangerous chemicals in a manufacturing process illustrates this point. Using inherently safer practices is an approach to designing safer chemical plants, storage facilities, and chemical processes. Three common risk-reduction strategies resulting in inherently safer practices are to (1) reduce the amount of hazardous material on-site, (2) substitute a less hazardous substance, and (3) use a less hazardous process or storage condition. If the less hazardous materials are on-site, the effect of a crisis is reduced: the Chevron Richmond Refinery reduced the amount of anhydrous ammonia it stored on-site and moved the storage facilities farther from the nearby residential area. If a nontoxic or less hazardous chemical can be substituted for a hazardous chemical, a risk can be eliminated or reduced: the Mt. View Sanitary District, a wastewater treatment facility, replaced three hazardous chemicals (chlorine, sulfur dioxide, and ammonia) with an ultraviolet light system to disinfect wastewater. Changes in the chemical process used or the state in which a chemical is stored can reduce a hazard: acrylate producers have switched from manufacturing with the Reppe process to the safer propylene oxidation process, and Dow Chemical switched from using liquid chlorine to the less hazardous gaseous form.

Using inherently safer practices is one among a variety of approaches for eliminating or reducing risk. Another common effort is training, and topics related to risk aversion can range from chemical safety to e-mail use. The exact action taken by an organization to reduce a risk varies according to the actual risk (Lerbinger, 1997). For instance, many companies face computer rather than chemical risks. Antivirus software, firewalls, and employee Internet use policies are ways to prevent risks. Consider the threat of viruses, such as the one known as Melissa, that could damage an organization's computer systems and databases. Cognos Corporation, a software developer, knew that the Melissa virus contained a file that was over 25K in size. The company set a 25K limit on incoming messages to keep Melissa out. Managers acted quickly; within one hour of identifying the risk, a policy was created and relayed to employees along with a rationale for the new policy (Meserve, 1999). The basic process involves determining whether the risk aversion is possible and then implementing the risk aversion program.

When a risk becomes manifest, a crisis can occur. Failure to reduce the risks associated with the startup of the isomerization unit at Texas City manifested itself in an explosion that killed 15 workers and injured over 170 others at the BP facility. Crises often create new risks. The oil from the Deepwater Horizon oil platform explosion in 2010 triggered multiple crises for those in the tourism and fishing industries in the Gulf of Mexico and beyond. Moreover, crisis communication may require the discussion of risk and the need to engage in risk communication, "a communication infrastructure, transactional communication process among individuals and organizations regarding the character, cause, degree, significance, uncertainty, control, and overall perception of risk" (Palenchar, 2005, p. 752). Risk communication is essentially a dialogue between the organization creating the risk and the stakeholders who are asked to bear the risk. Organizations explain what the risks are and what can be done to protect people from the risk, while stakeholders explain their concerns about and perceptions of the risk.

Issues management, reputation management, and risk management all can contribute to crisis scanning. Combined, the three functions provide a broad radar system for detecting warning signs. The challenge for crisis managers is to integrate the three organizational functions into an effective crisis-sensing mechanism, which is the focus of Chapter 4.

■ INTERRELATIONSHIP AMONG THE PROACTIVE MANAGEMENT FUNCTIONS

I must admit that it is a bit artificial to talk separately about the connections between crisis management and issues management, crisis management and risk management, and crisis management and reputation management. In reality these four proactive management functions are tightly interconnected, which is illustrated in Figure 3.2. A tetrahedron is a geometric figure composed of four triangles that has three triangles meeting at each vertex or connecting point. A simpler way to describe a tetrahedron is as a three-sided pyramid. Each of the four connecting points on the proactive management tetrahedron (PMT) represents one of the four proactive management functions. Changes in any one of the four functions can affect the others.

Reputation is the broadest concept because it involves any information a stakeholder receives about an organization. It follows that efforts to manage crises, risks, and issues can affect a reputation. We have already discussed how crisis harms reputations, but the same can be true for risks and issues. For instance, a reputation may deteriorate if an organization exposes stakeholders to unwanted risk or supports the resolution of an issue that stakeholders oppose. In turn, those risks and issues can then become crises.

Risks can become issues as people seek governmental help to control the risk. Consider the earlier laxative example. The ingredient was a risk, people wanted the government to take action on the risk (issues management), and the FDA banned the ingredient/risk, sparking a crisis and affecting reputations. Because of the strong connections, it is

Figure 3.2   Proactive Management Tetrahedron

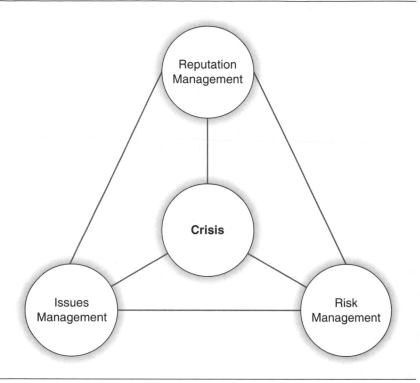

important that crisis managers have a familiarity with issues management, risk management, and reputation management. The value of these proactive management functions extends well beyond crisis prevention to the other stages of crisis management.

■ CONCLUSION

Crisis management works best when it includes avoiding or preventing crises. Issues management, risk management or aversion, and reputation management all can be used to avoid crises or at least their most dire consequences. Some issues can evolve into crises; issues management can be used to prevent such crises. Risks have the potential of becoming crises; risk aversion is used to lessen the chance. A threat to a reputation can be identified and resolved; by understanding and working with one another, the organization and its stakeholders can resolve reputation-related problems early on, before they escalate into crises. For example, customer complaints can be corrected before customers become outraged and publicly protest about a product or service.

DISCUSSION QUESTIONS

1. While this chapter separates issues, risk, and reputation management, the three areas are interrelated. How can a risk become an issue, an issue become a risk, a risk threaten reputation, or an issue threaten reputation? How do you see these three functions being interrelated?

2. How do you think perception gaps form? Does this inform how you would correct a perception gap?

3. What does it mean to say a risk can develop into a crisis?

4. Is it accurate to say that reputation management is the larger concept because of how the other functions can impact it?

5. Would you argue for an organization to create a separate department to manage these functions? Why or why not?

4

The Crisis
Prevention Process

C risis prevention is proactive crisis management. The goal of crisis prevention is to avoid a crisis. Crisis managers take actions designed to eliminate a crisis threat or to reduce the likelihood of the threat manifesting into a crisis. Issues management, risk management, and reputation management all provide ideas for developing crisis prevention. Drawing from these areas, this chapter provides details as to what comprises crisis prevention.

The crisis prevention process is a combination of signal detection and correction. Signal detection attempts to find crisis warning signs, while correction is designed to reduce or eliminate the threat. Combined, the two form the five-step crisis prevention process: (1) identify the sources to scan, (2) collect the information, (3) analyze the information, (4) take preventative action if warranted, and (5) evaluate the effectiveness of the threat reduction. The first three steps involve signal detection, and the last two involve correction. Elements of the three proactive management functions can be combined to create a comprehensive crisis prevention program. The structure of this chapter follows the five-step crisis prevention process.

■ IDENTIFY THE SOURCES TO SCAN

Issues and reputation management emphasize external threats, while risk management has more of an internal focus. Their different foci are reflected in the typical sources that each function scans for threats.

Sources used in issues management, risk management, and reputation management can be combined to provide a comprehensive set of sources that crisis managers should scan.

Environmental scanning is a tool that is popular in issues management (Gonzalez-Herrero & Pratt, 1996; Heath, 1997; Heath & Nelson, 1986; Pauchant & Mitroff, 1992). Basically, environmental scanning means watching the environment for changes, trends, events, and emerging social, political, or health issues. The information is used to guide organizational decision making to plot future actions (Lauzen, 1995). Unfortunately, environmental scanning strategies used by organizations are not well developed. Still, crisis managers must consider the sources involved in external scanning that would be helpful in locating warning signs.

External scanning uses both traditional print and online sources. In fact, most traditional sources can now be found online as well. A common method used to monitor the environment is to watch, listen to, or read both traditional and online news sources (Coombs, 2002; Heath, 1988). The news media include leading or elite newspapers (e.g., *New York Times, Wall Street Journal, Washington Post*), news and business magazines (e.g., *Time, Newsweek, Fortune*), and television news programs, such as the evening news and TV news magazines (e.g., *60 Minutes, 20/20*). Of special interest is information about crises in similar organizations. Case studies of similar organizations in crisis are a valuable resource for crisis managers, allowing crisis teams to learn from someone else's crisis rather than their own (Pauchant & Mitroff, 1992).

Other useful publications include trade journals, relevant medical or scientific journals and Web sites, newsletters, and public opinion surveys. The trade outlets are likely to carry stories about crises suffered by similar organizations. The trade journals, other publications, and Web sites provide information about issues the industry is facing as well as industry-specific complaints. All can help to identify possible crises for individual organizations within that industry. Medical or scientific journals and Web sites may contain studies that could affect how people view an industry. The dangers of cholesterol and concerns over the link between cell phone use and automobile accidents are examples of pertinent study topics. The public's first exposure to these two health concerns was through medical and scientific publications, not the news media.

Newsletters include reports published by special interest groups, foundations, and government agencies. Each can indicate potential threats to an organization. Special interest publications inform organizations about the concerns of activist stakeholders and indicate if anger is being focused on their industry or their specific organization. Foundations can identify emerging issues. Government publications and online portals offer insights into possible regulatory or legal changes identify emerging issues. For example, the *Federal Register* has information about potential regulatory changes, the *Congressional Record* and *Congressional Quarterly Weekly Report* provide information about new legislation, and the *Congressional Quarterly Researcher* provides information about salient issues in U.S. society. Public opinion surveys can indicate changes in attitudes, lifestyles, and values (Heath, 1997).

Individuals are another source of environmental information. Crisis managers should focus on two broad categories: public opinion experts and the organization's own stakeholders. Public opinion experts, like the published data, provide insights into public attitudes, lifestyles, and values. Stakeholders can tell the organization how they feel about issues and organizational actions (Heath & Nelson, 1986). It is easy to become overly dependent on the mass media and to forget about people as resources for environmental information.

Information spreads on the Internet by ways other than the conventional media or publication sources. Discussion groups, message boards and forums, Web pages, dedicated complaint sites, blogs, microblogs, content-sharing sites, aggregators, and social bookmarking and social networking sites are information sources that should not be overlooked. As noted in Chapter 2, online communication vehicles can be divided into traditional Web sites and social media. Social media has drawn the most interest recently because of its ability to spread information quickly (dna13, 2010).

Social media is easy to use, and I would bet you have already created some social media yourself. Using social media is simply the ability to post content (e.g., messages, videos, images) to the Internet that other people can access. All a person needs is Internet access and the ability to use a keyboard. Admittedly, most social media is of little interest to anyone. However, it is a potentially powerful form of word-of-mouth information distribution (Laczniak, DeCarlo, & Ramaswami, 2001). Word of mouth is recognized as serious force that can shape consumer decisions; hence, it should not be ignored (Blackshaw & Nazzaro, 2004). Consider how concerned organizational leadership can be with attack sites—Web sites designed to criticize an organization (Holtz, 1999). As noted in Chapter 3, tuning in to social media can be a very effective way to listen to stakeholders. Again, most social media is irrelevant to an organization, so crisis managers must carefully identify the social media most relevant to their concerns or hire firms such as Nielsen BuzzMetrics to collect social media data for them. Refer back to Chapter 3 for a more detailed discussion of the categories of social media to consider.

Consider the power of social media in this example. As of this writing, if you typed www.killercoke.org into your Web browser, you would arrive at the Killer Coke Web site. As the name implies, the site is hostile toward the Coca-Cola Company and supports the Campaign to Stop Killer Coke. So how is Coke a killer? The site maintains that security forces in Colombia have kidnapped, murdered, and tortured members of SINALTRAINAL (National Union of Food Industrial Workers) who work at Coca-Cola bottling plants. The claim is that these Coca-Cola plants hire violent, paramilitary security guards who commit these atrocities. The Coca-Cola Company disputes this claim. However, the Web site is composed of testimonials, photographs, and resources attacking the company. A key element of the campaign in the United States is to target college campuses. Students pressure their school's administration to terminate vending contracts with Coca-Cola. Michigan State University, Rutgers University, and Hofstra University are but a handful of the schools that have ended contracts with Coca-Cola. Killer Coke moved from the Internet to the business press when *BusinessWeek* did a feature on the campaign in January 2006 ("'Killer Coke' or innocent abroad?", 2006). The Killer Coke campaign continues to pressure Coca-Cola through lost contracts, and the Internet is the epicenter of this effort.

The Internet is more than a source of fear for an organization though. It is a resource that can be used to anticipate and respond to potential problems. An organization concerned with human rights, for example, can peruse a variety of human rights–oriented Web sites and blogs or follow human rights organizations on Twitter to get a feel for stakeholder sentiments and the development of human rights issues. These insights can guide actions designed to prevent possible crises.

The Internet is a source that organizations should not overlook. The Internet user population continues to grow, making it an increasingly important environmental information resource. The Internet serves as a dual information source: it can be used to access information also found in print or broadcast form, and it can be used to collect information unique to social media.

Risk management examines sources that have more of an internal focus. Total quality management systematically assesses the manufacturing process in order to improve quality. Part of that process is to locate sources of defects (Milas, 1996), which can trigger the need for recalls (Mitroff, 1994). Environmental crisis exposure includes pollution abatement actions and threats to the environment posed by an organization. Polluting can lead to accidents, lawsuits, protests, or regulatory fines. Legal compliance audits make sure that an organization is complying with all federal, state, and local laws and regulations. Failure to comply can result in lawsuits or fines. Financial audits review the financial health of the organization, which can indicate financially oriented crises such as shareholder rebellion.

Traditional insurance coverage indicates risks worth insuring against. Insurance risks include liability exposure, criminal exposure, and worker compensation exposure. All three areas can produce lawsuits and extremely negative publicity. Natural disaster exposure identifies what Mother Nature might do to the organization. An organization's managers must know if facilities are at risk of crises caused by floods, earthquakes, or volcanoes—natural actions typically not covered by insurance.

Safety, maintenance, and accident records reveal minor problems that could become crises. These records should be examined for patterns. Organizations have what are called near misses—something bad that almost happened. A series of near misses runs the risk of escalating into a major crisis. If there are a number of near misses, say, small hand injuries with a piece of equipment, it is possible that a major injury, such as amputation or death, could also occur. Action should be taken in the prevention phase to break the pattern of minor accidents. Similarly, a history of the same safety violation indicates that a major accident and injury could occur. Obviously, safety precautions are designed to prevent accidents and injuries. Unheeded, the workplace becomes unsafe and ripe for these troubling and preventable events (Komaki, Heinzmann & Lawson, 1980).

Employee use of the Internet and e-mail also are sources of risk. Misuse of these online communication tools can result in information leaks, computer viruses or worms, discrimination and harassment lawsuits, or reduced bandwidth capacity. Concerns over online risks have led most companies to create Internet and e-mail use policies and to utilize software designed to monitor employee online behavior. A 2006 study found that 38% of large companies in the United Kingdom and the United States hired people to read worker e-mails (Trotto, 2006). Online use policies lack any real meaning if the organization cannot effectively determine whether their policies are being violated. The monitoring software can block access to inappropriate Web sites, review all e-mails for inappropriate language, or record and evaluate all employee Web activity in terms of business-related and non-business-related site visits. Organizations assume unnecessary risk if they do not have and enforce employee Internet and e-mail use policies.

Product-tampering monitoring examines the manufacturing process and packaging for susceptibility to product tampering. Product tampering leads to recalls and lawsuits. Behavior profiling identifies the characteristics of potentially dangerous employees, typically those who may become violent. Violent employees can trigger workplace violence crises. Ethical climate surveys assess the organization for temptations and cultural blinders to problems. Such blinders are located by examining management attitudes and values about important concerns, such as sexual harassment. A weak ethical climate can encourage organizational misdeeds, such as check fraud, sexual harassment, or racial discrimination (Mitroff & McWinney, 1987; Soper, 1995).

Very few people have not heard of Enron and its fall from the list of most admired to most reviled corporations. At heart, the Enron tale is a story of an organization's culture precipitating a crisis. As Enron was winning honor after honor from the business press, its culture was characterized as aggressive. It was among the companies described as Most Admired, Best to Work For, and Most Innovative. However, an aggressive culture also made for a risk-taking culture. The company rapidly expanded into areas it knew little about. The expansion was required because Enron needed to keep its earnings high in order to maintain a strong stock price. Members of Congress referred to this as a "culture of greed" ("Lawmakers Blast Enron's 'Culture of Corporate Corruption,'" 2002).

Enron's risk taking had its downfall. Top management, led by Kenneth Lay, Jeffrey Skilling, and Andrew Fastow, had become arrogant and overly optimistic. They believed Enron could not fail, and its risk taking intensified. But Enron did begin to fail, and this meant revenues would drop. Being aggressive, top management engaged in very creative and illegal bookkeeping methods to hide losses and to feature gains. They crafted a fake financial front that cost investors billions of dollars when the company went bankrupt (Schuler, 2002). Enron's aggressive actions led it to ignore ethics in the pursuit of higher stock prices and profits (Brewer, Chandler, & Ferrell, 2006). It is safe to say that Enron was an ethically challenged organization; it had a morally bankrupt ethical climate. A similar fate can befall any company that fails to monitor and correct its own ethical climate and aspects of its culture that can promote rather than retard crises.

The sources for reputation monitoring are not well developed, but Table 4.1 identifies some logical choices, and they reflect the importance of stakeholders to reputation management, particularly the investor, customer, activist, and community stakeholders. Shareholder resolutions reflect the values and attitudes of those who own stocks. In 2006, Walmart investors rejected six different social responsibility shareholder resolutions, presumably because the resolutions did not reflect their priorities. Resolutions can reflect social concerns, such as

Table 4.1 Potential Crisis Sources to Monitor

Issues Management Sources		
TRADITIONAL		
News media: Newspapers, television news, news and business magazines Trade journals: Medical and science journals Newsletters: Government publications Public opinion polls: Public opinion experts Stakeholder actions		
ONLINE		
News and business wires Online newspapers, magazines, and trade publications Archives for professional associations, special interest groups, and government agencies Consumer-generated media: Web sites, blogs, and discussion groups Newsgroups		
Risk Assessment Sources		
Total quality management	Liability exposure	Natural disaster exposure
Environmental crisis exposure	Criminal exposure	Product tampering exposure
Legal compliance audits	Financial audits	Ethical climate surveys
Workers compensation	Safety, accident records	Behavioral profiling exposure
Internet use monitoring		
Reputation Sources		
Consumer-generated media: Web sites, blogs, and discussion groups Stakeholder comments sent to the organization		

support for the UN Global Compact (a set of 10 environmental and social principles), or financial concerns, such as resolutions preventing the "poison pill" as a takeover defense. Most resolutions are designed to address social concerns. Shareholder resolutions provide insight into how the stockholders feel about important issues or the organization itself. Stakeholder complaints and inquires help to detect discontent among customers and to discover rumors. Early identification of discontent means that the organization can act to resolve the problem and make a customer happy, maintaining a positive relationship with this stakeholder (Dozier, 1992). As the Pampers example in Chapter 2 illustrated, social media is ideal for finding and addressing stakeholder expectations that are relevant to reputations.

Profit-making organizations cannot survive without customers, which makes them a critical source for reputation signs. Organizations must identify when their actions place customers at risk and when customers are unhappy with organizational operations or policies. In October 1996, an *E. coli* outbreak linked to Odwalla juices killed 16-month-old Anna Gimmestad and sickened over 70 other people. Odwalla juice was not pasteurized at that time. Pasteurization kills bacteria, but natural juice makers felt it harmed the product. Odwalla began flash pasteurization after the incident. The company launched a quick recall and covered medical expenses for those who were stricken. In addition, Odwalla was one of the first companies to use the Internet as part of its crisis management. It has been praised for its quick and caring response (Baker, n.d.).

However, from a warning signs detection standpoint, Odwalla was a dismal failure. There were a number of warning signs prior to the October 1996 *E. coli* tragedy. Dave Stevenson, the head of Odwalla's quality assurance, had recommended using a chlorine rinse to increase the killing of bacteria. Senior executives rejected the idea and kept the far less effective acid-wash method. Even the supplier of the acid wash told Odwalla it was only 8% effective at killing *E. coli*. In the lawsuits that followed the outbreak, Odwalla admitted to more than 300 reports of bacterial poisoning prior to the 1996 event. Moreover, the U.S. Army had denied Odwalla access to military commissaries. Just four months before the outbreak, Army inspectors found an unacceptably high bacteria count in its sample and decided the risk was too high to sell in commissaries (Entine, 1998, 1999). Had Odwalla taken the warning signs seriously and either changed to the chlorine wash or switched to flash pasteurization, the 1996 outbreak would probably not have occurred.

One important source of concern is public criticism of the organization. Heath (1988) recommends that "all public criticism should prompt corporate leaders and operations managers to conduct studies to determine whether the charges are true and whether key publics are believing the allegations" (p. 105). Complaints can be found in inquires customers make to an organization or protests from activists. Inquiries may reveal an actual problem or a rumor, as people call to confirm the information they heard. Consider Nestlé's online confrontation with Greenpeace and others concerned about rainforests.

In the spring of 2010, Greenpeace began a campaign designed to force Nestlé to stop sourcing palm oil from Sinar Mas and other suppliers that illegally destroy rainforest as part of their efforts to extract palm oil. The campaign featured orangutans because rainforest destruction threatens their existence. There were protests in Europe, with people dressed as orangutans, but it was the Internet where the public complaints were there most active. People could visit the Greenpeace Web page titled *Ask Nestlé to Give Rainforests a Break,* a play on the commercial jingle for the company's Kit Kat candy bar. The site provided information and a parody video of a Kit Kat commercial in which the pieces of the candy bar were orangutan digits that dripped blood (Greenpeace, 2010). Even more impressive was the hijacking of Nestlé's Facebook page. Suddenly a little-noticed Facebook page was flooded with criticisms for the company's palm oil policies and killing of orangutans (Leonard, 2010). In March, Nestlé announced that by 2015 it would be using only certified-sustainable palm oil. But the public criticism continued and deemed Nestlé's action as too weak (Leonard, 2010). On May 17, 2010, Nestlé went further in response to its critics by announcing an alliance with The Forest Trust (TFT) to build responsible sourcing guidelines for palm oil and to help fight deforestation of the rainforests (*Nestlé Open Forum on Deforestation,* n.d.). Public pressure, amplified by social networking, created a crisis and forced Nestlé to change its palm oil policies.

Here's another example. Febreze is a fabric refresher manufactured by Procter & Gamble (P&G). One of its main selling points is its ability to eliminate pet odors. So when a rumor began circulating on the Internet that Febreze kills pets, there was reason for concern. Here is a sample message:

> There have been multiple instances of dogs and birds that have died or became very ill after being exposed to Febreze, a deodorizer/air freshener. Febreze contains zinc chloride, which is very dangerous for animals. Please do not use Febreze anywhere near your pets! If you have used it near your pets or on their bedding, clean the bedding area thoroughly to remove the Febreze, and move the animals away from the area. Please pass this information on to other pet owners/caretakers, before more animals are injured or killed, and find a safer method of odor control. (About.com, 2002, paras. 1–3)

P&G soon began receiving phone calls and e-mails asking if Febreze was safe around pets. The P&G response was "Yes!" The product had been tested and proved safe around dogs and cats. P&G created a special section of its Febreze Web site to debunk the myth. People were told of Febreze's safety and directed to testimonials from the National Animal Poison Control Center and the American Society for the Prevention of

Cruelty to Animals (*Hanging in the Febreze*, 2005). P&G used the consumer concerns to fight the rumor and protect the sale of Febreze.

■ COLLECT THE INFORMATION

Once potential environmental information sources are located, crisis managers face the challenge of gathering the information. Content analysis, interviews, surveys, focus groups, and informal contacts are among the most frequently used collection tools. Familiarity with these tools is an important crisis management asset.

When utilizing any print, online, or broadcast source, content analysis can be useful. It involves the systematic coding and classification of written materials, be they news stories, articles in other publications, or transcripts of focus groups or interviews. Effective content analysis requires the development of coding categories and expertise in using the categories. Coding categories are the boxes in which discrete pieces of information are placed. Each category needs a thorough written definition that indicates what is appropriate for it, and these categories must be mutually exclusive—no message should fit into more than one category (Stacks, 2002; T. D. Stewart, 2002). People who use the categories, the coders, must be trained in their use. Coders must be able to place similar messages in the same categories. This consistency is called *reliability*. Reliability allows different people to code messages consistently. Such consistency allows for comparisons of the coded data. Content analysis converts the written information into quantifiable data—the words become numbers that can be analyzed using statistics. Some examples may help to clarify the content analysis process.

Most organizations have established categories for accidents and safety violations. People are trained to understand the differences in the accident and safety categories so that they can accurately record these events. An organization can examine the data to see if certain accidents or safety violations have increased or decreased over time. For example, an organization might be interested in the number of falls in a particular area of the organization. Systematic coding of accidents permits an accurate analysis of the fall data. Similarly, organizations should develop categories for coding customer complaints. It is not enough to know the sheer number of complaints received; organizations should know the type and frequency of different varieties of complaints. By categorizing customer complaints, organizations can identify problem areas by the increase of complaints in those areas. If an airline receives increasing complaints about how canceled flights are handled, it needs to improve its customer service relative to canceled flights. Systematic coding allows for comparisons that could not be made if the written information had not been quantified. It is the recording and quantifying of the material that qualifies content analysis as a form of information collecting.

The first step in soliciting information from stakeholders is for the crisis team to construct a stakeholder map that lists all possible stakeholders (Grunig & Repper, 1992). Box 4.1 presents sample stakeholder maps that HP and Tesco use to guide their stakeholder engagement effort. Then the crisis team would identify the stakeholders

---

Box 4.1   Sample Stakeholder Maps

HP

Stakeholder engagement is integral to global citizenship, and HP works to build strong, mutually productive relationships with our diverse stakeholders. They include

- Communities
- Customers
- Employees
- Investors
- Legislators and regulators
- Industry analysts and media
- Nongovernmental organizations (NGOs)
- Suppliers
- Universities (Hewlett-Packard Development Company, 2010)

Tesco

- Customers
- Employees
- Investors
- Communities
- Suppliers
- Governments and regulators
- NGOs (Canadian Imperial Bank of Commerce, n.d.)

relevant to the most highly ranked crises. Interviews, surveys, focus groups, or key contacts can be used to collect information from stakeholders. Interviewers ask people questions about a particular subject in an organized fashion. The interviewers develop and follow an interview schedule. Preparation is essential. The person collecting the information must have an organized approach to the interview if it is to yield useful information (C. J. Stewart & Cash, 1997). Surveys collect information about people's perceptions, attitudes, and opinions. Surveys can be conducted by having people complete questionnaires or by having researchers ask stakeholders the questions. Focus groups are collections of specific stakeholders who are brought together to listen to and respond to questions as a group. Open-ended questions are used to encourage interaction and to probe the nature of people's beliefs. Key contacts are community, industry, or organization leaders who are selected because of their expertise on a subject. Using public opinion or issue experts is a form of key contact (Baskin & Aronoff, 1988).

■ ANALYZE THE INFORMATION

Collecting information about issues, risks, and stakeholder relationships is of no value unless the information is analyzed to determine whether it contains crisis risks. Analyzing information creates knowledge (Geraghty & Desouza, 2005). Crisis managers determine whether the information really does suggest a possible crisis. The premise behind finding warning signs early is to locate those that can significantly impact the organization and to take action to manage them (Dutton & Duncan, 1987; Gonzalez-Herrero & Pratt, 1996; Heath & Nelson, 1986). Analysis is the process of understanding if and how a warning sign might impact the organization (Heath & Nelson, 1986). Crisis managers need criteria for evaluating issues, risks, and reputation threats.

We can build threat assessment analysis around two factors: likelihood and impact. Likelihood is the probability that a threat will become a crisis. Impact is the effect the crisis can have on stakeholders and the organization. Typically, each threat is given a score from 1 to 10 for likelihood and threat, with 1 being *low* and 10, *high*. When crisis managers analyze the issue, risk, and reputation threats in terms of likelihood and impact, they can determine whether each threat warrants further attention and/or action. Likelihood and impact have slightly different means for the issues, risk, and reputation.

For issues, likelihood is the probability of an issue gaining momentum. An issue with momentum is developing and is more likely to affect the organization. Some indicators of momentum are sophisticated promotion of the issue, heavy mass media coverage, strong Internet presence, and a strong self-interest link between an issue and stakeholders. The 1989 anti-Alar campaign illustrates an issue with momentum. Alar is a chemical that was used to treat apples. Within a year of launching its campaign, the anti-Alar coalition headed by the Natural Resources Defense Council (NRDC) had caused Alar to be removed from use. The Alar issue had professionals crafting the publicity effort: sophisticated promotion. Celebrity appearances, including from Meryl Streep, helped to garner massive publicity: heavy media coverage. And Alar was treated as a threat to innocent children: a strong self-interest link between Alar and consumers (Center & Jackson, 1995).

Impact refers to how strongly the issue can affect either profits or operations. It involves the use of forecasting, which projects the potential effect of an issue on the organization. There are at least 150 forecasting techniques used in business. A detailed discussion of forecasting is beyond the scope of this book, but Coates, Coates, Jarratt, and Heinz (1986); Ewing (1979); and Heath (1997) offer more details on forecasting techniques. Organizations should use those forecasting methods with which they are familiar. Only issues with high impact would be considered crises because a crisis must be disruptive to or potentially disruptive to organizational operations.

For risks, likelihood is the probability that the risk can or will become an event—the risk will cause something to happen. This estimates the possibility of the risk being exploited or maturing into an event. Impact is, again, how much the event might impact the organization and its stakeholders. In this context, it includes disruption to organizational routines and potential damage to people, facilities, processes, or reputation (Levitt, 1997).

For reputation, the evaluation of likelihood and impact is not as clearly developed and a little more complex. Before evaluating likelihood and impact, crisis managers must determine if an expectation gap exists. As noted earlier, reputations are built around stakeholder expectations. Different stakeholder groups will have different expectations for organizational behaviors. For instance, investors want the organization to make money, employees want adequate pay and medical benefits, and community groups want the organization to be engaged in the life of the community. The point is that crisis managers must identify the expectations held by each major stakeholder group. Through research, they can isolate stakeholder expectations.

Once the expectations are known, crisis managers must determine whether the stakeholders perceive the organization as meeting those expectations: they search for gaps. Figure 4.1 illustrates two types of gaps. The first is based on performance; the organization is not doing what it needs to do to meet expectations. The second occurs when stakeholders fail to perceive that the organization is meeting expectations. Perception is the key. Even if an organization has made significant efforts to reduce pollution, if the stakeholders do not know about it, there is a gap.

If stakeholders have concerns based on expectation gaps, they can become a reputation threat by taking action against the organization and generating negative publicity. That threat is intensified by the various Internet communication channels (Conway, Ward, Lewis, & Bernhardt, 2007). Not all expectation gaps lead to crises. Moreover, no organization has the time, money, or personnel to address every

Figure 4.1   Expectation Gaps

Performance Gap: Organizational actions do not match stakeholder expectations.

Organizational Actions   Stakeholder Expectations

Perception Gap: Organizational actions do match stakeholder expectations, but stakeholders do not see the match.

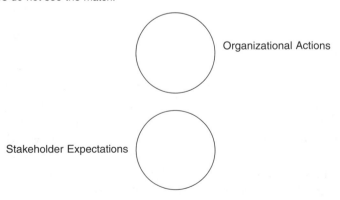

expectation gap. So what is an organization to do? The answer is to prioritize stakeholders and focus your resources on those that have the greatest potential to initiate crises. Crisis managers must be able to differentiate between mild and serious threats. The challenge is how to determine the likelihood and impact of an expectations gap. One option is to examine the salience of the stakeholder involved in the expectation gap. Stakeholders' salience, their importance to the organization, can then be converted into likelihood and impact scores. Stakeholder salience is a function of power, legitimacy, and willingness.

Power is the ability of the stakeholder to get the organization to do something it would not do otherwise. Power relates to the stakeholder's ability to disrupt organizational operations. Stakeholders who control essential resources or can form coalitions have strong power. Control over essential resources permits a stakeholder to disrupt organizational processes. For instance, employees can stop the production process or the delivery of goods and services. As mentioned earlier, in 1997, UPS drivers launched a strike that crippled the company's ability to deliver its primary service.

Coalition formation supplies power through numbers. As stakeholders join forces with one another, their power increases (R. K. Mitchell, Agle, & Wood, 1997; Rowley, 1997). An example would be an activist group that persuades shareholders and customers to join its efforts to pressure an organization for change. The combination of activists, customers, and shareholders was instrumental in convincing Levi Strauss to close its production facilities in Myanmar. Activists persuaded customers and shareholders that facilities in Myanmar contributed to human rights violations there. In turn, customers and shareholders questioned Levi Strauss's operations there. Levi Strauss felt that the stigma of human rights abuse was reason enough to leave Myanmar (Cooper, 1997). The Killer Coke campaign has followed a similar strategy. Alone, the activists would have little impact, but combined with shareholders and customers, they can exercise great power.

Stakeholder power is enhanced by the ability to take action against the organization. Stakeholders need resources (e.g., money) and skill in using communication channels if they are to put pressure on an organization (Ryan, 1991). Let us return to the NRDC's effort to ban Alar. The NRDC had money to hire professional communicators to develop a major publicity campaign promoting the danger of Alar. The campaign raised awareness of Alar danger from 0% to 95% in less than a month (Center & Jackson, 1995). Money and publicity skills created the perception of Alar as a cancer threat to children.

Legitimacy refers to actions that are considered desirable, proper, or appropriate according to some system. A stakeholder concern is more serious when it is deemed legitimate by other stakeholders. If other stakeholder see a concern as legitimate, they are likely to support the need to take action. Illegitimate issues are easy for other stakeholders to ignore because they are considered inappropriate or unimportant. Ignoring a legitimate concern makes the organization appear callous to the other stakeholders. They ask, "Why doesn't the organization address this reasonable concern?" Offending other stakeholders increases the risk of the threat spreading to additional organization–stakeholder relationships. Crisis managers should determine whether other stakeholders will view the concern as legitimate. This requires knowing the values and social responsibility expectations of various stakeholder groups (R. K. Mitchell et al., 1997).

Willingness refers to stakeholders' desire to confront the organization about the problem. A problem must be important for them, and their relationship to the organization must be relatively weak. Importance prompts stakeholders to take action. Why push a problem if it is unimportant? And stakeholders are less likely to pursue a problem when they have a favorable relationship with the organization. Once more, the Alar case illustrates the point. The NRDC considered Alar to be salient; it was the group's major concern at the time. The NRDC seemed to have no real relationship with the apple growers, the group affected most by the anti-Alar campaign. Documentation of the case makes no mention of the two sides ever meeting to discuss the concern prior to the launch of the NRDC's anti-Alar publicity campaign (Center & Jackson, 1995). A favorable relationship encourages both sides to seek a nonconfrontational approach to problem solving (Grunig & Repper, 1992).

Let us return to the Greenpeace–Nestlé palm oil case to illustrate power, legitimacy, and willingness. Greenpeace is an important activist organization that generated power by hijacking Nestlé's Facebook page and generating negative traditional media coverage and social media comments. Nestlé could not ignore the public relations pressure. Other stakeholders supported Greenpeace because the concern was legitimate. Most people feel we should protect the rainforests. Greenpeace's communication efforts showed that it was willing to exert pressure about the issue. Even after Nestlé made minimal effort to address the problem initially, Greenpeace kept the pressure on for two more months until there was significant movement on the deforestation concern.

Power, legitimacy, and willingness can be translated into impact and likelihood. High power and legitimacy indicate a strong impact. Stakeholders can disrupt the organization and are likely to be perceived by others as having a valid (legitimate) reason for doing so. Therefore, power and legitimacy can be used to establish an impact score. Legitimacy and willingness suggest a strong likelihood of occurrence. Willingness increases the chance of a stakeholder taking action, while legitimacy increases the possibility of other stakeholders supporting the action. Thus, legitimacy and willingness can be used to establish a likelihood score.

■ SUMMARY

By assessing the threat information, crisis managers create knowledge. That knowledge is an understanding of how important each threat might be to the organization. We can refine crisis threat assessment by creating a formula for calculating crisis threat values: Crisis Threat = Likelihood × Organizational Impact × Stakeholder Impact. For those who like abbreviations, we can write the formula as CT = L × OI × SI. Earlier in this chapter, issue and risk impacts were noted as involving both stakeholders and organizations. Crisis managers should think of both types of impact when assessing a crisis threat. A running theme in this book is the primary importance of stakeholder safety during a crisis. By incorporating stakeholder impact into crisis threat assessments, we further honor the commitment to stakeholder safety.

Combined, the first three steps in crisis prevention form the crisis-sensing mechanism, a systematic means of collecting crisis risk information built on three points: (1) locating the source of crisis risk information, (2) funneling the information to a central location, and (3) making sure the information is analyzed—converted into knowledge. Sources, collection tools, and evaluation criteria are the raw materials used to construct the crisis-sensing mechanism—the crisis radar and tracking system. No one crisis-sensing mechanism is right for all organizations. Each organization has quirks that must be accommodated, but some basic ideas can be offered.

The crisis-sensing mechanism can be viewed as knowledge management (KM). It finds and shares what is known by an organization or its external stakeholders. KM differentiates between *information* and *knowledge*. Information simply places facts in context, while knowledge analyzes the information so that it is usable by people in the organization (Halonen-Rollins & Halinen-Kaila, 2005; McKeen, Zack, & Singh, 2006). There is a close connection between KM and some aspects of crisis management; knowledge is essential to all phases of crisis management. In fact, "managing knowledge well is key to enhancing an organization's ability to deal with business crises" (Wang & Belardo, 2005, p. 7).

The crisis-sensing mechanism, a KM strategy, is a means of finding the knowledge an organization needs (Wang & Belardo, 2005). It attempts to create a repository of warning sign knowledge by locating, collating, and analyzing the crisis risk information or existing crisis knowledge.

Crisis sensing begins by determining what information-sensing mechanisms already exist in your organization. Avoid recreating the wheel. Review the issue management sources, risk sources, and reputation sources to see if they are comprehensive. Find out where your organization currently collects warning sign–related information or already processes it into knowledge. New procedures should be developed only if key sources are being overlooked. For instance, if no efforts are being made to scan relevant activist groups, add that as a source. A similar review should be undertaken for information-gathering techniques. Keep in mind that if you have the financial resources, you can hire vendors to help you scan, especially for issue and reputation information. Pay particular attention to how information and knowledge, such as publicity, are coded. A common weakness in information collection is a coding system that is too general and misses important details contained in the information (Denbow & Culbertson, 1985).

Consider this example that illustrates the importance of details. Let's say a retail store tracks its media coverage by collecting and analyzing news stories that mention the organization. A general coding system might simply count the total number of positive and negative comments about the retail store. The analysis provides a global evaluation of the reputation: is it favorable or unfavorable? No insight is provided into why the media image is favorable or unfavorable. A more specific coding system might include the following categories: sales staff, customer service, selection, merchandise quality, value and pricing, store appearance, and parking. The retail store would have separate evaluations for the seven categories. Store managers would know the exact areas where the store's reputation was strong and where it needed improvement.

Second, the organization must establish mechanisms and procedures for funneling relevant information and knowledge to the crisis manager or the crisis department. An organization should have at least one person who is dedicated full-time to crisis management (Coombs, 2006a). Crisis sensing is easier if there is an entire department, but many organizations are lucky to have one crisis manager. Crisis managers cannot process information they have not received nor attend to warning signs (knowledge) never encountered. Crisis managers must receive the scanning information and knowledge in a timely fashion and must carefully analyze the information for the warning signs. Various areas of the organization and possibly some vendors are likely to be responsible for different pieces of internal information and knowledge. Some organization units involved in scanning include operations and manufacturing, marketing and sales, finance, human resources, legal, customer communications and satisfaction, environmental and safety engineering, public relations and public affairs, engineering, shipping and distribution, security, and quality assurance.

The many organization units and vendors hired to scan must send this information and knowledge to the crisis team as soon as possible after they first receive and evaluate the information. The crisis manager becomes the center of a larger crisis-sensing mechanism. He or she must act as a functioning unit that is integrated within the flow of organizational activities, information, and knowledge exchange. Channeling information and knowledge sounds easier than it is. Consider that most organizations have difficulty collecting and analyzing information from customers (Halonen-Rollins & Halinen-Kaila, 2005). Now add information from a number of additional stakeholders, and your crisis-sensing mechanism becomes a real challenge.

Third, the crisis manager's assessment criteria for warning sign–related information must be carefully developed. This discussion provides general criteria for assessing issues, risks, and reputation threats. Crisis managers may wish to add their own organization-specific assessment criteria. The crisis team must determine which criteria they would like to use, develop additional criteria if need be, and determine precise definitions for the assessment criteria. Without precise definitions, the crisis manager is not able to apply the assessment criteria consistently. Last, the crisis-sensing mechanism must be tested to determine whether the various parts are integrated effectively. Running carefully selected and controlled information through the system is one way to assess the integration's effectiveness.

Walmart, for instance, has a crisis-sensing mechanism for staying ahead of crises. Jason Jackson, Walmart's director of emergency management, uses what he terms *watchdog positions*. The watchdogs monitor a variety of sources, including the Internet, news reports, and information from local stores, to identify possible disruptions to business. One source they monitor is weather, and Hurricane Katrina stands as testimony to the value of weather scanning. Before Katrina made landfall, Walmart had 45 trucks loaded with essential supplies ready for delivery. As Barbaro and Gillis (2005) commented at the time, "Wal-mart is being held up as a model for logistical efficiency and nimble disaster planning, which have allowed it to quickly deliver staples such as water, fuel and toilet paper to thousands of evacuees" (para. 4). When watchdogs find a threat, they relay that information to the emergency management team. The emergency management team evaluates the information and decides what action, if any, should be taken. Johnson conducts regular training and testing of Walmart's system (Rojas, 2006). The Walmart watchdogs concentrate on risk management and operational concerns, such as weather and security.

However, Walmart's crisis-sensing mechanism had not been tuned to issues management and reputation management. In 2005 and 2006, the company moved to improve both of these aspects through the hiring of external agencies and internal personnel. Walmart also launched its first-ever reputation advertising campaign during this period. This effort was designed to shore up the company's reputation with customers and employees (Hays, 2003). However, these issues management and reputation management efforts are not connected with the risk management efforts to build a comprehensive crisis-sensing mechanism. Walmart still has room to expand and to improve its crisis-sensing mechanism.

Crisis sensing can seem daunting, especially considering the need to scan so many sources. Organizations that can afford it can find assistance from monitoring services, which now cover traditional media and the Internet, including social media. Prominent monitoring services include BurrellesLuce, CyberAlert, and dna13. These companies aid in finding, retrieving, and even analyzing media, a large part of the external threat sources.

■ ACTION

Once threats have been evaluated, crisis managers determine whether to take action. Many threats are too minor and can be ignored. Crisis managers must determine what actions to take on the serious threats. One option is to monitor the threat if it does not pose an immediate danger. Monitoring involves following the development of the warning signs. The crisis team continuously collects and analyzes information about the warning signs, looking for changes that indicate whether the risk is becoming more or less likely to evolve into a crisis. The information sources, collection tools, and analytic criteria used in scanning are employed in monitoring. The key differences are a search for more detailed information and the continuous application of the search process in monitoring.

If a threat is serious enough, action is taken to diffuse it. Actions create changes that eliminate or reduce the likelihood of a warning sign becoming a crisis. Actions are taken to manage issues, to reduce risks, and to build or maintain reputations. A few examples will illustrate this point. Say that the issues management unit of a company learns of a proposal to tighten air quality standards. Action is taken to prevent or postpone the new regulation, thereby averting a possible plant closing while the plant implements ways to reduce emissions. Or a safety review finds that workers are not following the unloading directions for hazardous chemicals. A refresher training course is offered along with new, stricter safety procedures regulating the unloading of chemicals. The risk of a hazardous materials accident is reduced. And another: a number of complaints appear online about chain guards falling off a chain saw. Customers are offered replacements and design changes made to prevent the guards from falling off. Accidents and a major conflict with customers are averted, and the reputation is maintained. The exact nature of the action will depend upon the nature of the threat and best options for trying to reduce or eliminate that threat. Refer to Chapter 3 to review the principles that guide action in issues management, risk management, and reputation management.

■ EVALUATION

Evaluation monitors the threat to determine whether the action taken to address it had any effect. Without monitoring, the organization does not know if the change has been effective—has it reduced or eliminated the chance of a crisis? For example, an organization would want to know whether the new safety procedures and policies made the workplace less hazardous. The only way to know if safety has improved is to monitor workplace behaviors. If workers are now engaging in safer behavior— fewer violations of safety procedures—then the safety changes are working. Never assume any change is for the better. Some changes produce no results, while others may intensify the warning signs or risks, thereby moving an organization closer to a crisis. Monitoring involves a regular review of any changes designed to reduce warning signs. The review determines the effectiveness of the changes and whether any additional modifications are warranted (Pauchant & Mitroff, 1992).

To evaluate the results of issues management, the final resolution of the issue is examined. Evaluation consists of comparing the actual resolution of the issue to the intended or desired one. Success is measured by how closely the actual resolution matches the desired one

(Jones & Chase, 1979). In the earlier examples, the railroad and pharmaceutical issue managers were successful. The trucking legislation was defeated, and the government stopped pressing for direct-to-consumer regulation—the actual and intended resolutions were a match. Evaluation does not end with the issue's resolution. Issues are cyclical, and they have the potential to reappear. For example, the health care debate of the 1990s is much like the debate that took place in the 1940s and 1950s. During his first term, President Clinton introduced the idea of health insurance for all Americans. The government would help to insure Americans who were currently uninsured for various reasons. In the 1940s and 1950s, President Truman advocated national health insurance. His idea was to make health insurance a reality for all Americans through government assistance. The national health insurance issue may disappear for a while, but it never dies. In 2009, President Obama began a strong push for healthcare reform, and in March 2010, Congress passed healthcare reform. However, opponents vowed to make it an issue in future elections (Dunham, 2010). The cyclical nature of issues means an issue should be reexamined at least annually to see if it is gaining new momentum and might once again threaten the organization (Crable & Vibbert, 1985).

The evaluation of risk management—risk aversion, to be more specific—is an ongoing concern. Periodic reviews of the risk are conducted to determine the effectiveness of the risk aversion program (Pauchant & Mitroff, 1992). Evaluation compares the level of risk before and after the risk aversion program is implemented. The review is continued to determine whether the program works over time. Was the risk reduction a statistical aberration, or has the lower level of risk been maintained over the course of the program? The risk must be monitored continually to ensure that the threat does not reemerge.

For specific problems, stakeholders have stated what the concern is and have probably offered advice on how to solve the problem. If the organization decides to take action, management should ask the disgruntled stakeholders if the resolution was satisfactory. The feedback from stakeholders will serve as the measure of success.

Success in closing an expectation gap is determined by whether stakeholders perceive the organization as meeting expectations. The organization and stakeholders must cocreate meaning—they must share a similar interpretation of the organization's performance on the desired expectations—for expectation gaps to be closed (Botan & Taylor, 2004). The most effective way to determine whether an expectation gap has been closed is to use surveys to assess stakeholder perceptions of expectation performance before and after efforts are initiated to close the gap.

The survey provides the evaluative data necessary to determine whether stakeholder perceptions have changed. For example, one item can ask stakeholders to rate on a scale of 1 to 7 (7 being the highest), "Does the organization reflect your concern for the environment?" If the original evaluation was 2.5, a post–communication effort score of 4 would be considered a success, indicating that stakeholders see greater similarities between their concerns and the organization's behavior.

■ PARACRISIS

As noted in Chapter 2, crisis prevention raises the idea of paracrises, which occur when crisis managers must publicly manage a crisis threat. The effort to manage the crisis threat frequently mimics a crisis response. Paracrises are likely to occur for rumors, challenges, and product harm. These three are most likely to have stakeholders publicly question an organization's ability and warrant a public response to the crisis threat. The public connection is obvious for rumors and challenges, as illustrated in Chapter 2. A product harm case is instructive at this point. Maclaren makes baby strollers. Parents do love their babies and try to keep them from harm, so when reports began to emerge online that some children in the United States were having their fingers pinched, cut, or even amputated when parents were folding up the strollers, Maclaren issued a recall by sending out repair kits. The repair kit involved a safety guard that could be placed over the hinge. The online concerns created awareness of the product harm. In fact, when the threat is product harm, a paracrisis and a crisis fuse and illustrate how paracrises blur the distinction between precrisis and crisis communication. A few reports of injuries are a crisis threat, and crisis managers must decide when that threat is really a crisis and warrants corrective action. It should be noted that Maclaren said the injuries were from improper use of the stroller—children should not be so close when a parent is folding it. Moreover, the recall only pertained to the United States. The same product was sold and used in Europe, but the stroller threat was not deemed at the crisis level for Europe.

■ CONCLUSION

A crisis prevention program is a valuable part of the crisis management process. The crisis team uses the warning signs from signal detection to target situations that could become crises. The team then takes actions designed to eliminate or reduce the likelihood of the warning signs developing into crises.

But prevention is not as easy as it sounds. Finding potential crises is a type of warning environment, and a warning environment involves ambiguous information and penalties for incorrect actions. Possible crises can be hard to detect, and failure to do so can result in a crisis. Unfortunately, organizational politics can complicate or even block efforts to reduce risks. (Chapter 7 offers suggestions for combating resistance to preventative actions.)

Ideally, crisis teams must remember to monitor their corrective actions on a regular basis to determine whether preventative actions have produced the desired effects. However, an organization cannot count on avoiding all crises. Hence, the need remains for crisis preparation, which is the subject of Chapters 5 and 6.

DISCUSSION QUESTIONS

1. Locate and read information about fair-trade coffee. Do you think it is an idea that will gain additional support among coffee growers? Is Starbucks wise to increase its support for fair-trade coffee?

2. What barriers do you see to organizations taking preventative measures? How might they be overcome?

3. What are some organizational barriers to creating a crisis-sensing mechanism? How might you overcome those barriers?

4. How is social media changing crisis prevention?

5. What recommendations would you make to a small organization about how best to monitor the online environment?

6. Does it make sense to distinguish between traditional Web sites and social media, or should we treat all online communication channels the same?

7. Why is it useful to include impact evaluations for both stakeholders and organizations?

8. Do you agree or disagree with Maclaren's choice not to recall the strollers in Europe?

5

Crisis Preparation: Part I

D uring crisis preparation, organizations ready themselves for the inevitable crises that will befall them. Organizations should not fall victim to hubris and assume that their preventative measures will protect them from harm. All organizations should prepare to handle crises by addressing six concerns: (1) diagnosing vulnerabilities, (2) assessing crisis types, (3) selecting and training a crisis team, (4) selecting and training a spokesperson, (5) developing a crisis management plan (CMP), and (6) reviewing the crisis communication system. This chapter covers the first four points, and Chapter 6 is devoted to the CMP and the communication system.

■ DIAGNOSING VULNERABILITIES

As noted at the beginning of this book, an array of potential crises can happen to an organization. However, every organization has specific crisis vulnerabilities (Fink, 1986), which are a function of the organization's industry, size, location, operations, personnel, and risk factors. For example, a hotel must ensure the safety of hundreds of people who are in an unfamiliar building, and food producers run the risk of contamination that can poison their customers. Different types of organizations are prone to different types of crises. Location should not be overlooked, either. Location dictates which natural disasters are likely to strike. In addition, if your organization is near a facility that could have a serious crisis, such as a chemical leak, or be a strategic target for terrorists, that facility's crisis can become your crisis. Crisis managers must identify the crises for which their organizations and some neighbors are most vulnerable. Vulnerabilities affect the development of the CMP (Pauchant & Mitroff, 1992).

Vulnerabilities typically are assessed using a combination of likelihood of occurrence and severity of damage. Crisis managers start by listing all possible crises that could affect their organizations. The list of potential crises can result from brainstorming by the crisis management team or an assessment done by a consultant (Barton, 2001). Once a final list of potential crises is developed, each crisis should be assessed. A common approach is to rate each crisis from 1 to 10 for likelihood and impact (with 10 being the strongest score; Fink, 1986). Here is a quick review of the criteria we developed when evaluating crisis threats in Chapter 4. *Likelihood* represents the odds that the crisis might happen. *Impact* is the amount of damage a crisis can inflict on an organization. The crisis manager then multiplies the likelihood and impact ratings to establish a final crisis vulnerability score. The higher the score, the greater the potential damage (Barton, 2001; Fink, 1986). Crisis managers should focus their attention on crises that have the highest vulnerability scores. Summaries of the crisis assessments are often included in the CMP.

■ ASSESSING CRISIS TYPES

The list of potential crises for organizations is extremely long. It includes accidents, activist actions, boycotts, earthquakes, explosions, chemical leaks, rumors, deaths, fire, lawsuits, sexual harassment, product harm, strikes, terrorism, and whistle blowing, to name but a few. There is a point to the laundry list of crises—an organization faces different threats, not just one. Different crises can necessitate the use of different crisis team members, emphasize different stakeholders, and warrant different crisis response strategies. For instance, a product harm crisis is not the same as a rumor. A crisis involving product harm requires the organization to respond to those who were hurt, tell consumers how to return the product, and inform shareholders of the financial impact of the recall. A rumor requires a response designed to present the truth to consumers and to stop the source of the rumor.

While crises possess different characteristics, they tend to cluster into identifiable types (Coombs & Holladay, 2001). A variety of crisis typologies can be found in the crisis writings (e.g., Egelhoff & Sen, 1992; Lerbinger, 1997; Marcus & Goodman, 1991; Pearson & Mitroff, 1993). These typologies have been synthesized into one master list:

Natural disasters: When an organization is damaged as a result of the weather or "acts of God" such as earthquakes, tornadoes, floods, hurricanes, and bad storms

Workplace violence: When an employee or former employee commits violence against other employees on the organization's grounds

Rumors: When false or misleading information is purposefully circulated about an organization or its products in order to harm the organization

Malevolence: When some outside actor or opponent employs extreme tactics to attack the organization, such as product tampering, kidnapping, terrorism, or computer hacking

Challenges: When the organization is confronted by discontented stakeholders with claims that it is operating in an inappropriate manner

Technical-error accidents: When the technology utilized or supplied by the organization fails and causes an industrial accident

Technical-error product harm: When the technology utilized or supplied by the organization fails and results in a defect or potentially harmful product

Human-error accidents: When human error causes an accident

Human-error product harm: When human error results in a defect or potentially harmful product

Organizational misdeeds: When management takes actions it knows may place stakeholders at risk or knowingly violates the law

It would be impossible for an organization to prepare a CMP for every single crisis, but it can prepare CMPs for the major types it may face. Organizations should have crisis portfolios composed of CMPs for the primary types of crises they might face. Because of the similarities of the crises within each type, one CMP can be used to address any crisis within a particular crisis type (Pauchant & Mitroff, 1992). The crisis portfolio prepares an organization to cope with a wide array of crises.

The organizational vulnerabilities and crisis types can help crisis managers construct their crisis portfolios, addressing the specific crises that could affect the organization. Here is the way to proceed. First, organize the list of potential crises by type. Second, select at least one crisis from each type. Select those with the highest vulnerability rating.

The highest-rated crisis in each crisis type becomes part of the crisis portfolio. Third, develop variations of the CMP for each of the crises in the portfolio.

■ SELECTING AND TRAINING A CRISIS MANAGEMENT TEAM

The crisis management team (CMT) is a cross-functional group of people in the organization who have been designated to handle any crises and is a core element of crisis preparation. Oddly, the American Management Association (2003) found that only 56% of companies with CMPs had a dedicated crisis team. Typically the CMT is responsible for (a) creating the CMP, (b) enacting it, and (c) dealing with any problems not covered in it. The team crafts the CMP after thoroughly researching its organization's vulnerabilities. As just discussed, the CMP planning includes anticipating the most likely crises to befall an organization (Pauchant & Mitroff, 1992). To develop the crisis plan, the CMT needs information about different crisis types and all information about potential crises (scanning) and actions being taken to prevent crises (prevention). Any background information relevant to crises is helpful when the team is writing the CMP.

A second CMT responsibility is to enact the plan during simulated or real crises. CMPs must be tested to see whether they work by running the entire organization, certain departments, or just the crisis team through drills and simulations. The simulations help the CMT discover any holes in the CMP or weaknesses in the team (Pauchant & Mitroff, 1992; Regester, 1989). The CMT is responsible for implementing the CMP during real crises as well. We must remember that CMPs are contingency plans. This means that a CMT must be able to adapt to situational experiences and not just mindlessly follow a CMP (Fink, 1986; Littlejohn, 1983).

This brings us to the third major responsibility of the CMT: dealing with factors not covered in the CMP. It is impossible for a CMP to anticipate all possible contingencies in every crisis. During an actual crisis, the CMT must be able to provide counsel on, and resolve issues not dealt with in, the CMP (Barton, 2001; Regester, 1989). It falls to the CMT to make the necessary decisions when a crisis presents an unanticipated challenge. A CMP is an outline, not a road map, for how to manage a crisis. The CMT must fill in the details.

Development of an effective CMT is essential to the crisis management process. The best CMP is worthless if the team cannot fulfill its crisis duties (Wilson & Patterson, 1987). An effective CMT is developed through careful selection and training. Selection involves choosing the people best suited for the tasks, whereas training helps people improve their skills and become more proficient at performing tasks (Goldstein, 1993). Careful selection and training produce more effective workers; that is why organizations spend millions of dollars a year on each.

Functional Areas

CMT selection is not as simple as finding the people best qualified to work on the team. Selection is complicated by the need to have specific functional areas within the organization represented on the CMT. The dominant selection criterion in the crisis management writings is the functional approach. It posits that team members must represent specific functional divisions or positions within the organization, including legal, security, public relations or communications, operations or technical, safety, quality assurance, human resources, information technology, finance, government relations, marketing, and the CEO or representative (Barton, 2001; "Creating the Best," 2003). The logic behind the functional selection is that certain knowledge bases (e.g., operations, legal), skills (e.g., media relations, public relations), and organizational power sources (e.g., CEO) are required on a CMT. For instance, a crisis team often needs to integrate technical information about the organization's operations, assessment of legal concerns, and information collected by security when enacting a crisis plan. Furthermore, media relations skills are needed when addressing the press, and the CEO or a representative legitimizes the crisis team within the organization and empowers the team to take action. Human resources can address compensation issues for employees during a crisis, and financial can project the costs of the crisis.

The composition of the CMT should reflect the nature of the crisis. One example would be that a product harm crisis is unlikely to involve information technology, but a computer-hacking crisis would. The core members of the crisis team are typically operations or manufacturing, legal, public relations or communication, security, and CEO or representative. Keep in mind that a CMT may not be the best place for a CEO during a crisis. That is why a representative with authority is recommended. In some cases, the full-time dedicated crisis manager will have executive-level decision-making power.

Task Analysis

The key to selection and training is the identification of the characteristics (knowledge, skills, and traits) people need to perform their jobs (Goldstein, 1993). *Task analysis* is the technical term for identifying the key characteristics needed for job performance. A task analysis of crisis management should isolate the characteristics required by crisis team members. Once tasks are identified, the knowledge, skills, and traits needed to perform each task should be determined. Through interviews with crisis managers and an analysis of crisis management writings, four specific tasks have been isolated: (1) group decision making, (2) working as a team, (3) enacting the CMP, and (4) listening (Coombs & Chandler, 1996). Table 5.1 summarizes the task analysis.

Very little information exists about the characteristics of crisis team members. The discussions tend to be vague or limited. The personal characteristics mentioned in the literature include being a team player, having decision-making ability and listening skills, and being able to handle stress (Barton, 2001; Dilenschneider & Hyde, 1985; Littlejohn, 1983; T. H. Mitchell, 1986; Regester, 1989; Walsh, 1995). Unfortunately, little detail is provided about what actually constitutes these characteristics—the knowledge and skills needed to meet them. The following sections are dedicated to providing specific information about the tasks, knowledge, skills, and traits that make for an effective crisis team member. The tasks serve as the organizing point for the explanations.

Group Decision Making

Crisis management is a group decision-making process (Fink, 1986; O'Connor, 1985; Olaniran & Williams, 2001; Williams & Olaniran, 1994). Decision making involves selecting an option to meet the needs of the situation or reaching a judgment. The three primary responsibilities of the CMT all involve decision making. As previously mentioned, the team decides what goes into the CMP (Pauchant & Mitroff, 1992; Wilson & Patterson, 1987), when and how to enact it (Mitroff, Harrington, & Gai, 1996; Walsh, 1995), and how to extemporaneously handle those factors not covered in the plan. If crisis management is decision making, the knowledge, skills, and traits associated with group decision making should be essential to the effective performance of a crisis team.

Determining how to handle a crisis is an example of dynamic decision making and is characterized by time pressure, risk, and a changing situation. Researchers find that decision making in a crisis follows one of three styles: intuitive, rule based, or analytical.

Table 5.1   Crisis Team Task Analysis

Task Statement	Knowledge	Skills	Traits
Work as a team to facilitate the achievement of crisis team goals	1. Understand various styles of conflict resolution 2. Understand components of an ethical conflict resolution	1. Ability to use cooperation-based conflict management style 2. Ability to apply components of ethical conflict resolution	1. Cooperative predisposition
Apply the crisis management plan (CMP) to crises in order to facilitate an effective organizational response	1. Understand how to use the CMP 2. Understand specialized information of one's functional area 3. Understand mechanisms for coping with stress 4. Understand mechanisms for coping with ambiguity	1. Ability to follow directions given in the CMP 2. Ability to supply area-relevant information 3. Ability to use the mechanisms for coping with stress 4. Ability to use the mechanisms for coping with ambiguity	1. Stress tolerance 2. Ambiguity tolerance
Make the necessary group decisions to effectively solve the problems encountered by the crisis team	1. Understand the critical vigilant decision-making functions 2. Understand the value of argumentation 3. Understand how to structure arguments 4. Understand the value of group participation	1. Ability to apply the elements of critical vigilant decision making 2. Ability to create arguments 3. Ability to speak in groups	1. Argumentativeness 2. Willingness to speak in groups
Listen to others as a means of collecting information	1. Understand the steps to effective listening	1. Ability to use the steps to effective listening	

The intuitive method is derived from naturalistic decision making, how people use experience to make real-world decisions. Recognition-primed decision making is a form of intuitive decision making that has been applied to crisis management. The decision makers use their experience to recognize cues in crisis situations and to react. This is more than so-called gut instinct. The decision makers use their experience to gauge the situation and evaluate whether their past experiences are appropriate. The advantage of intuitive decision making is its speed and the limited negative effects of stress (Flin, 2006). It's safe to say that intuitive decision making seeks a viable solution rather than the most optimal one.

Rule-based decision making involves finding a rule that can be applied to events in the crisis. There is an assumption that a set of rules does exist. Government reporting requirements and actions are examples of existing rules that crisis managers can use. For instance, the government has a checklist for executing a product recall. However, most crisis situations cannot be managed with a list of rules. There simply are not enough rules to address all the possible factors a crisis team might encounter. Rules are useful for novices, but there is always the risk of applying the wrong rule. A rules approach would work well for deciding when to enact the CMP, however.

Analytical decision making is the type most commonly used in training. Decision makers are taught a process for making decisions. The focus is on identifying and evaluating options. Analytical decision making is thoughtful and requires time, and some feel it is ill suited to crisis decisions (Flin, 2006). However, the analytical approach is perfect for creating a CMP and has its place in crisis decisions, especially the decision about whether or when to enact the CMP. A well-trained crisis team can use processes like vigilance in a short period. The following discussion of vigilance is an analytical approach to decision making. An extended discussion of vigilance is offered because it is such a valuable tool for the crisis team.

Group decision-making research has consistently found vigilance to be valuable in making effective decisions and avoiding ineffective decisions (Hirokawa, 1985, 1988; Hirokawa & Rost, 1992). Vigilance is a form of critical thinking. Critical thinking can be defined as the "disciplined process of actively and skillfully conceptualizing, applying, analyzing, synthesizing, or evaluating information gathered from, or generated by, observation, experience, reflection, reasoning, or communication, as a guide to belief and action" (Paul & Nosich, n.d., para 5). Critical thinking involves learning and applying skills used to evaluate information. Vigilance applies critical thinking to group decision making by emphasizing the need for careful and thorough analysis of all information related to a decision (Hirokawa & Rost, 1992; Olaniran & Williams, 2001; Williams & Olaniran, 1994). Analysis is a process of dissecting a whole into its parts in order to examine something in more detail.

Hirokawa and Rost (1992) identified a specific set of four critical vigilant functions that aid the decision-making process: (1) conducting problem analysis, (2) evaluating alternative choices, (3) understanding the important positive aspects of an alternative choice, and (4) understanding the important negative aspects of an alternative choice. Each of these skills is a corrective for a factor that could contribute to faulty decision making. A decision is threatened when a group fails to a see a problematic situation or fails to identify its correct cause. The group must analyze and assess the problem thoroughly and systematically. The group must understand what it is supposed to accomplish.

A decision is also threatened if the group improperly evaluates the alternative choices for solving a problem. Three critical vigilant decision-making functions address the evaluation of alternative choices. The group identifies appropriate standards for evaluating alternative choices, and discusses and specifies criteria for evaluating the alternative choices. Then the group applies the criteria to consider the important positive aspects of each alternative choice, identifying and seeking clarification of these positive aspects. Finally, the group applies the criteria to understanding the important negative aspects of each alternative choice, identifying and seeking clarification of the negative aspects. Research in laboratories and in the field has found these three critical vigilance decision-making functions to be related to higher-quality decisions in groups (Hirokawa & Rost, 1992).

Vigilance is a composite of a variety of knowledge (K), skills (S), and traits (T). First, group members must know some process for evaluating situations (K) and be able to apply these processes (S) to their situations. Second, group members must know how to develop the criteria to evaluate decision alternatives (K) and be able apply these criteria (S). Third, group members must be able to argue for thoroughness of analysis and to present their views on the matters being discussed (S). Arguing, in this context, refers to giving reasons for and against a proposal, not fighting or having an emotional disagreement (Foundation for Critical Thinking, 2009). Group members must be motivated to use their skills if analysis is to be thorough (Hirokawa & Rost, 1992). This requires groups to continually argue for thoroughness. Group members must be willing to argue their positions (T), since group decisions become less effective when members do not voice concerns and allow one perspective to dominate the group's discussion (Hirokawa, 1985,

1988; Rancer, Baukus, & Infante, 1985). Group members are required to have the skills for argumentation and the disposition to argue (the argumentativeness trait).

Communication apprehension is the fear or anxiety some people feel in a communication setting. A team member with a high level of communication anxiety in a group setting is unlikely to fully contribute (Richmond & McCroskey, 1997) and will likely be silent and let others do the talking. As a result, communication apprehension can cause the team to lose the valuable knowledge that that team member was to bring to the team.

Working as a Team

Members of the crisis team must be able to work together as a group. They must be able to function in a cooperative manner in order to maximize the gains for themselves and others (T. D. Daniels, Spiker, & Papa 1997; Paton & Flin, 1999). Some people are naturally cooperative, while others are competitive (Baron, 1983). Part of working together is resolving the conflicts that inevitably occur within groups (Kreps, 1990; O'Connor, 1985). Conflict happens when people are interdependent with one another but have different goals, which may prevent team members from reaching their goals (L. L. Putnam & Poole, 1987). People in groups often disagree and can blame one another for the disagreements, but conflict can be beneficial to a group. Vigilance is fostered through conflict, including by arguing different perspectives. However, it is important to remember that cooperation is the key to conflict becoming productive rather than destructive (Kreps, 1990).

People seem to have preferred conflict styles, the typical modes they use to handle disputes (L. L. Putnam & Poole, 1987). There are systems for identifying conflict styles (Daniels et al., 1997; Kilmann & Thomas, 1975), and the key is to emphasize the use of cooperation-based conflict styles in crisis team deliberations.

Enacting the Crisis Management Plan

The crisis team must be able to enact the CMP. For this reason, groups train by reviewing and practicing the CMP. Creating the CMP should give the team members greater understanding of the plan (Barton, 2001; Wilson & Patterson, 1987). This is where each team member's functional organizational area becomes important. One reason to appoint a team member is his or her particular knowledge of a functional area that is important during a crisis (e.g., legal, media relations, investor relations). The knowledge and skills of these functional areas are important to executing the crisis plan effectively. Stress enters the crisis management equation most fully during the execution of the plan (Dilenschneider & Hyde, 1985; Shrivastava & Mitroff, 1987). When the crisis team faces deadline pressures and needs to deal with ambiguous information, the stress it experiences increases (O'Connor, 1985). Part of enacting the CMP is managing the concomitant stress and ambiguous information. Stress can hinder job performance (Baron, 1983), and ambiguity can create stress (Tsui, 1993).

Listening

Crisis team members frequently use the skill of listening. Collecting information when creating or enacting the CMP often means that team members must listen to others. Working together to make decisions requires listening to the others in the group. Obviously, listening is an important part of many tasks. However, many crisis managers feel that listening is important enough to be considered as a separate, distinct task.

Implications for Crisis Team Selection

As crisis expert Andy Podolak (2002) notes, "every crisis management program begins with a competent crisis management team" (para. 1). As mentioned earlier, team members must bring certain area-specific knowledge and skills to the crisis team, which will facilitate the execution of the crisis plan—the functional approach to selecting team members. However, as Shrivastava and Mitroff (1987) note, crisis team members also should have a set of general crisis management skills. The knowledge, skills, and traits in Table 5.1 represent a set of such general skills that are vital to the effective operation of a crisis team. The full range of knowledge, skills, and traits should be considered when identifying those people most likely to contribute positively to a crisis team. Assessment is vital in the screening of crisis team candidates. An organization may be in a position to choose among a number of people to represent a functional area. For instance, there might be a pool of five people from operations who possess the requisite skills and knowledge from their area. Only one person from operations is needed, and the organization wants the person best suited for work on a crisis team. The assessment instrument would indicate which of these potential candidates best matches the demands of being a crisis team member, particularly in terms of traits, because people can learn to cope with the limits of their traits but not to develop completely new ones.

It is possible to develop profiles of desirable and undesirable crisis team members from the traits shown in Table 5.1. A desirable member would be low in communication apprehension in groups, high in cooperation, high in ambiguity tolerance, moderate in argumentativeness, and well equipped to handle stress. The desirable profile would show that the crisis team member can work under stress, is not bothered by the ambiguity of a crisis, will work with the team to find the best solution, is willing to express opinions and ideas, and is willing to argue the merits and weaknesses of various solutions. An undesirable profile would describe a person high in communication apprehension in groups, high in competitiveness, low in ambiguity tolerance, high in verbal aggressiveness, and poorly equipped to handle stress. The undesirable team member functions poorly under stress, feels increased stress in ambiguous situations, works poorly in problem solving by fighting, and may be unwilling to contribute ideas and opinions. Combining the functional and task-based approaches results in being able to select the most competent crisis management team.

Applications for Training

Crisis experts frequently mention the need to train crisis teams (e.g., Augustine, 1995; Mitroff et al., 1996; Pauchant & Mitroff, 1992; Walsh, 1995; Williams & Olaniran, 1994). In any job, a person must possess the necessary knowledge and skills to perform effectively. Current training practices include a group review of the CMP and crisis drill (Wilsenbilt, 1989). Box 5.1, which is derived from the Federal Emergency Management Agency's (FEMA) recommendations for training, describes the basic forms of crisis exercises. The types of training are presented in a progression from simplest to most complex. Each requires additional preparation and places greater demands on the crisis team. Natural disasters, workplace violence, and accidents are the most likely crises for which a full-scale exercise is required. The other crises typically do not require going into the field or using equipment; thus, a functional exercise would be the most complex training. A crisis team needs to work its way up to functional and full-scale exercises through the orientation seminars, drills, and tabletops.

Discussions of crisis team training are dominated by proponents of practice based on running simulations of crises (Augustine, 1995;

| Box 5.1 | Training Options for Crisis Management |

Orientation Seminar: An overview of the crisis management process. The crisis team reviews roles, procedures, policies, and equipment.

Drill: A supervised exercise that tests one crisis management function, such as employee notification or evacuation.

Tabletop: A guided analysis of a crisis situation. A facilitator leads the team through a discussion of what they would do in a particular crisis situation. This exercise does not have the time pressures of a real crisis.

Functional Exercise: A simulated interactive exercise. This can be done in a large meeting room. It tests the complete crisis management system and unfolds in real time to create crisis pressures. The team will need to interact and coordinate with the groups it would encounter in a crisis, such as first responders. The team should conduct one functional exercise a year.

Full-Scale Exercise: The simulation of a real crisis as closely as possible. People are on-site and in the field. The actual equipment and people that would be used in a situation are deployed. There will be simulated injuries as well. Full-scale exercises are time-consuming and expensive, so they should only be done every few years.

Birch, 1994; T. H. Mitchell, 1986; Pauchant & Mitroff, 1992; Regester, 1989; Walsh, 1995). There is sound logic to this application; simulations enable the CMT to determine how well it can enact the CMP and how the plan might be improved. Part of group training is determining whether the team can accomplish group tasks (Goldstein, 1993). Crisis simulations emphasize group tasks, with their focus on enacting the CMP. Decision making is a critical group-level task that demands training attention. While managers know how to make decisions, the decision-making dynamic changes in a team, especially one that must make time-pressured decisions based on limited information. Training can improve the decision making of teams and of crisis teams. One promising training tool is thinkLet. It is a set of facilitation techniques that can aid decision making during a crisis. Some techniques are as basic as brainstorming options and using a straw poll to have group members evaluate options against a single criterion. Work on collaborative teams and crisis teams has shown that thinkLet can facilitate and improve team decisions (Kolfschoten

& Appelman, 2006; Kolfschoten, Briggs, de Vreede, Jacobs, & Appelman, 2006).

While useful, the group-level approach to training overlooks the need to train individuals in skills needed to complete CMT tasks. People need individual knowledge and skills to function as effective team members (Paton & Flin, 1999; Stohl & Coombs, 1988). Williams and Olaniran (1994) note that crisis team members must be trained in specific crisis duties, which include the individual-level knowledge and skills needed to be effective team members.

Individual-level assessment would be composed of the knowledge, skills, and traits listed in Table 5.1. The type of assessment of each team member indicates specific areas in which that person is strong or weak and identifies a person's specific training needs. Training should be specific; people should be trained only in those areas in which they are deficient. A crisis team assessment system not only determines a person's strengths and weaknesses but also evaluates a person's progress in acquiring knowledge and skills (Goldstein, 1993). The initial assessment is the benchmark or baseline against which subsequent assessments are compared. Specific training modules should be developed for each of the major knowledge and skills important to a crisis team. When needed, modules designed to help people cope with the limits of specific traits could be added, such as a module designed to develop listening skills.

A 2006 study found that 80% of crisis managers learned how to function in this role on the job. That means only 20% had any training in crisis management (*New Survey Finds Crisis Training*, 2006). A study of the *Fortune* 1,000 found that less than one-third of organizations with CMPs ever tested them (Levick, 2005). A study by the American Management Association (2003) found that only 50% of U.S. companies with CMPs have engaged in any type of crisis training in the past year. This suggests that even many organizations that have CMPs and CMTs are not truly prepared to face a crisis. How can an organization know whether its team members can perform or whether the CMP will work if the team has not trained using some form of crisis exercise? A crisis exercise seeks to simulate a crisis for educational purposes. Team members should know that the purpose is learning, not being critiqued, when they engage in exercises. It is important to create an atmosphere that is supportive rather than punitive in order to maximize the educational benefits of the crisis exercise.

It bears repeating: CMTs need training. Effective training requires the inclusion of both individual-level and group-level knowledge and skills. Crisis exercises are excellent ways to test group-level knowledge and skills. However, part of evaluating the crisis exercise should be dedicated to examining individual-level skills, a point that is missing in most current discussions of crisis team training. Remember, if a team does not exercise, an organization does not really have a dependable CMT or CMP.

Special Considerations

CMTs have two special considerations they may need to address: coordination with external agencies and the need for a virtual team. An organization may find that its crisis is part of a larger disaster, a large-scale event that may require government intervention and involve multiple organizations and agencies. Crises are smaller in scope and may involve just one organization. Disasters include acts of God and acts by humans, such as terrorism and major hazardous material releases. Hurricane Katrina taught organizations not to count on government agencies coming in to help them. However, CMTs may need to coordinate their efforts with firefighters, police, emergency medical teams, or the Red Cross. In disasters, agencies are supposed to follow the incident command system, more specifically, the national incident command system (NIMS; see Box 5.2). CMTs should consult the FEMA Web site, which contains the complete NIMS training module. While FEMA may be unreliable during some disasters, it offers very good online training. By being familiar with NIMS, CMT members will understand the basic language and chain of command needed to function within the NIMS environment.

Box 5.2   National Incident Management System (NIMS)

NIMS was developed by the Department of Homeland Security to allow for easier integration of agencies (public and private) that respond to disasters. The system provides a common set of incident command procedures, multi-agency coordination, standardized command and management structures, mutual aid, and public information procedures. The idea is that responders from different jurisdictions and disciplines can work together more effectively to respond to disasters, both natural and terrorist initiated. Government responders from federal, state, local, and tribal jurisdictions are required to take NIMS training, which is standardized as well. Nongovernment responders, such as corporations, are encouraged to understand NIMS. This is part of a larger effort to maximize the use of private resources during a disaster. NIMS did not seem to perform well during Hurricane Katrina, but it had not been in place for very long. Knowledge of the structure and terminology of NIMS would help crisis teams during disasters, as they would fall under the purview of NIMS at that point.

The second special consideration is the possibility of virtual teams. A virtual team does not meet in a designated crisis control center. Instead, members are assigned tasks, share information, and make decisions via the Internet and telephone with no face-to-face communication. The team uses mediated communication instead. Most virtual teams are really partially distributed teams (PDTs), which involve a mix of people, some in a shared location and some in remote locations. Some team members would be in the same room or area of the field and able to interact face to face while others would be in one or more different geographic locations and linked via mediated communication (Hiltz, 2006). Team members on the scene of a crisis have the ability to interact with team members in various geographic locations. A PDT may be needed if an organization has lost all possible crisis control center locations or needs to assemble a team that is geographically dispersed and travel time would be prohibitive for managing the crisis. Also, PDT members can begin managing a crisis as soon as they have been contacted. Any team member can begin to execute individual tasks as soon as she or he is notified. If a team has to wait until members arrive at the crisis command center to begin discussions, the team is losing time. In contrast, a PDT can be having team discussions as the members are traveling to their respective locations. However, a PDT increases the risk of problems for the team because any communication technology failure could doom the team. Still, it is worth considering the option of training for virtual teams or PDTs (*The Well-Provisioned War Room*, 2005).

■ SELECTING AND TRAINING A SPOKESPERSON

The spokesperson is the voice of the organization during the crisis. As such, the spokesperson is a very important and specialized function within the crisis management team. A poorly trained or unskilled spokesperson merely exacerbates the crisis situation (Donath, 1984; T. H. Mitchell, 1986). Again, selection and training require the identification of tasks and the knowledge, skills, and traits associated with those tasks. The discussion of the spokesperson begins with an analysis of the spokesperson's role and responsibilities during a crisis, which provide a foundation for locating the requisite knowledge, skills, and traits.

The Spokesperson's Role

The primary responsibility of the spokesperson is to manage the accuracy and consistency of the messages coming from the organization (Carney & Jorden, 1993; Seitel, 1983). Message management is not an

easy task and usually involves more than one person. Every organization should have multiple spokespersons. While this may seem to con-
tradict the view that the organization speaks with one voice, really it
does not. First, one person cannot be relied upon to be available all of
the time. An individual might be on vacation thousands of miles away
during a crisis and unable to reach the crisis control center in time.
What if the crisis drags on for days, requiring round-the-clock efforts
from the CMT? No one person can perform effectively for 24 to 48
hours straight. Eventually, lack of sleep will take its toll on job performance. Therefore, each organization should a have pool of spokespersons, all selected and trained in advance of a crisis.

Second, it is an overstatement to equate the idea of one voice with
one person. The concept of an organization speaking with one voice
merely implies that the organization presents a consistent message.
Working together, multiple spokespersons can share one voice.
However, the teamwork so vital to the CMT becomes a premium here.
The media want to question authoritative sources during a crisis. No
one person in an organization is an authority on every subject. As a
result, an organization may have a number of people available during
one press conference. Each question is then answered by the person
most qualified to address it (Lerbinger, 1997). The key is preparation of
all spokespersons, including the sharing of all relevant information
and the coordination of the questions and spokespersons.

Clearly, the spokesperson must be able to work with the media by
listening and responding to questions. Listening is essential because
spokespersons cannot give appropriate answers to questions if they do
not hear the question correctly (C. J. Stewart & Cash, 1997). Answering
questions demands the ability to think quickly. Press conferences are not
slow-moving events. The spokesperson must be able to answer questions rapidly. Compounding all of this is the fact that the spokesperson
is doing the job in a time of high stress—the organization is in crisis and
the media want answers immediately. A spokesperson must be able to
handle stress well and not let it interfere with handling media inquiries.
The spokesperson is a member of the crisis team, so all the knowledge,
skills, and traits in Table 5.1 still apply. However, the big difference
between spokespersons and other crisis team members stems from the
need to work with the media.

Crisis experts continually recommend that the spokesperson have
media training, which usually means practicing responding to media
questions: the spokesperson goes through rehearsals (Nicholas, 1995;
Sonnenfeld, 1994). Furthermore, there is a variety of laundry lists for
what spokespersons should and should not do (e.g., Katz, 1987;
Lukaszewski, 1987; Pines, 1985). A sample list of spokesperson dos and

don'ts includes being truthful, never saying "no comment," being concise and clear, never losing one's temper or arguing with journalists, correcting errors or misinformation in questions that are asked, looking pleasant on camera, and appearing in control and concerned. While such lists are helpful, they fail to provide a systematic means of either selecting or training spokespersons.

I have helped organizations train spokespersons and determine who should and should not speak to the media. Trust me, not everyone can be an effective spokesperson.

Media-Specific Tasks of the Spokesperson

From watching television, we all recognize that some people are well suited to media appearances and others are not. Some people look good on television, and others look like criminals (Nicholas, 1995). One task of the spokesperson is to be appealing to the viewers, but this does not mean that the person must be physically attractive. Rather, he or she must present material in an attractive fashion. Media training is often vague in explaining how to do this. Similar to the section on CMTs, Table 5.2 summarizes the primary tasks of spokespersons along with the salient knowledge, skills, and traits necessary to perform the pertinent tasks.

A mix of content and delivery concerns confronts any spokespersons giving public presentations. Content concerns emphasize the information being presented. Spokespersons must disseminate accurate information about the crisis situation (T. H. Mitchell, 1986; Trahan, 1993). Spokespersons must also have command over the crisis-related information if they are to convey this information to the media and other stakeholders. However, poor delivery skills can prevent a message from being received accurately (Holladay & Coombs, 1994; McCroskey, 1997). Spokespersons must be skilled at presenting messages to the target stakeholders, in this case the media. In the following, each of the four spokesperson tasks are explained, along with an analysis of the task's connection to content and delivery.

Appearing Pleasant on Camera

The importance of appearing pleasant on camera does not stem from a superficial observation that the spokesperson should look good. Instead, being pleasant on camera reflects a set of delivery skills that helps the spokesperson achieve a number of important crisis objectives. Previously it was noted that the crisis management team must show concern and control during a crisis. Part of the perception of concern

Table 5.2   Spokesperson Media Task Analysis

Task Statement	Knowledge	Skills	Traits
Appear pleasant on camera	1. Understand the value of proper delivery	1. Strong delivery	1. Low communication apprehension
Answer questions effectively	1. Understand the danger of long pauses 2. Understand the steps to effective listening 3. Appreciate the danger of "no comment" statements 4. Understand the danger of arguing with reporters	1. Ability to think quickly 2. Ability to use the steps to effective listening 3. Ability to use phrases other then "no comment" when an answer is not currently known 4. Ability to stay calm under pressure	1. High stress tolerance 2. Low verbal aggressiveness
Present crisis information clearly	1. Appreciate the problems with jargon 2. Understand the need to structure responses	1. Ability to avoid the use of jargon 2. Ability to organize responses	
Handle difficult questions	1. Understand the characteristics of tough questions	1. Ability to identify tough questions 2. Ability to ask for questions to be reworded 3. Ability to preface tough questions in a tactful manner 4. Ability to challenge incorrect information in a question 5. Ability to explain why an answer cannot be answered 6. Ability to evaluate the appropriateness of multiple-choice responses in a question 7. Ability to respond to questions with multiple parts	1. Low argumentativeness

and control is developed through the way a spokesperson presents the crisis-related information. One way to better understand delivery is to consider it as part of communicator style, the way a person communicates; it reflects the way something is communicated (Norton, 1983). Communicator style also influences how the content of the message is interpreted. Style provides a frame for how people should view the content of a message (Holladay & Coombs, 1994).

Spokespersons should maximize the style elements that cultivate the perceptions of control and compassion. Compassion is developed through the attentive and friendly style elements. Attentive styles reflect empathy and listening. Being friendly suggests that a person is confirming and giving positive recognition to others (Norton, 1983). The attentive and friendly style elements help to cultivate the perception that the spokesperson is compassionate because compassionate people are empathetic and confirming. The dominant style elements mean a person is behaving in a confident and businesslike manner (Norton, 1983). The dominant style facilitates the perception that the spokesperson is in control of the situation.

Maximizing these three style elements requires attention to specific delivery factors. Spokespersons must learn to maintain consistent eye contact with the audience (looking at the audience or camera at least 60% of the time), use hand gestures to emphasize points, vary their voices to avoid a monotone delivery, be sure to change facial expressions to avoid being blank-faced, and avoid too many verbal disfluencies, such as *uh*, *er*, and *um*. Spokespersons should be trained to maximize these five delivery variables when they present material to the media and other stakeholders. Research indicates that these variables promote the perception of dominance, attentiveness, and friendliness as well as increase credibility (Burgoon, Birk, & Pfau, 1990; Holladay & Coombs, 1994). It is logical to conclude that spokespersons will be perceived more positively by stakeholders when maximizing these five delivery factors.

There is a flipside to delivery as well. Poor delivery leads to negative perceptions of the spokesperson. Poor delivery skills are often interpreted as signs of deception (de Turck & Miller, 1985; Feeley & de Turck, 1995). People doubt the believability of a message when these delivery factors are present: (a) weak eye contact, looking at people infrequently; (b) frequent disfluencies; (c) the use of abnormal hand or arm movements associated with fidgeting; and (d) overuse of hand gestures (de Turck & Miller, 1985; Feeley & de Turck, 1995). These are among the clues people look for when trying to detect deception.

Although delivery has always been an important part of the presentation of a public message (Heinberg, 1963; McCroskey, 1997), content can never be forgotten because good delivery does not make up for lack of content. Good delivery enhances the reception of a message; poor delivery detracts from it. Spokespersons should be trained to maximize the delivery factors that promote control and compassion while minimizing those that contribute to perceptions of deception. All of the delivery factors mentioned thus far can be taught. However, it helps if people do not exhibit the communication apprehension trait when speaking in public. While communication apprehension can be overcome, spokespersons who are not communication apprehensive start out at a higher delivery proficiency level. Media training for spokespersons should include efforts to make them aware of their delivery habits and to polish their delivery skills. Having trainees watch videos of their press conferences is an excellent method for improving delivery skills.

Answering Questions Effectively

Answering questions effectively means providing responses to the questions that are asked. Preparation is essential to effective answers. Spokespersons must know or be able to quickly retrieve the crisis information that has been collected to that point. Another part is listening to hear the question. Spokespersons should not answer the questions they wanted to be asked; they must hear and respond to the very questions asked by reporters. Remember, spokespersons can give introductory remarks or a short briefing before fielding questions. They can use that time to deliver the core crisis message from the organization.

Sometimes the spokesperson does not know the answer. The correct response is to admit what you do not know but promise to deliver the information as soon as you get it (Stewart & Cash, 1997). Remember the rule to never say "no comment." That phrase triggers two negative events. First, 65% of stakeholders who hear or see "no comment" equate it with an admission of guilt ("In a Crisis," 1993). As David Pendery, senior manager of public relations for Quiznos, said, "Anytime you decline to comment on a known crisis you'll appear naïve at best, incompetent at worst" (quoted in Hall, 2006, para. 3). Second, "no comment" is a form of silence, which is a very passive response. As Richard Levick (2005), of Levick Strategic Communications, noted, "There are two sides to every story, and when you say 'no comment' the media gets the entire story and you don't get your side of the story" (para. 14). In a crisis, being passive means that other actors in the crisis event get to speak and to interpret the crisis for your stakeholders (Hearit, 1994). The organization is allowing others who may be ill informed, be misinformed, or hold a grudge against the organization to define the crisis for stakeholders. An interpretation based on the wrong information or information supplied by an enemy can only hurt an organization's reputation.

A spokesperson also must be cordial and not argue with reporters (Mackinnon, 1996; Nicholas, 1995). Being cordial brings us back to the personality traits of a good crisis team member. A spokesperson should not be high in verbal aggressiveness or argumentativeness. Either trait can lead to a dispute with reporters. This does not mean that a spokesperson lets incorrect statements stand. Instead, she or he corrects any errors or misinformation before answering a question but should not debate the error or misinformation (Mackinnon, 1996). Handling stress is a part of answering questions, too. An inability to handle stress reduces a spokesperson's ability to answer questions effectively because too much stress erodes task performance in general. Stress is high during media encounters due to the time pressure, the need to answer multiple questions from a variety of reporters (Balik, 1995), and the awareness of the huge number of possible hearers or readers. Participation in a mock crisis press conference is the best way to get a feel for the challenges a spokesperson faces.

Presenting Crisis Information Clearly

Presenting information clearly focuses on the content of the response. As such, it is related to answering questions effectively but has a narrower focus: ensuring that the stakeholders are able to understand what is said. The spokesperson's answers must be clear and concise. *Clear* means the answer is free of organizational jargon and overly technical terms and details (Mackinnon, 1996). Jargon is meaningless to those outside of the circle using it (Nicholas, 1995); as a result, it only clouds an answer. Overly technical information produces the same hazy reception of the message. In addition, "technobabble" makes people think the organization is using jargon to avoid telling the truth. It is best to use only the necessary technical information and explain it in such a way that nontechnical people can understand it. PepsiCo's handling of its 1993 syringe scare exemplifies how to translate technical information. In June 1993, reports began to surface that syringes were being found in cans of Diet Pepsi. PepsiCo chose to focus on how it would be virtually impossible for a syringe to get into the can during

bottling. The company reduced its bottling process to easily under-
standable terms for the news media and its consumers. PepsiCo
believed and later proved the syringe scare was a hoax (Magiera, 1993;
Mohr, 1994; Weinstein, 1993; Zinn & Regan, 1993). Clarity is aided by
careful organization of a response (Stewart & Cash, 1997). An organized answer is easier to understand than a rambling one. Box 5.3 provides a short case of an organization that had difficultly presenting
information clearly.

Box 5.3   Merck's Technical Response

VIOXX is an anti-inflammatory drug used to treat arthritis and acute
pain. On September 30, 2004, Merck, the maker of VIOXX, recalled
the product from the market. Merck made the voluntary recall when
one of its clinical studies showed a connection between VIOXX and
cardiovascular events, such as heart attacks and strokes. A clinical
study uses careful control and treatment conditions to prove a
cause-and-effect relationship between two things. This particular
clinical study was designed to test the ability of VIOXX to help treat
colorectal adenomas. In this case, VIOXX seemed to cause cardiovascular events.

Shortly after the recall, many in the medical community claimed
Merck had known of the potential connection between VIOXX and
cardiovascular events for years. A study published in the *Journal of
the American Medical Association* (Mukherjee, Nissen, & Topol, 2001)
indicates that there was a connection. Now consumers have to wonder, "Should Merck have recalled VIOXX sooner?" Merck's answer
was no. The company explained that the published study was based
on a meta-analysis, which looks at a variety of studies for trends.
Meta-analyses do not have the strict control and treatment conditions found in a clinical study. From a research methods perspective,
other factors could have been responsible for the link between
VIOXX and cardiovascular events found in the study published by
the *Journal of the American Medical Association*. Merck said it acted
when it had clear cause–effect proof from a clinical study. Much of
the research methods jargon and details had been trimmed from
this description, but even this reduced version was highly technical.
Probably few of Merck's consumers had the depth of knowledge
needed to appreciate its argument.

Handling Difficult Questions

During a press conference, not all questions are of equal caliber. Watching any press conference on television makes apparent the frequent exceedingly long and complicated questions, questions that are multiple questions (asking for several pieces of information), tricky or tough questions, questions that are based on erroneous information, and multiple-choice questions with unacceptable choice options. These five examples, each of which has identifiable features, represent the difficult questions faced by a spokesperson. The spokesperson must learn to recognize difficult questions and to respond appropriately. Recognition involves practicing listening to questions delivered in the press conference format.

Recognition is easier than providing responses to tough questions. Still, there are response strategies for each of the five tough questions. For long, complicated questions, ask for the question to be repeated, rephrased, or explained. These strategies give the media representative a chance to improve the question's wording and clarity while providing the spokesperson with more time to construct a response. Multiple questions in one question can be handled in one of two ways. First, the spokesperson can choose which part of the question to respond to, selecting the part of the question that fits best with providing the organization's desired message. Second, the spokesperson can address all parts of the question. When responding to all or multiple parts of a question, the spokesperson should number each part and the answer to each part. The additional structure helps to clarify the answer for other audience members.

Questions that are tricky or tough need a tactful preface to the answer. The spokesperson must convey to the audience that the question is tough or tricky and that a longer-than-usual answer is needed to address the question. It may also be the case that the tricky or tough question cannot be answered, and the spokesperson must explain why (Stewart & Cash, 1997). A question based upon erroneous information must be challenged and corrected (Nicholas, 1995). The spokesperson must make sure that misinformation is removed from the crisis information being presented at the press conference. For multiple-choice questions, the spokesperson must determine whether the response options are fair (Stewart & Cash, 1997). Why should a spokesperson choose a response when the two options might have the organization categorized as being heartless or stupid? The spokesperson should explain that the options are unreasonable or inappropriate and develop an option that fits with the appropriate answer to the question.

Training helps a spokesperson identify and develop effective responses to difficult questions.

University Application: Possible Crises

As a student, you are part of your university's organization. A crisis on campus could affect you. One way to begin applying many of the concepts in this book is to use them to examine your university from a crisis perspective. Either as a group or individually, list the possible crises that could hit your campus. Consider the wide range of personnel, geographic, and operations risks. Your list will probably be longer than you first thought it would be.

Internet Considerations for Spokespersons

Social media has added a new wrinkle for the spokesperson: starring in your own videos. There seem to be plenty of corporate leaders appearing in YouTube videos to offer apologies to their stakeholders. Here are six examples: (1) Domino's CEO Patrick Doyle for the product-tampering video, (2) JetBlue CEO David Neeleman for trapping passengers in planes for up to 14 hours, (3) KFC President Roger Eaton for the Oprah grilled-chicken giveaway fiasco, (4) Mattel CEO Bob Eckert for three toy recalls in four weeks, (5) Maple Leaf Foods President/CEO Michael McCain for a *Listeria* outbreak, and (6) United Airlines CEO Jim Goodwin for stranding passengers. The need to appear pleasant on camera is magnified in social media. Stakeholders can replay the corporate message and post their comments and critiques. While Patrick Doyle and Domino's were praised for his YouTube apology, many of the YouTube comments were not favorable. Here is a sampling of the critiques:

- He isn't looking at the camera because he might burst into a laughter. I'm sure he doesn't believe his own words. As we speak, we don't know how many other sandwiches are in the process of being molested.

- Cmon the least the CEO can do is look at the camera direct and be more presentable (open collard shirt?). Where is the PR at? You guys are not on your job.

- Why Read Teleprompter SPEAK FROM THE HEART!

- Urgency with sincerity is key, not disingenuous crisis mode by reading teleprompters then publishing written statements . . . "we have no evidence the food was served . . . ."

- Should have looked into the camera or hired a proper teleprompter.

No corporate response video should go out if it does not appear genuine and sincere. Again, eye contact and other delivery factors that combat perceptions of deception are the keys. As any media trainer will tell you, not all managers are meant to be in video and effective videos take practice and, when it is your video, multiple takes.

■ CONCLUSION

The preparation phase of crisis management anticipates the occurrence of crises. The organization musters the resources necessary to effectively manage the crises that may befall it. Diagnosing vulnerabilities assesses the likelihood and impact of potential organizational crises, and crisis types are groupings of similar crises. An organization cannot prepare for all crises but can prepare for the major crisis types. The diagnosis of vulnerabilities and the information about crisis types are used to construct the crisis portfolio, the individual crisis plans for each of the major crisis types.

The crisis team is responsible for managing the actual crisis. Therefore, it is essential to carefully select and fully train each crisis team member. The spokesperson is a specialized role within the crisis management process and provides a vital link to stakeholders. Spokespersons also must be carefully selected and thoroughly trained. Failure to select and train crisis team members and spokespersons methodically is a recipe for disastrous crisis management. In addition, a crisis team is lost without a crisis management plan. Chapter 6 concludes our discussion of crisis preparation by focusing on the plan and the crisis control center.

DISCUSSION QUESTIONS

1. What other types of crises would you add to the list presented in this chapter?

2. In June 2005, a four-year-old boy died after riding Mission Space at Epcot Center in Disney World. Who at Disney would the news media want at a press conference? Would the CEO be a good choice? Why or why not?

3. What barriers are there to getting an accurate diagnosis of an organization's vulnerabilities? What can be done to overcome those barriers?

4. As a group, select a particular company and create a potential list of vulnerabilities it might face. Then try to assign values to each of those threats.

5. Do you agree or disagree that the delivery factors are useful in creating effective online videos during a crisis?

6. What would your strengths and weaknesses be as a crisis team member?

7. What would your strengths and weaknesses be as a crisis spokesperson?

8. What types of training do you think would be most useful for crisis teams? Why?

6

Crisis Preparation: Part II

I f an organization has done any crisis preparation, it is usually the drafting of the crisis management plan (CMP). While important, a CMP is not a magic insurance policy that protects an organization from a crisis. Nor is it a step-by-step set of instructions for what to do when a crisis hits. Laboring under either of these two assumptions will result in a rude awakening when a crisis does hit. An organization having a CMP it has never tested is no better off than an organization with no CMP. Both will stumble and lose precious time as the crisis management clock starts to tick. This chapter examines functional CMPs and the related crisis communication system that is necessary to navigate the waves of a crisis.

■ DEVELOPING A CRISIS MANAGEMENT PLAN

The core sermon preached by crisis converts is the need for a detailed, usable CMP. It must contain the information needed to manage a crisis but should not be overly long and cumbersome. Long CMPs look nice on shelves as they collect dust but are not practical when a crisis hits (Barton, 2001; Coombs, 2006a).

Value

As mentioned previously, crises are time-pressured events during which quick responses are essential. During a crisis, time should not be wasted finding needed background information, deciding who will do what, and trying to determine the sequence of events (Barton, 2001). A CMP helps to reduce response time by gathering these elements together beforehand. In addition to speed, the CMP helps create an organized and efficient response. With some framework in place, the chaos surrounding a crisis is reduced and the event is less stressful (Corporate Leadership Council, 2003). A CMP creates a system that can save lives, reduce an organization's exposure to risks, and permit remedial actions without embarrassment and scrutiny (Barton, 1995).

Many large organizations have recognized the need for CMPs (Barton, 2001; Lerbinger, 1997). Still, in 2005 only 60% of major companies had them, up from 53% in 1984 (American Management Association, 2003). The numbers indicate that the message is still not being heard by all organizations. Sometimes it takes a crisis to reinforce the need for a CMP. The phrase *better late than never* comes to mind. In reality, all organizations should have CMPs because all organizations are at risk of a crisis, no matter how careful they are about their policies and operations.

Components

For CMPs, bigger is not always better. A CMP must be manageable, not filling a large binder and difficult to use. The most desirable CMP is a short document that is user-friendly. CMPs can be placed in an easy-to-use flipchart format, bound at the top, and with each section having a different tab for easy identification. Additional options include keeping copies of the CMP on CDs, flash drives, or secure intranet sites. Whatever the format, the CMP should be considered flexible and usable (Coombs, 2006a).

The CMP is, at its roots, a communication document and involves identifying who to contact and how. Contact information is provided for team members and additional experts that might be useful to the team. In fact, some crisis experts refer to the CMP as the *crisis communication plan* (e.g., Barry, 1984; Fearn-Banks, 2001). A crisis communication plan is a major part of the larger CMP. A CMP also includes methods and means for documenting what is said and done during a crisis. It can include reminders, in checklist form, of key actions that typically are taken during a crisis. However, it is important not to rely on a checklist for things that must be done. Each crisis is unique, and the CMP is a reference tool, not a step-by-step formula.

Following are the main components typically included in a CMP:

1. *Cover Page.* This page identifies the document as the CMP, notes that the document is confidential, provides the most recent revision date,

and records the number of copies. The confidentiality statement reminds employees that the CMP should not be copied or shown to people outside the organization. Recording the number of copies is used to control how many are in circulation. The revision date allows for a quick check to determine how up-to-date the CMP is.

2. *Introduction.* This is a message typically written by the CEO. It is used to highlight the importance of the CMP and to persuade employees to take it seriously.

3. *Acknowledgment Form.* This form is a removable page that employees sign and return to human resources, where it is placed in their personnel files. It is a signed affidavit saying that each employee has read and understands the CMP. Having the signed documents in their personnel files encourages employees to take the CMP very seriously.

4. *Rehearsal Dates Page.* This page records when the plan has been practiced and is another check on how up-to-date the plan and the crisis team are. Each person holding a copy of the CMP is responsible for keeping this page current.

5. *First-Action Page.* This section lists the incident commanders, how to reach them, how to activate the CMP (who should place the calls), and when it should be activated (when a situation is defined as a crisis). This section is the means of starting the crisis management process.

6. *Crisis Management Team Contact Sheet.* The contact sheet lists the names and contact information of all the members of the team, their areas of expertise, any outside consultants that may be needed, and any outside agents that may need to be contacted, such as insurance or emergency personnel. The Crisis Management Team (CMT) Contact Sheet section indicates who to contact, tells why they are relevant to a crisis, and provides a variety of means for contacting each person. This document is sometimes called the crisis directory. It provides an easy-to-use system for identifying and reaching members of the crisis team.

7. *Crisis Risk Assessment Section.* Every organization should anticipate what crises it may face. The Crisis Risk Assessment identifies possible crises and evaluates the risk of each in terms of likelihood and impact. (Likelihood is the probability of the crisis occurring, while impact is the amount of damage [financial, structural, environmental, reputational, or human] the crisis could inflict on the organization.) The assessment overviews the variety of crises an organization may

most likely face, but it is not an exhaustive analysis of all possibilities. (Crisis assessment was detailed in Chapter 5.)

8. *Incident Report Sheets.* Crisis teams must keep accurate records of what has been done during a crisis. The Incident Report Sheets are tools used to record this vital documentation. Crisis teams need this information when evaluating their crisis management efforts, and the organization needs this information when handling lawsuits or government investigations triggered by the crisis. The documentation centers on identifying when the incident was first apparent, where the crisis occurred, when various people and organizations were contacted about the crisis, and what actions were taken by whom and with what result.

9. *Proprietary Information Section.* While crisis managers often preach full disclosure of information, there are some policies and factual information that organizations should not reveal. The Proprietary Information Section reminds managers that certain information is confidential and cannot be released to stakeholders without CEO authorization or review by legal council (Tyler, 1997). For example, an organization should never give away trade secrets that provide its competitive edge in the marketplace without an extremely compelling reason (Barton, 2001). On a related note, an organization should never release the names of victims until family members have been notified.

10. *Crisis Management Team Communication Strategy Worksheet.* Crisis managers must remember that communication is strategic—it serves a distinct purpose. This worksheet reminds CMT members what it means to be strategic and to document crisis actions. Crisis managers are prompted to consider who they are talking to (the exact stakeholder), to record the specific audience, to record the specific goal, to consider what they are trying to achieve with this communication goal, and to attach a copy of the actual message that was sent to the audience (Barton, 2001). Crisis managers can add other pertinent reminders that are specific to their organizations. For example, reminders about the use of specific technical terms can be added. A sample technical term reminder might describe the difference between *venting* and *releasing*. Each organization should develop its own set of additional reminders.

11. *Secondary Contact Sheet.* Stakeholders others than those listed on the CMT Contact Sheet may need to be contacted during a crisis. These

people may have information the organization needs or may need to be notified about the crisis. The Secondary Contact Sheet identifies the stakeholders to be contacted and who in the organization is responsible for communicating with them. Stakeholder type, contact name(s), organizational affiliation (if applicable), title, contact information, and documentation (when contact was made and by whom) should be included on the sheet.

12. *Stakeholder Contact Worksheets.* During a crisis, various stakeholders will be contacting the organization. Foremost among those are usually the media, but others may request information and need a response during a crisis. The Stakeholder Contact Worksheet section should begin with the specific procedures that should be used when a call is received (Barton, 2001). The procedures should specify where all calls should be routed and who will answer them. The focus typically is on identifying a spokesperson to respond to the media, a topic discussed in Chapter 5. However, the organization should not overlook other stakeholders who may be seeking information, such as community leaders, employees, employees' families, and investors. Although a lower priority than the media during a crisis, these other stakeholders have legitimate information needs. Neglecting them injures the organization–stakeholder relationship. Organizations must develop procedures for all stakeholders that might contact the organization, not just the media. In addition to having clear procedures, careful documentation is essential. To record this information, multiple copies of a Stakeholder Contact Worksheet should be included in the CMP. The worksheet should include who contacted the organization, when the contact was made, the channel used to make contact, the specific inquiry, the response, the follow-up that was promised, and details of that follow-up.

13. *Business Continuity Plan (BC).* One organizational goal during a crisis is to resume business as usual as soon as possible. This section details what the organization will do if the crisis damages the facility or vital equipment needed to conduct business. While this plan may be a separate document, the CMP must acknowledge and recommend its use when necessary. This section should include conditions for when the BC is to be used.

14. *Crisis Control Center Description.* When the CMP is activated, team members need to know where they should assemble. Some progressive organizations have developed special crisis control centers,

sometimes called *crisis command centers*. Team members know to go directly to the crisis control center when they are contacted.

15. *Postcrisis Evaluation Forms.* Once a crisis is over, the CMT must assess its efforts. (As Chapter 9 details, an organization must learn from its crises.) Since the crisis management effort is primarily an exercise in communication—information collection and dissemination—the evaluation form focuses on communication (Barton, 2001; Egelhoff & Sen, 1992; Fearn-Banks, 2001). The evaluation form contains sections on the notification system used by the CMT and its information collection efforts. The information collected through the form will help the CMT correct weaknesses and maintain the strengths of the CMP.

Including all 15 points need not make for an excessively long CMP. However, it is a formal document as opposed to a functional one. Key points of the CMP, such as 5, 6, 8, and 11, can be extracted to create a reduced version of the plan. This abbreviated version can be placed on pocket and wallet cards that all crisis team members are required to carry at all times. It is best to keep the CMP lean. If necessary, move some aspects of the CMP to a Crisis Appendix.

Crisis Appendix

Even the collection of 15 elements just discussed can become lengthy. As a result, you may wish to create a Crisis Appendix to supplement the core CMP. The appendix reflects a knowledge management aspect of crisis management. A Crisis Appendix is a crisis knowledge database that can contain precollected information, templates, and past crisis knowledge. For instance, a Crisis Appendix is an excellent place to store extended lists of potential experts and the documentation you will need for recording the team's actions.

The Crisis Appendix can contain the supplemental or background information you might need to know in a crisis, placed in an easily accessible format. An effective way to organize this information is to think of the questions you are likely to be asked in a crisis. What is your organization's safety record? When was your last product recall? How often is maintenance performed on the equipment in question? You can store answers and information related to these and other questions. Your precollected information will reflect your organization's crisis risks. That means you should precollect information related to the crises most likely to affect your organization.

Templates are prewritten statements that require only a few blanks to be filled in before they are released. A number of different news releases can be drafted ahead of time and approved by the legal department. The CMT simply fills in the details from the current crisis, such as date, location, number of injuries, amount of damage, and so on. Time is saved, as the core message is written and approved before the crisis. An organization should also store what it has learned from past crises and exercises. Chapter 9 elaborates on organizational memory and learning. The idea is that the organization uses past experience to guide current actions by repeating previous successes and avoiding past mistakes. Knowledge from past crises or exercises may be useful to current crisis management efforts, so it should be available to the CMT.

The templates should take advantage of the interactive nature of the Internet. Many companies now talk about social media releases, which attempt to maximize the interactivity offered by the Internet, especially social media. Toward that end, templates should include an RSS link and a share link. *RSS* stands for *really simple syndication.* It is a web feed that allows others to follow and publish your content. Figure 6.1 shows the symbol for RSS. A share link allows people to click on an icon, then select the social media they would like to use to share the information with others. For instance, if I want to share information that has a share link icon, I can connect it to my Twitter account. A message then appears as a tweet with a Web link to the information and some space for me to add my own comments. RSS and share links allows stakeholders to expand the reach of your crisis message by sending it to other stakeholders.

Figure 6.1   RSS Symbol

Source: feedicons.com

> ## University Application: Preparation
>
> Do you know what to do if the building you are in right now were to catch on fire? Of course you get out of the building, but where should you assemble? Is there a procedure for checking in or out once you evacuate? If you do not know this information, see if you can find it. A good place to start would be your university's Web site. What other emergency situations should you be prepared for on campus, and how has your university prepared you for them?

The CMP Is Not Enough

The danger of a CMP is that it can provide managers with a false sense of security. Some managers feel that if they have this plan in place, they are protected when a crisis hits. Three flaws challenge this assumption. First, the CMP is a general guideline for action; it represents contingencies. Crisis teams must adapt the plan to match a specific crisis. Mindlessly following a CMP in lockstep fashion is a recipe for disaster (Fink, 1986; Littlejohn, 1983). The team is invaluable in adapting the CMP to contingencies and for handling those factors never addressed in the CMP (Barton, 2001; Regester, 1989).

Second, the CMP is a living document. Organizations change, their operating environments change, and their personnel changes; thus, the plan must be updated regularly. At least once or twice a year, the CMP should be examined for necessary changes. Moreover, a crisis manager should review it weekly to see if updates are necessary.

Third, a CMP has little value if it is not tested and practiced in simulations or exercises. This point cannot be stressed too strongly. Practice reveals the holes or weaknesses that must be addressed before a real crisis occurs (Wilsenbilt, 1989). For example, at an airport in Texas, a serious flaw was discovered during the crisis drill for an airplane crash. Because airport personnel had the wrong radio frequency for contacting emergency personnel in the town, their radios were worthless during the drill. This is a common problem in disaster responses and was one of many problems during Hurricane Katrina. Changing the frequencies was a simple procedure, but the problem would not have been discovered in time without the drill. Fortunately, the drill rather than an actual crisis revealed this serious problem in the CMP. Furthermore, practice is the only way for team members to gain experience enacting the plan. Practice also builds team members' confidence that they can handle a crisis. The dangers of an unrehearsed team have already been addressed. Managers must not let having a CMP lull them into a false sense of security. An ongoing approach to crisis management should prevent this complacency.

Other Related Plans

Organizations should create emergency preparedness and business continuity plans that will interface with the CMP. If a crisis requires an evacuation or providing shelter-in-place, the emergency preparedness plan is in effect as well. How do the two plans coordinate with one another? This is a question that exercises can answer and can help to enable smooth coordination. Of particular concern is overlapping memberships or resource demands of the two plans. The CMP and emergency preparedness plan should complement one another and not compete in any way.

As noted in the 15 elements of a CMP, the BC outlines efforts that are to be taken either to keep the organization running during the incident or to return to normal operations as soon as possible after the incident. Again, the organization should determine whether overlapping membership or resource demands exist between the BC and the CMP. Also the BC and crisis team should coordinate messages. For instance, if an alternative location is used temporarily to maintain production, workers need to be told where and when to report for work. Suppliers and customers need to know if there will be a disruption in the supply chain, the extent of that disruption, and its estimated time span.

An excellent example of coordinating the CMP and BC was shown in response to the West Pharmaceuticals plant explosion in Kinston, North Carolina. West Pharmaceuticals told customers the length of time it would take before production in their other facilities would offset the loss of the Kinston facility. Employees were told they would be working at other facilities until the Kinston facility was rebuilt. Employees were instructed where they would go and how they would be rotated home every so many weeks to have time with their families.

■ REVIEWING THE CRISIS COMMUNICATION SYSTEM

With the personnel and CMP in place, crisis managers must make sure the physical setup of the communication system is prepared. Elements of the crisis communication system include the mass notification system, crisis control center, and the intranet and Internet. Preparation entails determining whether the crisis communication system is sufficient to meet the needs of the CMT and to verify that the system is operational—that it works.

Mass Notification System

There are times when the crisis team must send a simple message to large a number of people. This is called *mass notification.* Although mass notification typically involves employees, it also can include community members who need to be given safety information about evacuation or shelter-in-place. Mass notification is done through an automated messaging system, which sends a message by phone, text message, e-mail, or a combination of these to a preset list of people. The easiest way to engage in mass notification is to outsource it. A number of vendors, such as MessageOne, provide an array of automated messaging options. The crisis team can use automated messaging systems to inform employees that a crisis has occurred and warn the community about safety risks. The messages need to be short. Employees and community members should be told where to go to find additional information, such as a phone number, a Web site, or an internal intranet site for employees only. Community members should be informed of any safety risks as soon as possible. Moreover, it is critical that employees learn about the crisis from the organization, not the news media. The mass notification system may be used whenever the crisis management process demands a short message be sent to multiple people.

Crisis Control Center

The review of the CMP noted that organizations should have a crisis control center. Such a center serves many functions. It is a place for the CMT to meet and discuss the crisis, an information collection center, and a place for briefing the media. Ideally, the crisis control center is a separate area in the organization devoted solely to crisis management and equipped to meet the needs of the CMT. Large, geographically dispersed organizations should have crisis control centers at all major facilities. Multiple crisis control centers provide two benefits. First, a global company cannot expect to handle all crises effectively from one location. Extreme distances and time zone differences will hamper the crisis management effort. Second, multiple crisis control centers provide natural backups. If a crisis such as a fire or an earthquake were to destroy an entire facility, the organization could use one of its other crisis control centers. Large-scale crises, such as Hurricane Katrina, reinforce the need to have backups that are geographically distant from the site of the crisis. Some smaller organizations may use public relations agencies to house their crisis responses and use these agencies' facilities for the crisis control center.

To fulfill its various functions, the ideal crisis control center will have a scenario-planning room in which the CMT members can meet, a communication center for monitoring information (TV monitors, phones, computers, and wire service), and a press room for briefings. The crisis control center should be fully equipped and operational at all times. Part of being prepared is having backups for all the necessary equipment. The specific equipment will vary according to the needs of the specific organization. There must be sufficient equipment and backups for the center. The equipment must be checked regularly to ensure that it is in working order.

The crisis control center should also be stocked with food and drinks to keep the CMT going and have administrative support to help assist the team with basics tasks, such as making copies or taking inquiries. The crisis control center must have dedicated phones lines, redundant Internet access, wireless connectivity, and the ability to track the news media. It follows that information technology support is essential, too (*The Well-Provisioned War Room*, 2005).

Some crisis experts have argued that a crisis control center should be mobile or even virtual. A mobile center can be deployed anywhere. You do not have to worry if your facility is shut down, unless the mobile center was at the site of the crisis. A mobile unit would have the same equipment needs as the stationary crisis control center. The main difference is that there would be no media briefing room due to space limitations at a mobile site. However, media briefings could be handled in a separate mobile facility; rented space, such as a meeting room in a hotel; or outdoor space, weather permitting. Virtual and partially distributed teams can stay linked through wireless communication and the Internet. Even team decisions can be made through conference calls or online meetings. As noted before, the problem with virtual and partially distributed teams is the potential for equipment to fail. This risk is greatest for virtual teams because all communication is mediated. Partially distributed teams are preferable to virtual teams because you have the option to base your response from the traditional crisis communication center and to use technology to allow some team members to stay involved when they are in the field or cannot get to the crisis control center.

> ## University Application: Crisis Command Center
>
> Identify a location on campus that would make an excellent crisis command center. What makes that location an excellent choice? Next, create a list of all the equipment you believe should be in the crisis command center. Be sure to consider the need for backup or alternative equipment.

The Intranet and Internet

Intranets are custom-made for crises. They are like the Internet but are self-contained within an organization—only organization members have access to the information, and even then, access to sensitive information is limited to those with the proper clearance (Hibbard, 1997). The beauty of an intranet is the speed of accessing information for the CMT and other employees. The CMT can access information directly through a computer instead of through telephone calls. If the crisis team needs financial information, it can retrieve the information on the computer—no need to place a call. Collecting and analyzing information is crucial during a crisis. Crisis teams gather raw data, transform the data into usable information (create knowledge), store the knowledge, and communicate it to others (Egelhoff & Sen, 1992). An intranet is ideal for meeting these needs (National Research Council, 1996; Reeves, 1996). Motorola, for example, uses an intranet as part of its crisis management efforts. It stores crisis-relevant information (e.g., financial and product information) on its intranet and uses the system to facilitate the exchange of information during a crisis.

An intranet allows immediate access to data about the organization; it can store information, provide a site where the crisis situation and relevant information is updated regularly, be accessed by any employee, and allow communication to others in the organization via e-mail. Granted, not all crisis-relevant information can be collected via an intranet. For instance, interviewing witnesses to an accident in a facility must be done in person. However, any precrisis background data needed about the organization, such as product ingredients or safety records, can be located there (e.g., in a Crisis Appendix). Moreover, e-mail and an intranet are not always appropriate means of communicating crisis-related information to employees. Still, employee e-mail can be effective at times, and a regularly updated summary of crisis information allows employees to access what they want when they want it.

As noted previously, the Internet offers multiple channels with different applications for crisis communication. This discussion of the

Internet will be divided into two broad categories: (1) Web sites and e-mail and (2) social media. The separation is based on the primary use of e-mail and the Web to present information to stakeholders, while social media is dominated by stakeholders creating the content.

The Web allows outside stakeholders to access your organizational information. They can make e-mail inquiries or visit a Web page to do so. In situations when it is an appropriate channel, e-mail can be used to reach government officials, media representatives, activist groups, and many other stakeholders. The only limit is whether your target stakeholders have e-mail and you have the correct addresses. A Web page can contain updated information about the crisis. Again, stakeholders have the option of deciding what information they examine and when they examine it. As mentioned previously, Odwalla developed a Web page when it needed to recall some of its products in 1996. The voluntary recall and consumer communications were launched because of reports that people were becoming ill from E. coli in Odwalla fruit drinks (Thomas, 1999). The Web page identified the exact products under recall, how to return these products, and the reasons for the recall—the exact information customers needed to receive. Sample messages included Odwalla's completion of the recall (November 2), an update on the recall (November 1), confirmation that the Food and Drug Administration found E. coli (November 4), and condolences to the Denver family whose child died from E. coli poisoning (November 8). Taylor and Kent (2007) have been strong advocates of integrating Web sites into crisis communication.

An organization should also create a crisis dark site. A dark site is a section of a Web site or a completely separate Web site that has content but no active links. When a crisis hits, the CMT can activate the link, and the dark site becomes accessible. West Pharmaceuticals used part of its Web site for this purpose when the Kinston facility was destroyed. BP used a separate Web site to address the deadly 2005 explosion at its facility in Texas City, Texas. A significant amount of information can be placed on a crisis site before a crisis. Such information would include background information on the facility or product, photographs of the facility (for media use), maps of the facility, and links to relevant third-party experts (Corporate Leadership Council, 2003). Specific information about the crisis can be added as it becomes known. Again, templates or holding statements can speed the posting of information. The templates or holding statements are a series of fill-in-the-blank statements for the media. The focus is on basic information: what happened, where it happened, the cause if known, and next steps to be taken (Business Roundtable, 2002).

Stakeholders do turn to the Web to find information about a crisis. Yet oddly, researchers have found that only about 60% of organizations in crisis use the Web site (Perry, Taylor, & Doerfel, 2003). Failure to use the Web site in a crisis will become a greater liability for organizations because stakeholders increasingly use the Web as a means to get information quickly. If an organization does not address the crisis online, stakeholders may wonder why. There is a need to tell the organization's side of the story, and the Web site provides an ideal place to tell that story. Unlike the news media, company Web sites provide organizations with unlimited space to talk about the crisis. Chapter 8 returns to the need to tell "your side of the story."

Crisis management is moving toward using the Web more fully. Major agencies, such as Hill & Knowlton, Ketchum, and Burson-Marsteller, feature the Internet in their discussions of crisis management client services. Their focus is on preparing dark sites for clients and monitoring the Internet for crisis-related information. Integrating the Internet into the crisis management effort is becoming an expectation as the media and other stakeholders increasingly turn to the Internet when seeking crisis information (*Lackluster Online PR No Aid in Crisis Response*, 2002). Not having an Internet component to your crisis management effort may be viewed negatively by stakeholders.

Web sites also provide access to information outside of the organization. Some forms of external information required during a crisis can be drawn from them. In particular, government agencies provide information on regulations and reporting procedures. Other sources also might be relevant, depending upon the type of crisis being experienced. For instance, industry accident data are useful during an organization's own accident crisis. The CMT can also monitor what is being said about the organization and the crisis online, including via traditional as well as social media. As with monitoring the traditional media, the CMT needs to know what is being said and what the stakeholders know in order to determine the accuracy of the crisis information being disseminated and whether the organization's crisis message is getting through to stakeholders. The intranet and Internet can be valuable information processing and delivery tools when used properly during a crisis. Remember, the intranet and Internet do not make all other information gathering and dissemination tools and channels obsolete. Always use the channel that is most effective for the communication situation (Clampitt, 1991; Rupp, 1996).

Crisis teams can pre-prepare social media messages as well. The focus lately has been on blogs. C4CS, a strategic crisis communication consulting firm, recommends creating dark sites for blogs, or what they term *stealth blogs*. In other words, messages are written for the blogs but do not go live until the crisis hits (Wacka, 2005). Shel Holtz (2007), a recognized expert on social media, argues that crises are not the time to start a blog because a new blog has no following and probably will be ignored. We began discussing this point in Chapter 2 but expand on the point here. The counterargument, one that even Holtz notes, is that stakeholders are looking for information, so why not offer a blog? The logic is that if anyone sees the blog, it has contributed to the crisis management effort (Martine, 2007). However, the new blog will not serve as a mechanism for engagement or have that informal, authentic voice that an established corporate blog would have (Holtz, 2007). In fact, one recommendation is that crisis blogs not allow comments (Wacka, 2005). In essence, the blog becomes a Web site but is another location where stakeholders might find crisis information. So decide for yourself how much a new blog might help during your crisis.

During a crisis stakeholders will conduct online searches for information about the crisis. Search engines follow a logic, and altering words in crisis messages can help to achieve search engine optimization (SEO). During preparation, crisis teams should identify the key words that will be searched for, for each of the various crises the organization is likely to encounter. Make sure those key words are in your prewritten templates and that the list is available during the crisis for crafting messages. The organization also might consider arranging for paid search contracts to be in place. Both SEO and paid search options will increase the likelihood of stakeholders finding your information when they search online during the crisis (Wehr, 2007). Some search terms that stakeholders use during a crisis are benign and can be embedded in messages appearing online before a crisis. For instance, during product harm, stakeholders might search "safe+[the product name]." Swanson might use the term "Swanson+frozen dinner+safe" in everyday messages. Then during a crisis, searches again will feature existing messages from the organization. Contracts could also be in place for pay per click. The idea is that when a crisis term is searched, an ad linked to your crisis information will appear next to the search results (Oneupweb, 2007).

▪ STAKEHOLDERS AND PREPARATION

Stakeholders should be part of the prevention thinking and process. If crisis managers expect stakeholders to do some tasks during a crisis, stakeholders need to know what task to do and be confident that they can execute it. The most common tasks required for stakeholders during a crisis are the emergency measures of evacuation and shelter-in-place. Making sure that stakeholders are aware of what they should do (task knowledge) and feel that they can do it (self-efficacy) is a complex challenge. Cultural differences are one of the greatest barriers to task knowledge and self-efficacy. Heath, Lee, and Ni (2009) found that many people did not have task knowledge or self-efficacy for emergency tasks due to cultural issues. The awareness and self-efficacy efforts failed because the messages lacked sources similar to, and message sensitivity to, the target stakeholders. Stakeholders are more likely to be informed and have self-efficacy for emergency information if the message comes from a source similar to themselves and the message is sensitive to cultural factors (Heath et al., 2009). Risk communication can offer insights into how to help stakeholders develop task knowledge and self-efficacy (e.g., Heath & Palenchar, 2000; Palenchar & Heath, 2007). A more detailed discussion of risk communication is beyond the scope of this book, but crisis managers should know there are resources available if they are faced with these challenging tasks of preparing stakeholders.

■ CONCLUSION

The CMP and crisis control center complete the discussion of the six elements of crisis preparation. The CMP should be meticulously crafted before a crisis occurs, and the crisis communication system must be in working order. The CMP prescribes how and when to communicate during a crisis. An excellent CMP and CMT are useless if the physical structure of the communication system is not in proper working order. Calls cannot be made without working phones, and online data cannot be accessed without working computer stations and Internet connectivity. All preparation elements should be reviewed and updated regularly to maintain a state of readiness for crises.

DISCUSSION QUESTIONS

1. Would you choose to have a virtual crisis team? Why or why not?

2. What are the dangers of becoming overly dependent on the Internet or intranet during a crisis?

3. What crisis communication utility do you see in the various social media channels?

4. How might you change the list of required sections for a crisis management plan?

5. How might the structure of crisis management plans change as they become more digital?

6. Which side of the dark blog debate do you support? Why?

7

Crisis Recognition

An actual crisis puts an organization's crisis preparation to the test. We deceive ourselves into believing that crises are easy to spot. We think all crises are like giant icebergs in the North Atlantic on a clear summer's day, relatively simple to see and to avoid. It is true that crises are easy to locate when there is an obvious trigger event: a train derails, a natural gas pipeline explodes, *E. coli* is found in a frozen lasagna, an employee is wounded by a coworker, or some other identifiable event. The obvious crises make it easy to realize the need to implement the crisis management plan. However, not all crises are obvious.

As the definition of crisis in Chapter 1 noted, crises are symbolic as well as objective. People can disagree on whether a situation is a crisis. Some crises, particularly those involving conflicts with outside groups, are hard to see. As strange as this may sound, an organization may not even know it is in a crisis (Kamer, 1996). A situation becomes a crisis when key stakeholders agree it is a crisis. Unfortunately, some members of management may wish to deny that the organization is in a crisis even when stakeholders are screaming that it exists (Fink, Beak, & Taddeo, 1971; Pauchant & Mitroff, 1992). Similarly, management may refuse to take preventative actions to address warning signs. The first part of this chapter details how crisis team members might "sell" a crisis to top management in an organization. The recommendations hold true for selling warning signs, too.

To review, the crisis management team (CMT) begins to understand a crisis once they have uncovered it. The CMT engages in knowledge management. The team must collect accurate crisis data quickly (Darling, 1994; T. H. Mitchell, 1986). The crisis team analyzes the information to create the crisis-related knowledge that is used to (a) guide decision making and (b) create the messages sent to various stakeholders (whether internal or external). Without crisis-related knowledge, the team cannot make decisions or take actions to ameliorate the effects of the crisis. Actions include making statements to the media because this stakeholder is the most likely to pressure the organization for crisis information.

Members of the CMT must be aware of the problems associated with information collection, knowledge creation, and knowledge management. The second part of this chapter reviews research concerning the pitfalls associated with information collection, processing, and dissemination, along with ideas for combating these problems.

WHAT WOULD YOU DO? GLASS IN THE BABY FOOD

You work for Gerber, the baby food company. In the same month, there are reports of pieces of glass appearing in products produced by both Gerber and Beech-Nut, your competitor. An internal investigation and an investigation by the Food and Drug Administration can find no glass contamination at your facilities. Management strongly suspects product tampering. Reports of glass in Beech-Nut products appeared a week before reports of glass in Gerber's. It could be people trying to cash in on the product scare—they put the glass in hoping to get money from Gerber. Beech-Nut has just announced a product recall related to the glass.

- What do you recommend Gerber do, and why?

■ SELLING THE CRISIS

While more the exception than the rule, some crises are not obvious or easily accepted. A problem can be ignored or not deemed worthy of the label *crisis* (Billings, Milburn, & Schaalman, 1980). Whether a problem is defined as a crisis is significant; framing a problem as a crisis changes how the organization responds to it. When a problem becomes defined as a crisis, the organization expends more resources on it and works harder to discover an explanation for it (Dutton, 1986). Part of expending resources includes activation of the crisis management plan (CMP). While some crises may be hard to see, others are simply ignored.

As I've stressed, stakeholder perception matters during a crisis (Augustine, 1995; Frank, 1994; Higbee, 1992). If your customers define a situation as a crisis, it is a crisis, even if the dominant coalition (those managers in the organization who make decisions) chooses to initially define it as a noncrisis. We have to go no further than the Intel Pentium chip flaw fiasco to recognize the wisdom of these words. Intel knew in the summer of 1994 that the chip was flawed; it could make mistakes on certain advanced mathematical calculations. However, Intel ignored customer concerns about the flaw. The company even failed to grasp the significance of having the flaw posted on the Internet. After generating greater customer animosity, Intel eventually agreed that the situation was a crisis, and in December 1994, it replaced the defective chip (Gonzalez-Herrero & Pratt, 1996). It may fall to the crisis team to convince the dominant coalition to accept stakeholder perception that a crisis exists. A crisis is taken more seriously and is given more attention than a noncrisis. The issue for crisis managers becomes how to sell a problem as a crisis to the dominant coalition. The same concerns and advice hold true when the crisis manager is trying to convince others in the organization that a crisis threat requires additional attention.

Crisis Framing: A Symbolic Response to Crises

Organizational environments are filled with ambiguous events. Organization members must frequently decide whether something is important or try to determine why something happened (Fairhurst & Sarr, 1996). Crises are part of the ambiguity encountered by organizations. All problems within organizations are framed in some way. A *frame* is the way a problem is presented, the meaning one attaches to the problem (Fairhurst & Sarr, 1996). A frame affects interpretations of the problem by highlighting certain of its features while masking other features (Dutton & Ashford, 1993). There can be competing frames. For example, abortion has been framed as both freedom of choice and murder. Crisis managers need to create a frame that will provoke the most desirable response from top management. Three factors play a role in developing an appealing crisis frame: (1) the crisis dimensions, (2) the expertise of the dominant coalition, and (3) the persuasiveness of the presentation.

Crisis Dimensions

Crises vary along three dimensions: (1) perceived importance, (2) immediacy, and (3) uncertainty. Like warning signs, actual crises differ in the amount of loss that can occur and the likelihood of the loss if the CMP is not enacted. Failure to act can allow damage to spread to other areas of an organization, into surrounding communities, and to additional stakeholders. For instance, fire or toxic gas can spread to other parts of a facility or into the community, and shareholders can suffer when financial damage from a product harm crisis is not contained.

Perceived importance is related to the crisis assessment dimensions of impact and likelihood; it varies with the value of the possible loss (impact) and the probability of the loss (likelihood). The greater the possible loss or probability of loss, the greater the perceived importance of a crisis (Billings et al., 1980; Dutton, 1986). For instance, a faulty product that affects a few customers has less perceived importance than a faulty product used by hundreds of thousands of customers, if the potential harms from the defects are equal. Perceived importance is the key to framing warning signs. As has been discussed, crisis managers use likelihood and impact to rate warning signs (see Chapter 3). Similarly, crisis managers need to emphasize the danger of ignoring warnings when presenting them to the dominant coalition.

Immediacy refers to the time pressure involved with the crisis. Time pressure has two components: (1) how quickly the crisis will hit and (2) the degree of stakeholder pressure to take action. The sooner a crisis can produce harm, the greater its immediacy. A tampered product that endangers customers' lives has greater immediacy than an initial complaint about moral violations by an activist group. A tampered product places people in immediate danger, while moral violations tend to involve philosophical debates.

Comparing two cases will clarify the idea of immediacy. Early in 1990, an antiabortion group had urged Dayton Hudson Corporation to end its grant to Planned Parenthood (Kelly, 1990). In September 1990, Dayton withdrew its funding from Planned Parenthood. Dayton wanted to avoid being drawn into the abortion debate. Management felt that providing funding to Planned Parenthood could tie them to abortion. Women's groups were angered by the decision. Dayton officials had time to consider their options and to study consumer attitudes. The grant was eventually restored. The moral debate did not require immediate action. In contrast, Burroughs Wellcome Company experienced extreme immediacy when two people in Washington state died from taking cyanide-laced Sudafed 12-hour capsules in March 1991. Burroughs had to remove the products from the shelves and warn customers quickly (Dagnoli & Colford, 1991; Kiley, 1991). The product safety concern required immediate action.

Intense pressure from key stakeholders is another form of time pressure. When primary stakeholders (e.g., employees, customers) want action now, the crisis has immediacy. For example, the 1997 UPS drivers' strike gave the crisis immediacy. During the strike, UPS was delivering only 10% of its packages and losing millions of dollars (Sewell, 1997). A company cannot survive under such conditions. Pressure from employees gave the UPS crisis immediacy.

Uncertainty is the amount of ambiguity associated with a problem. The larger the amount of ambiguity surrounding a crisis, the greater its uncertainty. People are drawn to and have a need to reduce uncertainty. Organizations are no different (Dutton, 1986). Organizations need to know what is going on in their operations and why. How can a problem be corrected if it is not understood? Low-uncertainty problems can be explained and corrected using common organizational rules and procedures. High-uncertainty problems demand the type of extra attention crisis management can deliver. A comparison of similar crises helps to illustrate the power of ambiguity.

On December 10, 1995, American Airlines Flight 965 from Miami to Cali, Colombia, crashed into a mountain, killing 160 of the 164 people on board. On July 17, 1996, TWA Flight 800 from New York to Paris exploded 12 miles off the coast of Long Island, killing all 230 people on board. The Searchbank database listed five articles dedicated to Flight 965 and 141 for Flight 800. One reason for the different levels of media interest was the variation in ambiguity.

For Flight 965, investigators quickly identified the automated guidance system as the cause of the crash. The final report, released seven months later, confirmed that the plane was following the wrong directional beacon, causing the automated guidance system to fly the plane into the side of a mountain (Dornheim, 1996; McGraw, 1996).

The cause of Flight 800's explosion was investigated and debated for over 17 months. Missiles, terrorist bombs, lightning strikes, meteorites, and mechanical failures all surfaced as possible causes (Duffy & Beddingfield, 1996; Gray, 1996). The National Transportation Safety Board's final report ruled out all but mechanical failure. The evidence suggested that a small electrical charge ignited the fumes in an empty fuel tank that then exploded and destroyed the plane. More than 10 years later, the cause of Flight 800's crash is still being debated online. Flight 800 remains a mystery because of the ambiguity surrounding the explosion. The mystery helped to hold media and public attention for over a year. Furthermore, a Herculean effort went into discovering the mysterious cause of the explosion and reducing the ambiguity.

Ambiguity demands to be resolved. Organizations must expend extra effort and resources when crisis ambiguity increases. The CMP can focus the attention required by an ambiguous crisis. The easiest crisis to sell is one that is perceived as very important, is very immediate, and has high uncertainty. Crisis managers must maximize as many of the crisis dimensions as possible when they frame the crisis for the dominant coalition.

Expertise of the Dominant Coalition

Organizational politics creeps into crisis management. Part of successful politicking is in knowing the people with whom you are dealing. The management personnel that make up the dominant coalition will possess varying types of expertise, and their expertise affects their comfort zone for dealing with problems. Managers like to successfully solve problems. Not surprisingly, they are more likely to be successful when dealing with problems within their expertise—their comfort zones. Comfort increases because they can identify more easily with the problem. Crisis managers must be sensitive to the expertise of the dominant coalition when framing a crisis. The crisis frame should be adapted to the coalition by reflecting some aspect of their expertise (Dutton & Ashford, 1993). If the dominant coalition has financial expertise, the CMT should make sure the crisis frame includes a financial component. One way to tap expertise is to use jargon, the language of a profession. A message using jargon from the dominant coalition's area of expertise cultivates a sense of familiarity with the situation (Fairhurst & Sarr, 1996). While not a completely rational reaction, the dominant coalition will want to manage crises they feel they can resolve successfully. A crisis leads stakeholders to question the dominant coalition's competence. Successful crisis management restores the perception of the dominant coalition's competence, while failure further erodes it (Dutton, 1986; Pearson & Clair, 1998). Hence, top management prefers crises it can feel comfortable with. The same holds true for prodromes. Any Dilbert cartoon reminds us that the organizational world does not run on pure logic.

Persuasiveness of the Presentation

Crisis managers have an opportunity to convince the dominant coalition that a problem is a crisis, and they must use their persuasive skills when given this opportunity. People are persuaded by three basic factors: (1) credibility, (2) emotion, and (3) reason (Larson, 1989; Tan, 1985).

Credibility is a concept that is used in persuasion and is defined as the receiver's attitude toward the communicator. For crisis management, the organization is the communicator and the stakeholders are the receivers. Credibility is a very important concept because it has a significant effect on the persuasiveness of a message (McCroskey, 1997). Research has proved that credibility can be divided into two components: expertise and trustworthiness. *Expertise* is the communicator's knowledge about the subject. An expert organization will appear to be competent, capable, and effective (Kouzes & Posner, 1993). *Trustworthiness* is the communicator's goodwill toward or concern for the receivers. A trustworthy organization is truthful and ethical and considers the impact of its actions on stakeholders when making decisions (Allen & Caillouet, 1994; Kouzes & Posner, 1993). To be credible, crisis managers need to have a record of successful task completion demonstrating their expertise. Having a reputation as being honest enhances their trustworthiness (McCroskey, 1997).

Emotion centers on how the message is presented (McCroskey, 1997). To heighten the emotionality, a crisis should be presented in a dramatic fashion. A crisis is dramatic when it is novel. Vivid examples and stories help to create a dramatic presentation. The drama and emotion make the message easier to understand and more interesting, and they catch the attention of management (Dutton & Ashford, 1993; Larson, 1989). Management and other targets of persuasion do not evaluate information on the basis of emotion alone, however; they also rely on logic.

Reason, a rational appeal, stirs the intellect (Larson, 1989). The use of facts (verifiable information) and logical evidence persuades people. However, facts do not simply speak for themselves. Crisis managers can spin the facts by emphasizing the dangers of a situation. Lotteries sell tickets by telling people they cannot win if they do not play, not by reporting the odds against winning. To convince management of a crisis situation, crisis managers would feature information that supports the strong likelihood and impact of a crisis while downplaying information that erodes either. Both sides of the issue must be presented because one-sided arguments are ineffective with educated audiences, such as managers (Tan, 1985). Crisis managers who use emotions to capture the dominant coalition's attention must then use compelling rational evidence (e.g., statistics, expert testimony) to support the acceptance of the crisis (Dutton & Ashford, 1993). The message designed to sell the crisis or warning sign should begin dramatically with vivid stories and examples, then move to reasoned arguments to reinforce its acceptance.

A hypothetical example demonstrates the use of emotion and reason. Imagine you work for Juice-Is-Us, a fresh vegetable juice maker. Evidence suggests that a recent shipment of tomato juice could be tainted with *E. coli*. You want to have the situation treated as a crisis. One option is to state the statistical probability of *E. coli* contamination and to note that the effects would be bad for the company. Another option is to describe in detail the effects of *E. coli* on the human body. Retell an actual case of a person who suffered from it. Vivid examples and a story reinforce the dangers by bringing them to life. Next, present the information by noting the possibility of people contracting the disease, not the probability that they will not; spin the information. Add the possibility that regulatory agencies and law enforcement officials, such as the FBI, could investigate the situation. Last, reinforce your case with statistics about the likelihood of contamination, the potential number of consumers affected, and the potential financial and reputational impact of any *E. coli* poisonings or deaths. As you can see, the second option provides a much more persuasive argument for enacting the CMP.

Organizing the Persuasive Effort

Effective persuasion should draw upon theory. Theory tells crisis managers what factors to consider when trying to sell a crisis or crisis threat and how to organize their efforts. The Theory of Planned Behavior (TPB) is a commonly used persuasive theory. It argues that behavior is a function of behavioral intention or the readiness to perform a behavior. Behavioral intention is indicated by normative beliefs, subjective norms, perceived behavioral control, and control beliefs. Normative belief is the individual's perception of the behavior. Subjective norm is how relevant others feel about the individual's behavior. Perceived behavioral control is how easy or difficult the individual believes the behavior will be. Control beliefs are any factors that the individual perceives can facilitate or impede the performance of the behavior. What we need to do is translate TPB into selling a crisis or threat (Ajzen, 2002).

The individuals are the managers that need to accept that a crisis or threat needs action. The behavior would be the efforts to manage the crisis or threat. Crisis managers can sell the crisis or threat by concentrating on the subjective norm, perceived behavioral control, and control beliefs. Stakeholders are relevant to management; thus, crisis managers must emphasize how stakeholders would expect the organization to act on the crisis or threat. Perceived behavioral control is the easy part of managing the crisis or threat. Talking about the organization's expertise to handle the crisis or threat, in part by playing to the expertise of the dominant coalition, helps to build favorable perceived behavioral control. Finally, control beliefs are any barriers or resources related to improving the effort to manage a crisis or threat. Crisis managers must identify the resources and ways to overcome any barriers so that control beliefs become positive. This section can only scratch the surface of persuasion, but it does provide guidance to help crisis managers sell a crisis or threat to a reluctant dominant coalition.

Resistance to Crises

Not all problems rise to the level of crisis in an organization. As stated in the opening of the chapter, crises can be contested, symbolic issues. Natural disasters, malevolence, technical and human accidents, organizational misdeeds, and workplace violence tend to be obvious crises about which most stakeholders would agree on the interpretation. Challenges and rumors are two crisis types about which contrasting interpretations abound. At least one stakeholder group will see a crisis while the organization does not. The different interpretations can cause an organization to overlook a crisis. It is foolish arrogance to believe that only the organization can place the crisis label on a situation. Crisis interpretations are socially cocreated by primary stakeholders, secondary stakeholders (especially the news media), and the organization. If primary stakeholders believe a crisis exists, it does. Remember the Audi 5000 case from earlier in the book? Audi never did agree with customers over the sudden acceleration problems with the 5000. The contested crisis generated years of bad press and consumer ill will before Audi recalled the 5000 (Sullivan, 1990; Versical, 1987).

Karl Weick (1979, 1993) is a social psychologist who has studied crises and whose ideas have been applied to crisis management (Seeger, Sellnow, & Ulmer, 2003). Weick's (1979) model of information processing provides a theoretical explanation for crises being missed. He uses the term *enactment* to explain how people in organizations make sense of events such as crisis. The process begins when there is some change in the organization's environment—an event occurs. Through enactment, managers isolate pieces of information about that event for closer inspection. The managers then try to make sense of and give meaning to this information through the process of *selection*. (In knowledge management, this is when information is converted into knowledge.) Selection guides how the managers respond to the event. Last, *retention* explains what information the managers store for future use. Enactment is the key to the entire model. The information that is chosen for further attention shapes how managers see and react to their environment. If managers enact information that does not indicate a crisis, the organization will not respond to the event as a crisis. Weick's idea of enactment is that managers actively shape and create the environments to which they react by imposing their interpretations on the information. Managers may enact an event very differently from stakeholders and create a conflict over whether a crisis exists.

Crisis managers should evaluate all stakeholder claims that a crisis exists by examining or reexamining the information. First, they must determine whether the facts are correct. Are the claims accurate? Inaccurate claims should be corrected immediately, thereby diffusing the crisis. Second, if true, determine whether other stakeholders accept the interpretation of the situation as a crisis. Will more stakeholders in a particular group or other stakeholder groups support the crisis interpretation? In Audi's case, would more customers as well as government regulators see the sudden acceleration as a crisis? A crisis interpretation gains power and salience when it spreads among stakeholders. Crisis managers must decide whether the values and interests embodied in the crisis interpretation will appeal to other stakeholders. Such decisions require a clear understanding of one's stakeholders.

Here's an example. In 1990, Philip Morris was challenged for having a high number of billboards selling cigarettes in inner-city areas. The crisis interpretation painted Philip Morris as a racist organization that exploited minorities in the inner city, which worried the company. About 40 different demonstrations were launched against the company by Reverend Calvin Butts, an inner-city antitobacco advocate. Philip Morris ended the advertising campaign due to fear of a spreading crisis interpretation. It agreed to reduce the number of cigarette billboards in inner-city areas and to join a council that would examine outdoor advertising practices in such areas (Fahey & Dagnoli, 1990). The lesson to be learned here is that if crisis managers believe a crisis interpretation will resonate with other stakeholders, they must work to convince the dominant coalition to accept it as a crisis.

Another scenario involving a missed crisis is when the dominant coalition purposefully refuses to see one. Embezzlement and successful computer hackings are common crises that are purposely not seen. Even when internal or external audits discover embezzlement, most organizations hide it. The FBI believes that only 10% of all embezzlements are reported. Embezzlement is embarrassing, and many organizations fear that reporting it will encourage more theft or anger shareholders, clients, or customers (Strauss, 1998). Similar reasons exist for not disclosing computer hackings; organizations do not want to appear weak or vulnerable. However, some states, such as California, require disclosure of computer hacking that places individuals' identity at risk (Hopper, 2002). I have had firsthand experience with laws requiring this kind of disclosure. My mortgage company (ABN-Amro) was forced to tell me and other customers when its data tape containing mortgage information was misplaced by a package delivery service (DHL).

Each organization and industry has its own type of crises that are purposely ignored. The organization may take actions to address the problem but choose to keep the situation quiet to avoid involving most stakeholders. The organization is engaging in a form of cover-up. Any cover-up is dangerous; it could be exposed later and trigger a different and more severe crisis (Barton, 2001).

As mentioned, crisis managers can affect the acceptance or rejection of a crisis by how they frame its presentation to the dominant coalition. Crisis managers must have information to support the frame and articulate it in a compelling fashion. Frame development begins with information. Crisis managers need information that indicates that a problem is (a) important—damage will occur or become more severe by spreading, (b) immediate—there are pressures to act now, or (c) uncertain—there is ambiguity surrounding the situation. Any of these three can signal a crisis; if all three are present, it is a compelling situation.

To underline the importance of these points, let's review. Crisis managers should consider the dominant coalition's expertise and basic elements of persuasion when selling the frame. The dominant coalition must be familiar and comfortable with the crisis—see it as within their realm of expertise. Jargon is one way to link a crisis to the dominant coalition's expertise. Vivid stories and examples capture the dominant coalition's attention. The facts about the importance, immediacy, and uncertainty of the crisis are then offered to support the acceptance of the crisis label.

It falls to crisis managers to cure organizational blindness by convincing management to openly acknowledge a situation as a crisis. Crisis managers should sell a situation as a crisis because they believe that enacting the CMP will improve the situation and benefit the organization, its stakeholders, or both. Selling crises is even more difficult when the dominant coalition is purposely ignoring the crisis.

Organizations can be blind to warning signs as well, and the recommendations for selling crises can also be applied to selling prodromes. For instance, a semiconductor manufacturer ignored evidence for eight years that its lax operating procedures were poisoning workers. A lawsuit by 30 workers alleging widespread ills and workplace abuses brought the problem to light. The case was settled out of court (E. B. Smith, 1998).

■ CRISES AND INFORMATION NEEDS

Crises can be regarded as information-poor and knowledge-poor situations. A crisis begins as an unknown and must become a known. A typical crisis requires large amounts of information because initially little is known, it is a rapidly changing situation, and often the changes in the situation are more random than predictable. These factors indicate that the information demands of a crisis are complex (Barge, 1994). There is pressure on a crisis team to acquire information and to process it into knowledge quickly and accurately if the team is to operate effectively in a crisis. Understanding and coping with the information and knowledge demands of a crisis are part of crisis management.

Crises as Information Processing and Knowledge Management

Egelhoff and Sen (1992), Seeger et al. (2003), and Weick (1993) have all identified information processing as a major task during crisis management, while Wang and Belardo (2005) emphasize knowledge management as central to crisis management. These are complementary perspectives because information processing is how knowledge is created. *Situation awareness* is a term used to describe this information-processing and knowledge-creating aspect of crisis management. In general, situation awareness describes the point at which the crisis team feels it has enough information and knowledge to make a decision (Kolfschoten & Appelman, 2006). More specially, situation awareness involves perceptions of the situation and environment, comprehension of them, and the ability to project future states (Endsley, 1995). For the CMT, situation awareness indicates that the team has a perception and understanding of the crisis situation and the ability to predict the effects of the crisis and to determine what actions are needed to address it.

A sample crisis illustrates the process of moving from the unknown to the known and creating situation awareness. There is an explosion in an aerosol can facility. The crisis team should know the location of the explosion, the employees working in the area at the time, the chemicals involved in the process, and the exact tasks performed in the area of the explosion. What the crisis team does not know but needs to know includes who was injured, the nature and severity of the injuries, what emergency actions were taken after the explosion, the amount of damage to the facility, the need to suspend operations, and possible causes of the explosion. The crisis team collects information until they have the knowledge and information about the crisis necessary to make decisions.

The Unknown

The crisis begins with a trigger event or someone convincing management that a crisis exists. Either way, the organization is faced with a problem that now commands the CMT's attention and demands some resolution. The team's first task is to determine what they need to know about the crisis, what they already know, and what they do not know. What they need to know is the information and knowledge required to enact the CMP and to make decisions. What is already known would be the previously collected crisis information and knowledge. What they do not know is the difference between what is needed and what exists in the crisis data bank (all the previously collected crisis information and knowledge, including the CMP and Crisis Appendix). Understanding these three informational concerns allows the crisis team to assess how much they know and what they need to gather in order to cope with the crisis and to reach situation awareness. The team then must try to reduce what they do not know by collecting crisis-relevant information.

■ INFORMATION GATHERING

Information gathering should be an organized search, not a wild scavenger hunt. In fact, knowledge management strategies were created in large part to aid information collection and analysis. The crisis team must prioritize the information needs as well as know where to go and who to ask in order to collect the information (Clampitt, 1991). The team must prioritize the needed information because information needs are not equal. High-priority information should receive immediate attention and greater effort (Geraghty & Desouza, 2005). For example, during an industrial accident that vents dangerous gas, the crisis team must know the direction and intensity of the gas cloud before they worry about the cause of the gas venting. Each crisis will determine its own information priorities.

Knowing that certain information is needed is pointless if the team does not know where to get it. Links to organization members and external stakeholders become valuable when a crisis team requires information, because these links are the sources for the requisite information (Pearson & Clair, 1998; Wang & Belardo, 2005). It behooves a crisis team to know the sources of potential crisis-relevant information and knowledge before a crisis hits. Identifying sources of knowledge is known as a *knowledge map* and fits with the CMT contact sheet in the CMP. The idea of developing a crisis knowledge map is discussed shortly.

■ INFORMATION PROCESSING: THE KNOWN

Raw information is a starting point, not an end point, when trying to understand a crisis. The crisis team must determine what the pieces of information mean. What is typically called *making sense out of information* is information processing. Through processing the information, the team determines whether they have actually assembled the knowledge needed. Only by analyzing information can a team determine whether enough of the requisite knowledge has been collected to convert the unknown into the known. The crisis managers must determine whether they have enough knowledge to make effective decisions, whether they have reached situation awareness. If there is a knowledge deficit, the information gathering continues. If there is enough knowledge, decisions are made about what the organization will do and say about the crisis, which is the domain of Chapter 8.

■ INFORMATION-PROCESSING PROBLEMS

The crisis management literature treats information processing as a rather simple task. Crisis managers are told to mobilize their resources and to gather all possible information (T. H. Mitchell, 1986). We are led to believe that information is easy to collect and to analyze. However, this is not the case. Research in organizational and small-group communication has found consistent flaws that plague information collecting and processing as well as knowledge sharing (Halonen-Rollins & Halinen-Kaila, 2005; Stohl & Redding, 1987). By understanding the following flaws, crisis managers can construct better mechanisms for information collecting and processing: (1) serial reproduction errors, (2) the MUM effect, (3) message overload, (4) information acquisition biases, and (5) group decision-making errors.

Serial Reproduction Errors

Have you ever received a message that has traveled through three or four people before reaching you? The odds are that the message you received made little sense or was far from accurate. This distortion is known as the *serial reproduction problem* or *serial transmission effect*. The more people a message passes through before reaching its final destination, the greater the likelihood of the message being distorted (Daniels, Spiker, & Papa, 1997). Obviously, inaccurate information is problematic during a crisis. It leads to public embarrassment through misstatements to the media and dangerous miscues by a crisis team that has based its decisions on inaccurate information. Remember the emotional pain caused by wrong information during the Sago mine disaster in West Virginia in early January 2006?

The MUM Effect

One critical source of crisis-related information would be members of the organization. Not surprisingly, people in organizations have a tendency to withhold negative information completely (e.g., information that makes them look bad) or alter the information to make it less damaging (Stohl & Redding, 1987). This phenomenon is known as the *MUM effect*, acting to block the flow of negative or unpleasant information in an organization (Tesser & Rosen, 1975). Crises involve negative situations. Things have gone wrong and threaten the organization in some way (Barton, 2001). Organization members may be reluctant to provide negative information, especially if it could make them or their organization unit look bad.

Some people attribute the explosion of the space shuttle *Challenger* to the MUM effect (Goldhaber, 1990). The night before the *Challenger* launch, 15 engineers at Morton Thiokol argued against the launch. Morton Thiokol makes the solid rocket boosters (SRBs) that help to lift a space shuttle into orbit. The SRBs have O-rings (rubber circles) that seal gaps and prevent improper ignition of the solid fuels. The O-rings have no backup. If an O-ring fails, the solid rocket fuel can ignite improperly, explode, and destroy the vehicle. Everyone at NASA was aware of the potential consequences of an O-ring failure. The engineers felt the weather was too cold and would prevent the O-rings from functioning properly. (O-ring failure was determined later to be the cause of the explosion). Morton Thiokol originally refused to approve the launch. After another meeting, the decision was reversed, and Morton Thiokol green-lit the launch. Middle managers at NASA never told either Arnold Aldrich, the manager of the entire space shuttle program, or Jesse Moore, NASA's associate administrator responsible for the final launch decision, about Morton Thiokol's launch concerns (Boffey, 1986; Mecham, 1986; Sanger, 1986). We can speculate whether either of these two men would have stopped the launch had they known about Morton Thiokol's concerns. However, NASA managers illustrated the MUM effect by not relaying negative information to their superiors. No crisis team can afford to have negative information withheld or modified just to keep a short-term peace or to protect team members.

Message Overload

A common problem experienced by people in organizations is message overload, when people are given more information than they can competently manage (Geraghty & Desouza, 2005; Stohl & Redding, 1987). The risk of information overload is great during a crisis. As noted earlier, crises are information poor, which demands the collecting and processing of large amounts of information to compensate for this information void. The demand for information can produce a vast flow of data into the crisis team. However, the danger is that the information flow becomes overwhelming and blocks the process instead of helping to close the gap between the unknown and the known in the crisis.

Information Acquisition Biases

Because the amount of available information exceeds the human ability to make sense of it, people naturally use selective perception, which means we each focus on certain aspects of the information; we encounter and disregard the rest (Barge, 1994). Weick's (1979) idea of enactment is related to selective perception. The risk in crisis management is as follows: Early on in the crisis, crisis team members form impressions about the nature of the crisis. All subsequent information and knowledge are tested against this initial perception or crisis frame. The crisis team tends to seek information that confirms the initial impression while discounting information that contradicts this impression. Unfortunately, the initial perception may blind the crisis team to critical information and knowledge needed for its decision-making efforts. Another risk arises when members define any new crisis in terms of past crises (Barge, 1994). Rather than treating a new crisis as a novel event, a crisis team can simply view it as a version of some previous crisis. If the past crisis is a poor match, the crisis team applies the wrong template when it addresses the new crisis. The crisis team manages the wrong crisis because it mistakes the new crisis for the old one. In either instance, important nuances about the current crisis are lost. The crisis team discounts potentially important information because of the blinders from initial impressions or baggage from past crises.

These two information acquisition biases can be demonstrated by returning to the case of TWA Flight 800 discussed earlier in this chapter. Initial reports indicated that a bomb was responsible for the incident. The pattern of the blast and the discovery of microscopic PETN traces, a plastic explosive, on salvaged pieces of the plane were the best evidence. Investigators could have relied on their initial perceptions and examined only the circumstantial evidence supporting the bomb explanation. The remainder of the investigation could have ignored all other possible causes. Another reason to suspect terrorism was the similarity to the Pan Am Flight 103 bombing over Lockerbie, Scotland, in 1988. The radar tapes and the voice and flight data recordings of Flight 800 were very similar to those of Flight 103. Investigators could have examined all the remaining evidence through the lens of a previous crisis. As it turned out, Pan Am Flight 103's template was the wrong one to apply to TWA Flight 800 (Gray, 1996; Watson, 1996). Had either of these information acquisition biases been used, the investigators would have ignored the clues to the real cause of the explosion: mechanical failure.

Group Decision-Making Errors

Groups are prone to decision-making errors when they fail to use critical thinking skills. Critical thinking is a process of carefully evaluating information (Williams & Olaniran, 1994). Two tendencies contribute to poor group decision making. First, the group fails to see a problem or fails to identify the correct cause of the problem. The group is led to ignore problems or to solve the wrong problems. Second, the group improperly evaluates its alternatives for solving a problem (Hirokawa & Rost, 1992). Improper evaluation can lead the group to select an ineffective alternative for solving the problem. Both types of errors result in poor decision making. In each instance, the root cause of the error can be traced to the careless handling of information.

Summary

The purpose of reviewing information-gathering and -processing errors was twofold. First, the errors highlight how difficult information gathering and processing can be. Crisis team members should not underestimate these problems. Second, realization of the problems can help to develop more effective information-gathering and -processing mechanisms for crisis teams. The information gathering and processing should become more effective when the crisis team is trying to counter those errors.

■ INFORMATION-PROCESSING MECHANISMS

Information-processing mechanisms are designed to aid crisis teams in both the collecting and processing of crisis-relevant information. These mechanisms involve both structural and procedural elements. The structural elements focus on how to collect information, and the procedural elements on how to prevent or reduce processing errors.

Structural Elements

Let me stress once again that crisis managers need to access sources that have information (potential knowledge) they might need during a crisis. Crisis managers must seek out needed information that is not part of their previously assembled crisis database. Communication consultants recognize the value of networks (i.e., relationships with other people), when collecting information. Stronger networks lead to better information gathering and more accurate understanding of problems (Barge, 1994; Clampitt, 1991; Geraghty & Desouza, 2005). Crisis management teams must develop connections they can use to collect crisis-related information. I call the system the *crisis knowledge map*, and it is composed of external and internal stakeholder networks.

The *internal stakeholder network* consists of the people within the crisis team's organization. The foundation of this network stems from the networks of the individual team members. Their contacts and information sources become the team's sources. The crisis team then looks to expand the list by asking each contact for others who may know about the subject (Barge, 1994). The crisis team should formalize the information by developing a list of contacts for various types of information that might be needed during a crisis, developing an internal stakeholder section for a Crisis Knowledge Map Directory. The Crisis Knowledge Map Directory lists multiple contacts for various types of information the team may need. It can be an appendix to the CMP or a separate document. The Crisis Knowledge Map Directory starts with a listing of the expertise required, which is a way of categorizing people by the type of knowledge they possess. The expertise designation is followed by basic contact information: name, organization and title, phone numbers, pager number, fax number, and e-mail. Multiple contact points are important because if one fails, another can be tried until the person is contacted.

The *external stakeholder network* is composed of people outside of the crisis team's organization. Common members would include customers, government officials, suppliers, distributors, community members, competitors, and investors (Pearson & Mitroff, 1993). Any external stakeholder could be a part of this network. The Secondary Contact Sheet from the CMP is an essential resource. It provides contact people for all stakeholder groups—and it indicates who in the organization handles each particular stakeholder. The crisis team converts the information from the Secondary Contact Sheet into an external stakeholder section for the Crisis Knowledge Map Directory. The structure of the external section parallels that of the internal section. The difference is that the external section would include the contact person(s) for the various stakeholder groups. The crisis team would have the option of direct contact with the external stakeholder or use of the organization's contact person(s). A contact person is helpful when a positive relationship has been established. The stakeholder should be more open with the contact person given the history of a positive relationship with that person versus having no relational history with a member of the crisis team. The open relationship should make it easier for the contact person to solicit higher-quality information from the external stakeholder.

During a crisis, it is critical to track the amount and movement of crisis-related information and knowledge within the organization. *Crisis information logs* are a useful tool for doing this. Logs are a record of when a crisis team member makes an information request and the result of that request. By logging information requests and receipts, the crisis team knows what information it has and what information it still needs. The log starts with the standard concerns: the time and date of the request, what is requested, requested from whom, the channel used to make the request, and requested by whom. Once this information is received, it is recorded along with the name of the person who received the information. Administrative support staff can help keep the crisis information logs. The CMT needs administrative support to help with this and other tasks during the crisis management process.

Once again, the next step is to evaluate and process the information into knowledge. Team members must decide whether any follow-up information is needed and whether the received information is sufficient. The log notes when the information was processed (knowledge created) and by whom. Accepted criteria for evaluating information are clarity, timeliness, and depth. *Clarity* means that the information has one interpretation, not multiple interpretations, and people can easily understand what the message means. *Timeliness* means that the information is current and received when needed. *Depth* means that the information seems complete—it answers the questions asked (Barge, 1994).

A hypothetical example demonstrates clarity, timeliness, and depth. Imagine that a hurricane hits the central manufacturing facility of your power tool company. The CMT wants to know when operations will resume. Does the team want to hear "in a reasonable amount of time" (lack of clarity) or "in five to six days" (clarity)? The CMT needs to know what alternatives are available for maintaining production. Does the team want a business resumption plan that has not been revised in three years (is not timely) or a current business resumption plan (timely)? Last, the CMT needs to know about injured workers, people who were on duty when the hurricane struck. Does the team want to learn there were 10 injuries (lack of depth) or the exact names of those injured and the extent of their injuries (depth)? The CMT works best when it receives quality information.

Precision should be stressed in the logs. The information is to be recorded as it is received and not summarized or modified. Precise written records help to eliminate some of the factors that promote serial reproduction errors. Also, having a written record reduces the number of sources used to transmit a message, which again reduces the likelihood of serial reproduction errors.

The crisis information log records when information is requested, when it is received, and whether it has been processed. Time and date help to assess the timeliness of information. Channels are useful in evaluation. The log can help to evaluate the extent to which specific channels were effective in requesting and sending information. Noting who the information was requested from helps to determine if better sources could be used in the future. The source of the information indicates the believability of the information, due in part to the credibility of the source. The log also tracks if, when, and by whom the information was processed. Overall, the log helps the CMT monitor its information-collection and -processing efforts. Crisis teams must collect and store accurate information about the progression of events in a crisis because such documentation is central to postcrisis evaluation, crisis-related lawsuits, and governmental investigations triggered by the crisis.

Procedural Elements

The procedural elements are all actions that can be taken to overcome various information-processing problems. A priority system is one way to combat information overload by using selective criteria to establish the perceived importance of information (Geraghty & Desouza, 2005; Stohl & Redding, 1987). Prioritization is a multistep process involving evaluation, storage, and retrieval. When incoming information is logged, it is also evaluated. A simple priority system might use three categories: (1) immediate, (2) routine, and (3) miscellaneous. *Immediate* refers to information the crisis team requires for pressing decisions or actions. *Routine* is the basic information a crisis team typically needs during the course of a crisis management effort. *Miscellaneous* is information that is received, has no apparent value, but does have some relationship to the crisis.

Routine and miscellaneous information is stored until the crisis team has time for or need of it. Information might be stored on paper, electronically, or both. Retrieval involves extracting the desired information from the information queue. Storage and retrieval require categorizing the information by topic. The information is assigned a general topic area and a list of key subjects that it covers. The process is similar to cataloging books in a library. Chapter 9 provides additional recommendations for storage and retrieval.

Allowing the crisis team to focus on high-priority information reduces the message load, thereby decreasing information overload. The message priority system should reflect the crisis team's information needs. A contaminated food recall crisis can illustrate and clarify the priority process. Top priorities at the start of a food recall include identifying affected consumers, locating the source of the contamination, and informing consumers about the recall. Information related to any of these three topics would be categorized as immediate during the initial phase of the crisis. Suppose the crisis team received the following information: (1) results of production facility inspections, (2) newspaper stories about the company's crisis management efforts, (3) projected costs of the recall, (4) confirmation that the recall information is being reported in the news media, (5) projections on lost market share, (6) estimated recovery time, (7) confirmed cases of consumer illnesses, (8) consumer reactions to the recall, and (9) Internet newsgroup discussions linking the recall to a government conspiracy.

Information chunks 1 (inspection results), 4 (confirmation of recall in the news media), and 7 (cases of illness) would be recognized as immediate priority. In each case, the information relates directly to the initial priorities of the crisis team. Information chunks 2, 3, 5, 6, and 8 would be routine priority. Eventually the crisis team will need to assess the financial damage (3 and 5), estimate the recovery time (6), and evaluate their crisis management performance (2 and 8). Information chunk 9 is miscellaneous because there probably is no government conspiracy here, but the information does pertain to the crisis. When a lot of information is being received and the risk of information overload is high, crisis teams would benefit from an information priority system.

Data splitting is a technique used to combat information acquisition bias. By this method, information is divided into smaller units for more effective analysis. The crisis team can examine these units of information more carefully because they are easier to examine in detail. In addition, smaller units act to break patterns that could feed into pre-existing information-processing biases (Barge, 1994). In terms of the

TWA Flight 800 case, data splitting would include considering the flight data and radar records separately before placing each into the larger picture of the investigation.

Unfortunately, there is no simple technique for handling the MUM effect. The only proven means is an open communication system in which people engage in the candid disclosure and receipt of facts, even if it is bad news (Redding, 1972). Openness is developed through trust and past interactions with one another (Barge, 1994). Crisis team members must work to earn the trust of organization members and demonstrate that there will not be negative sanctions for passing along information that indicates member mistakes or errors. In a similar way, open and positive relationships with external stakeholders facilitate the flow of accurate information from outside sources (Grunig, 1992).

Group decision-making errors can be combated through vigilance and the devil's-advocate technique. The discussion of crisis team selection touched on vigilance, a form of critical thinking. The four primary elements of vigilance are (1) problem analysis, (2) standards for evaluating alternative choices, (3) understanding the important positive aspects of an alternative choice, and (4) understanding the important negative aspects of an alternative choice. These four elements counter the two group decision-making errors. Problem analysis counters the failure of the group to identify the correct cause of the problem, while standards for evaluating alternative choices and understanding the important positive and negative aspects of an alternative choice compensate for the group improperly evaluating alternatives for solving the problem (Hirokawa & Rost, 1992). The devil's-advocate technique ensures that some group member always voices opposition to a group's plan. The opposition is supposed to lead the group to reevaluate their decisions and reminds the group to examine weaknesses they may have glossed over originally (Barge, 1994).

Training

Stress can be the enemy of the crisis team. While stress can enhance performance by making people more alert and causing them to react faster, it can also create problems such as freezing, misplaced aggression, and ignoring new tools and techniques. Training helps to reduce stress and promote team dynamics that mitigate stress. Part of crisis team training can be on stress-proofing team members. People can learn techniques to help reduce stress in pressure situations. When a team has an open and supportive climate, stress is reduced. Part of training can reinforce the value of open communication and the value of cooperation and support for team members (Paton & Flin, 1999). Training is critical to team learning. In times of stress, people retreat to what is comfortable. New tools and techniques for crisis communication will not be used if team members do not feel comfortable using them before a crisis. The team will ignore the new tools and techniques and go back to what they know. New tools would include new software, hardware, or decision support techniques such as thinkLet (Kolfschoten & Appelman, 2006). If it's important for a crisis team to integrate a new technology or technique into their work, then make sure the members are familiar and comfortable with using it (Hiltz, 2006).

WHAT WOULD YOU DO? SPRINT AND THE BABY

A local NBC station in Los Angeles, California, reports that Sprint refused to help parents whose 10-month-old child was in the backseat of a stolen car. The Cochrans were loading their car in their Riverside, California, driveway. They had placed the child in the car and had returned to get their second child when the thieves struck. The parents claimed that Sprint would not provide global positioning information from the parents' cell phone unless proper channels were used. The story also said that Sprint needed a $25 fee to be paid before they would even help the authorities. The child and the car were recovered safely less than two hours after the theft. Bloggers were irate with Sprint and helped to spread the story.

- Why would this event be a reputational crisis?

Sprint's policy is that law enforcement personnel, not the regular consumer, must submit a faxed request to get access to global positioning data. The process takes only a few minutes. The policy is necessary because people could use the global positioning data for stalking or child abductions. There is no fee for law enforcement. Clearly, the customer representative did not know or understand the policies.

- What can Sprint do to alleviate this crisis and prevent a repeat of this kind?

■ CONCLUSION

A crisis cannot be managed effectively if an organization is blind to its details. At times, crisis team members will have to sell a crisis to the dominant coalition before action can be taken to resolve the crisis. This chapter began by offering suggestions for crisis selling. Once the existence of a crisis is recognized, information must be collected and processed into knowledge vital to successful management of the crisis. Crisis teams need accurate and timely information if they are to have the knowledge they need to make effective decisions quickly. While it sounds easy, numerous problems can hinder information gathering and processing. But there are techniques that crisis management teams can adopt to improve their information-gathering and -processing capabilities. Taken together, the material in this chapter prepares crisis teams for identifying a crisis and processing information into the knowledge needed to resolve it.

DISCUSSION QUESTIONS

1. Bribery and computer hacking are two crises that are often unreported. What other crises are organizations likely to hide? What types of information does a university prefer that potential students not have?

2. Organizations keep saying how much customer service means to them. Why are so many crises caused by not paying enough attention to consumers?

8

Crisis Response

Once a crisis hits, the crisis team must work to (a) prevent it from spreading to unaffected areas of the organization or the environment and (b) limit its duration (Mitroff, 1994). Communication presents unique challenges during the response phase. Internally, the crisis team must collect and process information in order to make decisions, which were discussed in earlier chapters. Externally, stakeholders must be informed about the crisis and actions must be taken to address it, including reporting the organization's progress toward recovery. The advent of social media has added to the challenge.

Discussions of external crisis communication must include form and content. *Form* is how the response should be presented. *Content* is what is said.

■ FORM OF THE CRISIS RESPONSE

The form of a crisis response is mentioned more frequently in the crisis management writings than any other topic. The crisis response includes the first public statements the spokesperson makes about the crisis. This first statement typically is delivered through the mass media or the Internet, hence the concern in crisis management with media relations and the Internet (e.g., Barton, 2001; dna13, 2010; Lerbinger, 1997). The focus on the initial response stems from the fact that first impressions form quickly and color the remainder of stakeholders' reception of the crisis communication efforts (Sen & Egelhoff, 1991). In any crisis,

WHAT WOULD YOU DO? BP AND TEXAS CITY: ACT 2

You are the spokesperson for BP, and it is about an hour into the crisis. The crisis team is assembled in the designated crisis control center. Local fire crews and BP's own fire crews are dealing with the flames. Local emergency crews are on the scene attending to the injured. The crisis team has learned that there are fatalities. A construction trailer near the explosion was hit hard. Many of the injured and killed were contractors working for BP; they were in the trailer. The local and national news media have sent crews to the site. The flames and smoke will make for dramatic visuals on the news. The crisis team will hold a briefing in a few minutes.

- What information are you likely to have that you can share with the news media?

- What questions do you anticipate being asked but cannot answer at this time?

- How will you handle those questions?

stakeholder information needs occur simultaneously with the crisis team's information needs.

In terms of the form of crisis communications, recommendations are to be quick, consistent, and open. It is important to keep in mind that crisis communication transpires in times of stress. Stakeholders will not be at their best for receiving information. Research suggests that people's ability to process information is reduced by up to 80% during emotionally charged situations (Gilman, 2004). Crisis teams must take care to craft and send crisis messages so that they can be clearly and easily understood.

Responding Quickly

The terms *quick* and *quickly* are common when describing an effective crisis response. The need for speed in crisis communication continues to escalate as technology accelerates the spread of information, thereby actually reducing the amount of time a crisis team has for responding (Barton, 2001). The media report crises very quickly, including posting the stories online by media outlets or by so-called citizen journalists. In some cases, the key stakeholders affected by the crisis learn about it from media or online reports before they have been officially notified, creating a bad situation for the organization. The quicker the stakeholders can hear about a crisis from the media, the quicker the crisis team must respond. Emergency room physicians talk about the "golden hour." Dr. R. Adams Cowley coined the phrase because he felt if he stopped the bleed and restored blood pressure within the first hour, he could save the patient. Some experts treat crises like medical emergencies (Friedman, 2002) and subscribe to a similar one-hour rule when providing the initial crisis response.

Obviously, speed increases risks. As the crisis team must act quickly, it can make mistakes. The primary risk associated with speed is the potential for inaccuracies (C. A. P. Smith & Hayne, 1997). Johnson & Johnson committed a quickness mistake when handling the original Tylenol product-tampering crisis. In 1982, seven people in the Chicago area died from taking cyanide-laced Extra-Strength Tylenol capsules. A reporter asked if cyanide was used in the Tylenol manufacturing facility, and the Johnson & Johnson spokesperson responded that there was no cyanide in the plant that produced Tylenol. The statement was in error; the testing laboratories at the production facility did use cyanide. At the time of the press conference, the spokesperson did not have all the relevant information, and the error was corrected as soon as it was discovered (Berg & Robb, 1992; Leon, 1983; Snyder, 1983). But speed does not have to mean mistakes, and the benefits of a rapid initial response far outweigh the risks.

It is accurate to say that a crisis creates an information void. Nature abhors a vacuum. Any information void will be filled somehow and by someone. The media have deadlines, so they are driven to fill the information void quickly. And media demands trigger a chain reaction. The media are going to report on a crisis. Stakeholders may find that the news media are their primary or initial source of crisis-related information (Fearn-Banks, 2001), with the Internet increasing in use as well (*Lackluster Online PR No Aid in Crisis Response*, 2002). If the crisis team does not supply the initial crisis information to the media, some other groups will, and they may be ill informed, misinformed, or motivated to harm the organization. The information void can become filled with rumor and speculation, not facts (Caruba, 1994). Whatever the case, the initial crisis information may well be incorrect and may intensify the damage created by the crisis. A quick response helps to ensure that stakeholders receive accurate crisis-related information and hear the organization's side of the story.

Silence is a very passive response and reflects uncertainty and passivity, the exact opposite of what an organization should be attempting to create. A silent response suggests that an organization is not in control and is not trying to take control of how it or the crisis is perceived by stakeholders (Hearit, 1994). Silence allows others to take control of the situation (Brummett, 1980) and define the crisis for stakeholders. A quick response helps to create the impression of control and is necessary to get the organization's definition of the crisis—its side of the story—into the media and out to the stakeholders (Heath, 1994; Kempner, 1995; T. H. Mitchell, 1986). From the stakeholders' viewpoint, a quick response demonstrates that the organization is taking action and is capable of responding to a crisis (Darling, 1994; Maynard, 1993). Conversely, a slow response makes an organization appear to be incompetent (Donath, 1984). Control is important to credibility; it is part of the organization's expertise. A crisis indicates a lack of control in and by the organization (Heath, 1994). A quick response is a first step in reasserting organizational control and reestablishing organizational credibility (Augustine, 1995).

Stealing thunder illustrates the benefits of a quick response. Researchers have found that organizational managers and the organization are viewed as more credible when the organization reported the crisis before other sources, that is, by stealing thunder (Arpan & Pompper, 2003; Arpan & Roskos-Ewoldsen, 2005). The measure of credibility used in the studies overlaps with the organizational reputation instrument used in many other crisis studies, which is based on credibility assessments related to trustworthiness (Coombs & Holladay, 2002). Therefore, we can conclude that a quick response does have reputational protection benefits.

However, there are limits to being able to respond quickly. In some crises, it takes time to collect and process the necessary information. Large-scale accidents produce great confusion. A January 1998 explosion at a Sierra Chemical dynamite manufacturing facility 10 miles east of Reno, Nevada, exemplifies the limits to quickness. Initial reports on January 7 listed eight injured, three known dead, and two missing. A report later that same day listed six injured, five missing, and no confirmed deaths. The next day, officials had the final count: six injured and four missing, presumed to be dead. It seems one of the five people originally listed as missing had not reported to work on January 7 (Ryan, 1998; "Several Missing in Nevada Explosion," 1998). There was a repeat of the speed error problem during the 2006 Sago mine tragedy in West Virginia. Relatives were told that all the miners were alive, when in fact only one survived. This fateful error added to the suffering of the families and townspeople.

It is important to acknowledge that it takes time to collect some types of information.

[A crisis team might have to appear before the media or post information online with an incomplete story. That is OK. There is no sin in telling the media the crisis team does not know something but will provide the information as soon as possible. Consider a variation of the Sierra Chemical case: the crisis team decides to delay a press conference until it has all of the information about the explosion. In the meantime, the local news media are telling people about suspected causes. Perhaps a disgruntled, former employee claims the accident was due to mismanagement. Mismanagement is the explanatory theme reported as a likely cause of the blast because no other reasons are forthcoming. The initial news stories have Sierra Chemical responsible for the workers' deaths and injuries. This theme frames the thinking of reporters and other stakeholders. Speculation and rumor inadvertently become crisis fact, at least for a while. Better to have the spokesperson saying that the cause or extent of damages is still under investigation than stakeholders being fed inaccurate information.

Lack of information and knowledge coupled with the need for a fast response can beget two media communication "sins." The first is "no comment." The danger is that stakeholders hear "we're guilty" instead of "no comment" (see Chapter 5's discussion of spokesperson training for more on "no comment" statements and silence.) Better to say that the information is not yet available but will be reported to the media as soon as it is received. This brings up the second sin: not delivering on the information promised to the media or other stakeholders (Birch, 1994; Gonzalez-Herrero & Pratt, 1995). A good organization–stakeholder relationship is built on trust, and trust requires an organization to deliver on its promises. Failure to provide promised information damages the organization–media relationship, thereby eroding the organization's credibility with the media. If information is promised, it had better be delivered in some way.

Speaking With One Voice: Consistency

The organization must deliver consistent messages to stakeholders, and a unified response promotes consistency. As mentioned previously, consistency does not mean having just one person speak for the organization every time there is a public statement, as some crisis experts recommend (Carney & Jorden, 1993). Rather, speaking with one voice means coordinating the efforts of the official spokespersons and discouraging other organizational members from becoming unofficial spokespersons (Seitel, 1983). Chapter 5 detailed this point in its discussion of the spokesperson. The crisis team must ensure that the team of spokespersons is well prepared to ensure consistency in their responses. Spokespersons sharing the same information base are more consistent than those who do not. As noted in Chapter 5, message maps help to establish consistency when there are multiple spokespersons (Covello, Minamyer, & Clayton, 2007). Consistency is essential to building the credibility of the response. A consistent message is more believable than an inconsistent one (Clampitt, 1991; Garvin, 1996).

There is no way to ensure the consistency or accuracy of messages from unofficial spokespersons, and these can be any employee the media happen to persuade to answer questions. The crisis management plan (CMP) specifies the process for handling inquiries, which should be reinforced to employees so that they fight the urge to speak for the company. It is hard for employees to resist the opportunity to be on the local news. A camera crew appears as an employee is leaving work. The employee has a chance to be on television. Why not comment on the crisis? Most employees are not aware of the perils of talking to reporters who are thirsty for a scoop. Again, speculation and rumor can enter the media through comments made by unofficial spokespersons. And of course, employees will talk to friends and family about the crisis. The best defense against inappropriate employee comments is to keep employees informed. They should receive timely updates through a mix of the intranet, mass notifications, and briefings. If employees understand the crisis, they can better articulate it to the media, friends, and family. The CMP and crisis training can help to avoid inconsistency.

Openness

The openness of an organization is a multifaceted concept. Openness means (a) availability to the media, (b) willingness to disclose information, and (c) honesty. A spokesperson should answer inquiries in a timely fashion, immediately if the information is available. In a crisis, the focus is on the media, but other stakeholders may ask or demand that their questions be answered, especially if social media is being used. Neighbors of a facility may want to know how a chemical leak might affect them, or investors might want to know the financial impact of the crisis. If an organization uses social media in its crisis response, stakeholders might expect interaction, meaning that they are likely to ask for information and expect a response. The foundation for availability should have been developed prior to the crisis, especially with respect to blogs and microblogs. The organization should have a history of being responsive to the needs of stakeholders. During a crisis, this responsiveness takes the form of spokespersons or other crisis team members making every reasonable attempt to respond to questions promptly. Reasonableness is an important qualifier.

As I've mentioned, sometimes the situation does not allow for an immediate response. When delays are necessary, tell stakeholders why the question cannot be answered and when they might be able to expect a response (C. J. Stewart & Cash, 1997). Never let a request go unacknowledged, or you risk damaging the stakeholder–organization relationship. Communication with stakeholders is a two-way process. You must honor their requests if you expect them to accept the organization's messages.

A typical struggle in crisis management is between the legal perspective for limited disclosure of crisis-related information and the public relations perspective for full disclosure (Fitzpatrick & Rubin, 1995; Kaufmann, Kesner, & Hazen, 1994; Twardy, 1994; Tyler, 1997). The choice actually is on a continuum between saying as little as possible (limited disclosure) and revealing everything the organization knows about the crisis (full disclosure). Cautious full disclosure is preached heavily in crisis management circles (Kaufmann et al., 1994). However, full disclosure is rarely possible or advisable. Some crisis-related information may be proprietary, covered by privacy laws, involve company policies, or be otherwise sensitive. This means some information cannot be disseminated publicly. At other times, full disclosure could exacerbate a crisis by escalating the direct and indirect costs of litigation. Direct costs involve the amount of money awarded to plaintiffs, while indirect costs include trial costs, personnel matters, lost work time, deaths, serious injuries, and possible regulatory changes (Kaufmann et al., 1994). Organizations must consider their responsibility to stockholders, creditors, and employees as well as to victims (Tyler, 1997). Simply put, there are times when an organization must protect its financial assets. Crisis managers choose what level of disclosure to employ during a crisis. Today, issues of disclosure may be called *transparency*. Transparency involves the availability of organizational information to stakeholders. The more transparent the organization, the more information stakeholders have about that organization and the easier their access to that information (Gower, 2006). Stakeholders may ask how transparent an organization is when it comes to crisis information.

The disclosure debate raises the question of honesty. A common rec-ommendation for crisis managers is to be honest and not lie to stake-holders. Stakeholders are angrier when an organization lies about a crisis than when an organization simply has a crisis (Caruba, 1994). Limited disclosure—not revealing critical information—is not meant to be a form of deception. In fact, an organization should fully disclose any and all information about a crisis if there are risks of further harm or even death resulting from the crisis. Limited disclosure should not be used as a form of stonewalling. It should be used to disclose only the information stakeholders need to know. Of course, what stakehold-ers need to know is difficult to define, and each crisis management team should establish guidelines for when it will utilize full or limited dis-closure. (See Kaufmann et al., 1994, and Tyler, 1997, for discussions about the ethics and procedures for using limited disclosure.) Remember, lack of honesty seriously damages organization–stakeholder relationships, destroys the organization's reputation, and can lead to massive mone-tary awards against the organization in future lawsuits (Fitzpatrick, 1995).

■ CONTENT OF THE CRISIS RESPONSE

What is actually said during a crisis has serious ramifications for the success of the crisis management effort. As mentioned, key goals in the crisis management process are to prevent or minimize damage, main-tain the organization's operations, and repair reputational damage. Clear communication is essential to each of these goals. Crisis response content can be divided into three sequential categories: (1) instructing information, (2) adjusting information, and (3) reputation manage-ment. The first messages must present instructing information, fol-lowed by adjusting information, then reputation repair (Sturges, 1994). I would argue that instructing and adjusting information are the foun-dation for any crisis response. In fact, many crises can be managed effectively without even utilizing reputation management. Again, clar-ity is a concern because emotions will reduce stakeholders' ability to process information.

Instructing Information

Instructing information focuses on telling stakeholders what to do to protect themselves physically in the crisis. People are the first priority in any crisis, so instructing information must come first. When a crisis hits, stakeholders need to know how the crisis will or might affect them. They should be told if there is anything they need to do in order to protect themselves physically. They may need to know how to evacuate an area, find adequate shelter-in-place, boil drinking water, go somewhere for assistance, or return a defective product (Sturges, 1994). Instructing information satisfies the needs of both the stakeholders and the crisis team. The stakeholders receive the information they require to protect themselves; the crisis team cultivates the perception that the organization is once more in control of the situation.

Product harm and accidents illustrate the need for instructing information. Products can be defective and place the users at risk. Here's an example. In May 2010, Hoover recalled over 100,000 vacuums because they posed a shock hazard. The retractable cord was not properly routed, allowing it to loosen, thus creating a shock and a fire hazard. Hoover received three complaints of burned carpet and one report of a consumer burning a hand. The Hoover Web site provided extensive details about the recall, including the exact model numbers. There were also a number of images, including video, to help people identify the model number on Hoover vacuums (Techtronic Floor Care Technology, 2010).

Here's another example. On average, 40,000 people each year must be either evacuated or sheltered in place because of a chemical release (Kleindorfer, Freeman, & Lowe, 2000). In October 2009, 65 homes in Freeport, Texas, had to be evacuated due to a leak in a pipeline at a Dow Chemical facility. Dow workers went door to door within a six-block radius of the facility to notify community members of the need to evacuate. Dow made special arrangements for Joe Diaz because he was disabled and required dialysis. Dow transported Mr. Diaz to a hotel in a van and had a dialysis machine set up in the hotel where Dow was housing the displaced residents (*Dozens Evacuate After Chemical Leak*, 2009).

Instructing information is a natural fit with message maps. Crisis managers can anticipate the type of questions/concerns stakeholders may have related to physical protection and develop message maps for them. Crisis managers want stakeholders to follow the instructing information, so the message map emphasis on clarity and simplicity is ideal.

The Consumer Product Safety Commission (CPSC), which provides vital information about product recalls in the United States, illustrates the value of instructing information. Each recall announcement includes the product's name, the hazard it presents, incidents/injuries, a description of the product, the model number and where to locate it on the product, where the product was sold, the remedy, and contact information should consumers need additional information.

The announcements also include pictures of the products to help consumers determine whether they have that product. Some products even have videos that illustrate the hazard and how to locate the model number. Box 8.1 provides a sample CPSC product recall announcement. Social media is integrated into the CPSC instructing information efforts; video can be found on YouTube, images of recalled products are uploaded to Flickr, and people can follow the CPSC on Twitter. More traditional online channels are used as well; consumers can sign up for e-mail alerts about recalls or link their Web sites to the CPSC Web site.

Business continuity creates a second type of instructing information—how the crisis affects business operations. As noted in the CMP discussion, business continuity plans outline what the organization will do to maintain operations and to restore business as usual. Various stakeholders must receive information about the implementation of the business continuity plan. For example, maintaining operations may involve renting equipment, using different facilities, and even hiring other employees. In terms of business continuity, this is known as *interim processing* (Myers, 1993). All the people and vendors necessary to get the interim processing phase up and running must be contacted and given specific instructions. Moreover, employees, suppliers, and distributors must know how the interim processing affects them. When and where do employees report to work? When and where are deliveries to be made? Is the supply chain disrupted, and if so, how long is that expected to continue? These are critical questions that the crisis team must answer through instructing information. Once business is restored to normal, the relevant stakeholders must be informed of the change as well (Myers, 1993).

At this point, the crisis team must consider connecting with employee assistance programs. Employees need to know such instructing information as how they will be paid during the crisis and how benefits information will be processed. Human resources people are important crisis team members when it comes to handling employee assistance concerns.

Adjusting Information

Adjusting information helps stakeholders cope psychologically with the crisis. Stress is created by the uncertainty and potential harm of a crisis. On a basic level, stakeholders need to know what happened: the *what, when, where, why,* and *how* of the crisis (Ammerman, 1995; Bergman, 1994). Stakeholders are reassured when they know what happened. Moreover, they want information about what is being done to

Box 8.1	**Consumer Product Safety Commission Recall Announcement**

Walmart Recalls General Electric Coffee Makers Due to Fire Hazard

WASHINGTON, D.C.–The U.S. Consumer Product Safety Commission, in cooperation with the firm named below, today announced a voluntary recall of the following consumer product. Consumers should stop using recalled products immediately unless otherwise instructed. It is illegal to resell or attempt to resell a recalled consumer product.

Name of Product: General Electric–branded 12-cup digital coffee makers

Units: About 900,000

Importer: Walmart Stores Inc., of Bentonville, Ark.

Hazard: The coffee maker can overheat, posing fire and burn hazards to consumers.

Incidents/Injuries: Walmart has received 83 reports of overheating, smoking, melting, burning and fire, including three reports of minor burn injuries to consumer's hands, feet and torso. Reports of property damage include a significant kitchen fire and damage to countertops, cabinets and a wall.

Description: This recall involves General Electric–brand 12-cup coffee makers sold in white or black. The digital coffee maker has programmable functions and plastic housing. The GE logo is printed on the base of the coffee maker and the model number is printed on the bottom of the base. Model numbers included in the recall are: 169164, 169165.

No other models are included in this recall.

Sold exclusively at: Walmart stores nationwide from March 2008 through January 2010 for about $30.

Manufactured in: China

Remedy: Consumers should immediately stop using the recalled coffee makers and return the product to any Walmart for a full refund.

Consumer Contact: For additional information, contact Walmart at (800) 925-6278 between 7 a.m. and 9 p.m. CT Monday through Friday, or visit the firm's website at www.walmart.com

Source: U.S. Consumer Product Safety Commission.

WHAT WOULD YOU DO? **DIAMOND PET FOODS AND TOXIC DOG FOOD: ACT 1**

In late 2005, reports began to surface of dogs suffering from aflatoxin in their food, with at least 76 dying from it. Aflatoxin is a fungus on corn that can damage a dog's liver. The Food and Drug Administration found that all of the stricken dogs had been eating Diamond pet food. The company tests all corn shipments for aflatoxin and rejects shipments that test too high. Diamond Pet Foods decided to recall the related dog food products.

- What type of instructing information would consumers need?

- What other messages would you include in your crisis response and why?

- What would you do to help make sure pet owners hear of this recall?

- What other groups might be willing to help get your message to owners?

prevent a repeat of the crisis and to protect them from future crises. Communicating action taken to prevent a similar crisis is known as *corrective action*. Corrective action reduces psychological stress by reassuring stakeholders that their safety is a priority (Sellnow, Ulmer, & Snider, 1998). Stakeholders are reassured when they know the crisis situation is being controlled. Adjusting information furthers the perception that the organization has regained control of the situation. It is desirable to present corrective action as early as possible in the crisis response. The limitation to corrective action is that it may take time to develop. The cause of a crisis may take weeks or months to uncover (Ray, 1999). Corrective actions cannot be developed until the cause is known. If an attempt is made without solid knowledge, it is speculating, and that violates a basic *don't* of crisis communication. If crisis managers speculate and are wrong, they appear to be deceptive or incompetent.

A variation of corrective action is the *renewal response strategy* (*rhetoric of renewal*), which takes a positive approach to crisis communication. The focus is on rebuilding confidence and restoring the organization, not on assigning or averting blame (Seeger & Ulmer, 2001;

Sellnow, Seeger, & Ulmer, 2002; Ulmer & Sellnow, 2002; Ulmer, Sellnow, & Seeger, 2006). Ulmer's (2001) study of Malden Mills's recovery from a devastating fire illustrates renewal. The owner, Aaron Feurstein, pledged to rebuild the mill and to pay workers until it was rebuilt. For renewal to work, the organization needs a favorable reputation, or the promises of renewal will ring hollow. The renewal pledge must be consistent with the organization's core values (Ulmer & Sellnow, 2002). Though limited as to when it can be employed, renewal can be a very powerful and positive crisis response for psychological adjustment. We return to renewal efforts in Chapter 9.

Employee assistance programs are critical for adjusting information. Crises are traumatic incidents that can produce debilitating levels of stress. Traumatic stress incidents overwhelm a person's ability to cope. Seeing people injured or killed in accidents, workplace violence, or natural disasters all qualify as traumatic stress incidents. Immediate and long-term interventions, such as defusing and debriefing, may be necessary to help employees and perhaps other stakeholders adjust properly. Defusing sessions are conducted immediately after the crisis and provide a framework to help people cope. Debriefing sessions are therapeutic interventions at the group or individual level. Any type of traumatic stress response should be handled by qualified professionals.

Crises have the potential to create an entirely new class of stakeholders: victims. These are the people who have suffered physically, mentally, or financially from the crisis. For instance, employees may be injured in an industrial accident, customers may be traumatized by the violence in an accident, or investors may lose dividends due to the costs of a recall or a drop in stock prices. Victims expect an organization to express concern for them (Patel & Reinsch, 2003; Sen & Egelhoff, 1991). Expressions of concern make victims feel better about the crisis and hold less animosity toward the organization (Cohen, 2002; Kellerman, 2006). Expressing compassion does not mean an organization necessarily admits responsibility, though. Rather, the spokesperson expresses sympathy and concern for the victims. Sympathy can be expressed without incurring the liability associated with taking responsibility for a crisis (Fitzpatrick, 1995; Tyler, 1997). The key is that the expression of concern cannot include an overt statement accepting responsibility. However, lawyers may still try to use expressions of concern against an organization in court. Texas, California, Florida, and Massachusetts all have laws that prohibit statements of concern from being used as evidence to prove fault in civil cases (Cohen, 2002; Fuchs-Burnett, 2002).

Crisis managers can extend expressions of concern and sympathy by holding memorials for those who were killed in the crisis, or other events in honor of those who were injured. When a memorial is held soon after the crisis, it will be viewed as part of the crisis response. West Pharmaceuticals honored the six people killed in its Kinston, North Carolina, facility shortly after the blast. The memorial service was titled "A Service of Healing and Remembrance." Transocean held a memorial service for the 11 employees lost on the Deepwater Horizon oil rig in the Gulf of Mexico while efforts continued to stop the well from spewing oil into the ocean. Memorial services put some action behind the expression of sympathy and provide a mechanism to promote grieving and healing. The idea of memorials and the ability to help those emotionally affected by crises is developed further in Chapter 9.

Reputation Management

Reputations are threatened during any crisis. Research in marketing and public relations has begun to explore how crisis response strategies can be used to protect a reputation during a crisis (Coombs & Holladay, 2004, 2005; Dean, 2004). The belief is that communication (words and actions) affects how stakeholders perceive the organization in crisis (Allen & Caillouet, 1994; Benoit, 1995, 1997; Hearit, 1994, 1996, 2001). A variety of crisis responses strategies have been identified by researchers (e.g., Allen & Caillouet, 1994; Benoit, 1995). The crisis situation is recognized as an important influence in the selection of strategies (Benson, 1988; Bradford & Garrett, 1995; Coombs, 1995; Hobbs, 1995). The key is knowing when to use a particular strategy. The problem has been in understanding when to use a particular strategy for a specific crisis situation. Attribution theory has been offered as a useful framework for fitting the crisis response to the crisis situation (e.g., Bradford & Garrett, 1995; Coombs, 1995, 2004b; Dean, 2004).

The Situational Crisis Communication Theory (SCCT) is part of a growing body of research that applies attribution theory to crisis management (Ahluwalia, Burnkrant, & Unnava, 2000; Dawar & Pillutla, 2000; Dean, 2004; Folkes, Koletsky, & Graham, 1987; Härtel, McColl-Kennedy, & McDonald, 1998). In public relations, the SCCT has used attribution theory to develop and test a set of recommendations for using crisis response strategies. Attribution theory is based on the belief that people assign responsibility for negative, unexpected events (Weiner, 1986). Clearly, crises are unexpected and negative, so

WHAT WOULD YOU DO?

BAUSCH & LOMB AND RENU WITH MOISTURELOC: ACT 2

It is April 10, 2006, and the Food and Drug Administration and Centers for Disease Control and Prevention have posted a warning about Fusarium keratitis on their Web sites. The messages note that ReNu with MoistureLoc was used by 26 of 30 people interviewed about having infections. The messages also note that Bausch & Lomb has stopped producing and shipping ReNu with MoistureLoc and that investigations so far have shown no proof that the product causes the infection. At this point, there has been no recall of the product. However, large retailers, such as Walmart, Walgreens, CVS, and Rite Aid, are pulling the product from their shelves. Bausch & Lomb tells people about stopping shipments, informs people about the warning signs of a Fusarium keratitis infection, and reminds people to properly clean their contact lenses. Messages from the American Optometric Association reinforce the Bausch & Lomb message by saying improper cleaning can lead to Fusarium keratitis.

- Do you agree that this is the right response from Bausch & Lomb?

- From the retailers?

- What do you like or dislike about the response from Bausch & Lomb?

- From the retailers?

A slight complication appears. The government and news media report that similar outbreaks of Fusarium keratitis hit Singapore and Hong Kong in November 2006. Bausch & Lomb voluntarily suspended sales of ReNu with MoistureLoc in those countries.

- Does that change your response at all if you are Bausch & Lomb?

they provoke attributions of responsibility. In turn, these attributions shape how a stakeholder feels and behaves toward the organization. SCCT utilizes attribution theory to evaluate the reputational threat posed by the crisis situation and then recommends crisis response strategies based upon the reputational threat level.

To appreciate the SCCT recommendations, we need to define a set of crisis response strategies and explain how the reputational threat posed by a crisis is assessed.

■ CRISIS RESPONSE STRATEGIES

Crisis response strategies represent the actual responses an organization uses to address a crisis. As has been mentioned, communication has both verbal and nonverbal aspects. Hence, crisis response strategies involve the words (verbal aspects) and actions (nonverbal aspects) the organization directs toward the crisis (Allen & Caillouet, 1994; Benoit, 1995).

Crisis response strategies were first examined as apologia or the use of communication to defend one's reputation from public attack (Ware & Linkugel, 1973). Since crises threaten reputations, it was believed that organizations would use apologia to defend their reputations (Dionisopolous & Vibbert, 1988). A number of crisis critics have applied the apologia strategies or stances to understand how organizations defend their reputations during a crisis (Hearit, 1994, 1996, 2001, 2006; Hobbs, 1995; Ice, 1991).

But apologia offered a rather limited number of crisis response strategies, and a belief grew that strategies other than those found in apologia were being used in crisis responses. The number of strategies was expanded by examining the concept of *accounts.* Accounts are statements people use to explain their behavior when that behavior is called into question. A crisis response can be a form of account. Similar to apologia, accounts involve protecting one's reputation from a threat (Benoit, 1995).

Benoit (1995, 1997) has developed a list of 14 *image restoration strategies* based on apologia and account research. Allen and Caillouet (1994) used impression management and accounts to develop a list of 20 *impression management strategies* that an organization might use. Impression management is based on the idea that communication can be used to strategically shape the public reputation of an organization. Organizations use the impression management strategies, what I term *crisis response strategies,* to repair reputational damage from a crisis.

Trying to specify the exact number of crisis response strategies is a losing proposition (Benoit, 1995). A more productive approach is to identify the most common strategies and to organize them in some useful fashion. Table 8.1 offers a list of 10 common crisis communication

Table 8.1   Crisis Response Strategies, by Posture

Denial Posture	
Attacking the Accuser	The crisis manager confronts the person or group that claims that a crisis exists. The response may include a threat to use force (e.g., a lawsuit) against the accuser.
Denial	The crisis manager states that no crisis exists. The response may include explaining why there is no crisis.
Scapegoating	Some other person or group outside of the organization is blamed for the crisis.
Diminishment Posture	
Excusing	The crisis manager tries to minimize the organization's responsibility for the crisis. The response can include denying any intention to do harm or claiming that the organization had no control of the events that led to the crisis.
Justification	The crisis manager tries to minimize the perceived damage associated with the crisis. The response can include stating that there were no serious damages or injuries or claiming that the victims deserved what they received.
Rebuilding Posture	
Compensation	The organization provides money or other gifts to the victims.
Apology	The crisis manager publicly states that the organization takes full responsibility for the crisis and asks forgiveness.
Bolstering Posture	
Reminding	The organization tells stakeholders about its past good works.
Ingratiation	The organization praises stakeholders.
Victimage	The organization explains how it too is a victim of the crisis.

strategies that was derived by selecting those that appeared on two or more lists developed by crisis experts.

SCCT organizes crisis response strategies by determining whether the intent of the strategy is to change perceptions of the crisis or of the organization in crisis. As shown in Table 8.1, the strategies have been grouped into four postures, clusters of strategies that stakeholders perceive as similar to one another (Coombs, 2006b). The denial strategies seek to remove any connection between the crisis and the organization. An organization will not be affected by a crisis if it is not involved in or responsible for the crisis. The denial posture involves attacking the accuser, denial, and scapegoating strategies.

The diminishment strategies attempt to reduce attributions of organizational control over the crisis or the negative effects of the crisis. If the attributions for control of the crisis are viewed less negatively, the reputational threat to the organization is reduced. The diminishment posture consists of excusing and justification strategies.

The rebuilding strategies try to improve the organization's reputation. The words said and actions taken are designed to benefit stakeholders and to offset the negative effects of the crisis. The rebuilding posture involves compensation and apology. Apology is a complicated response, so Box 8.2 provides additional details. The denial, diminishment, and rebuilding postures also represent varying degrees of accommodation, the amount of concern the response shows for victims. This reflects the amount of responsibility an organization is perceived to have accepted for the crisis (Coombs, 2006b).

Box 8.2   The Apology

Apology is the most complex and perhaps controversial of the crisis response strategies. It is critical to differentiate between full and partial apologies. A full apology must acknowledge the crisis, accept responsibility, include a promise not to repeat the crisis, and express concern and regret (Kellerman, 2006). A partial apology is typically just an expression of concern and regret. Why the split? The answer is legal liability. Accepting responsibility results in organizations losing lawsuits related to the crisis. If an organization says it is responsible, it must pay in court. As noted earlier, the expression of concern or regret does not carry the same liabilities (Cohen, 2002). A person must be careful when using the term *apology*. That is why full apology is specified and treated as separate from an expression of concern.

The bolstering strategies are supplemental to the other three postures. They also seek to build a positive connection between the organization and the stakeholders. This posture comprises the reminding, ingratiation, and victimage strategies. These three focus on the organization, so they would seem rather egocentric if used alone, which is why they are considered supplemental. We should assume crisis managers will not use just one crisis response strategy. Within limits, crisis response strategies can be used in a variety of combinations. Clearly, this is the case with bolstering since it is a supplemental strategy. The limit is combining denial with either diminishment or rebuilding because that creates contradictions. Denial argues that there is no crisis, while diminishment and rebuilding accept that there is a crisis.

Evaluating Reputational Threat

Three factors are used in SCCT to evaluate the reputational threat presented by a crisis: crisis type, crisis history, and prior reputation. These factors are applied in a two-step process. The first step is to determine the crisis type, the frame that is used to interpret the crisis (see Chapter 5 to review the list of crisis types or frames used in SCCT). Research has found that each crisis type creates predictable attributions of crisis responsibility among stakeholders (Coombs & Holladay, 2002). Table 8.2 organizes the frames according to the levels of crisis responsibility they evoke. The victim cluster produces very little crisis responsibility for the organization. Stakeholders see the organization as a victim of the crisis, not the cause of the crisis. The accident cluster produces low attributions of organizational crisis responsibility. The crises are seen as largely uncontrollable by the organization and unintentional. The preventable cluster produces very strong attributions of organizational crisis responsibility. The organization willfully engaged in behaviors that led to the crisis (Coombs, 2005; Coombs & Holladay, 2001).

Crisis responsibility can be a threat to an organization's reputation because stronger attributions of crisis responsibility produce greater reputational damage (Coombs, 2004a; Coombs & Holladay, 1996, 2004). To determine the crisis type, look to see what cues are present and being used to describe the crisis. Most crises will fall easily into one of the types. If the crisis type is ambiguous, the crisis team can attempt to shape which frame is selected. However, it is possible that the crisis team and stakeholders may disagree on the crisis type. If this is the case, the crisis team should seriously consider adopting the stakeholders' frame.

Table 8.2   Crisis Types, by Level of Responsibility

Victim Cluster: Very little attribution of crisis responsibility

Natural disasters
Rumors
Workplace violence
Malevolence

Accidental Cluster: Low attribution of crisis responsibility

Challenges
Technical-error accidents
Technical-error product harm

Preventable Cluster: Strong attributions of crisis responsibility

Human-error accidents
Human-error product harm
Organizational misdeeds

The second step in assessing the reputational threat is to modify the initial assessment based upon crisis history and prior reputation. If an organization has had similar crises in the past, the current crisis will be a much greater reputational threat (Coombs, 2004b; Coombs & Holladay, 2004). The crisis history compounding the threat of the current crisis is known as the *Velcro effect* (Coombs & Holladay, 2002; Klein & Dawar, 2004). Organizations with a history of crises attract additional reputational damage, just as Velcro attracts lint. Similarly, an unfavorable prior reputation intensifies the reputational threat as well (Coombs & Holladay, 2006). So what does this really mean? If an organization has a history of crises or a negative prior reputation, stakeholders will treat a victim crisis like an accidental crisis and an accidental crisis like an intentional one. In turn, crisis managers must adjust which crisis response strategies to use (Coombs, 2006a; Coombs & Holladay, 2002).

Once the reputational threat is assessed, the crisis team selects the recommended crisis response strategy. SCCT posits that as the reputational threat increases, crisis teams should use more accommodative strategies. Research using nonvictim stakeholders has found support for the SCCT-recommended strategies (Coombs & Holladay, 1996, 2004). Table 8.3 lists the crisis response recommendations from SCCT.

It is important to understand how stakeholders perceive crises and crisis response strategies. SCCT takes an audience-centered approach to crisis communication, considering how stakeholders react to the crisis situation and crisis response strategies. SCCT goes far beyond the typical case study approach to crisis communication that many feel has limited the field's development (Ahluwalia et al., 2000; Coombs & Schmidt, 2000).

Table 8.3   Situational Crisis Communication Theory Recommendations for Crisis Response Selection

1.	Provide instructing information to all victims or potential victims in the form of warnings and directions for protecting themselves from harm.
2.	Provide adjusting information to victims by expressing concern for them and providing corrective action when possible. Note: Providing instructing and adjusting information is enough of a response for victim crises in an organization with no crisis history or unfavorable prior reputation.
3.	Use diminishment strategies for accident crises when there is no crisis history or unfavorable prior reputation.
4.	Use diminishment strategies for victim crises when there is a crisis history or unfavorable prior reputation.
5.	Use rebuilding strategies for accident crises when there is a crisis history or unfavorable prior reputation.
6.	Use rebuilding strategies for any preventable crisis.
7.	Use denial strategies in rumor crises.
8.	Use denial strategies in challenges when the challenge is unwarranted.
9.	Use corrective action (adjusting information) in challenges when other stakeholders are likely to support the challenge.
10.	Use reinforcing strategies as supplements to the other response strategies.
11.	The victimage response strategy should only be used with the victim cluster.
12.	To be consistent, do not mix denial strategies with either diminishment or rebuilding strategies.
13.	Diminishment and rebuilding strategies can be used in combination with one another.

With the threat to lives and property presented by a crisis, a focus on reputation may seem shallow. SCCT acknowledges that people are the first priority in a crisis. Only after instructing and adjusting information is provided should crisis managers turn their attention to reputation concerns. Reputation protection is a valuable aspect of crisis communication. Organizations invest a substantial amount of money and effort into building reputations.

Effects of Credibility and Prior Reputation on Crisis Response Strategies

Two additional points must be considered when discussing the crisis response strategies because they affect their use: credibility and prior reputation. As noted previously, credibility is composed of expertise and trustworthiness. Expertise is the organization's knowledge about the subject. An expert organization will appear to be competent, capable, and effective (Kouzes & Posner, 1993). Trustworthiness is the organization's goodwill toward or concern for its stakeholders. A trustworthy organization is truthful and ethical and considers how its actions will affect its stakeholders (Allen & Caillouet, 1994; Kouzes & Posner, 1993).

Although not referred to directly, credibility is an underlying theme in much of the crisis management literature. Two common refrains noted by crisis experts are that an organization must (1) establish control during a crisis and (2) show compassion during a crisis (e.g., Carney & Jorden, 1993; Frank, 1994; Sen & Egelhoff, 1991). When examining what is meant by control and compassion, a strong similarity is found with the expertise and trustworthiness dimensions of credibility. Control includes having accurate and complete information about the crisis (Bergman, 1994; Caruba, 1994; Kempner, 1995). Having such information shows that the organization is an expert about the crisis. Compassion means showing concern and sensitivity for those affected by the crisis (Higbee, 1992; T. H. Mitchell, 1986), which is consistent with trustworthiness. People trust an organization that seems to have their best interests in mind. Thus, crisis experts have indirectly argued the importance of credibility during crisis management.

Believability is essential during any type of crisis event because there always can be competing interpretations. For this reason, crisis experts repeatedly emphasize that an organization must get its side of the story or version of the crisis out quickly (e.g., Heath, 1994; Kempner, 1995). However, this advice has a hidden premise—it is assumed that stakeholders will believe what the organization says. The importance of believability is heightened when the crisis hinges on the stakeholders choosing between competing versions of the crisis story. In some crises, the accepted version will determine the success of the crisis management effort and affect the amount of damage inflicted by the crisis. Challenges and rumors are two types of crises that rest on the selection of competing crisis stories (Lerbinger, 1997). A closer look at challenges and rumors will clarify the importance of credibility to crisis management.

A challenge occurs when a stakeholder calls an organization's actions into question. The stakeholder claims that the organization is acting in ways that are inappropriate. Other stakeholders must decide whether to accept the claim of wrongdoing or to accept the organization's claim that its actions are appropriate (Lerbinger, 1997). Challenges are marked by ambiguity; there are some reasons why both sides may be correct. The ambiguity stems from the challenges being based on either morals or questions of product or service quality. A moral challenge is tied to some set of moral principles, such as a code of conduct. The UN Global Compact that recommends universal social and environment principles for companies is an example of such a code. A moral challenge does not involve the violation of any law or regulation. What is violated is a set of standards some stakeholders believe the organization should adhere to. Some examples include not buying fur because of the inhumane treatment of animals or not buying oil from Nigeria because of the Nigerian government's human rights abuses. The potential for a moral challenge is great since the world is composed of many diverse groups with conflicting views of appropriate conduct. During a moral challenge, stakeholders support the side that is the most believable or credible to them.

A challenge related to the quality of a product or service derives its ambiguity from how the data that measure quality are interpreted or from competing data sets that lead to different conclusions about the product or service quality. The Audi 5000 sudden-acceleration case exemplifies the ambiguity that can be associated with interpreting quality data. For a number of years, Audi 5000 drivers reported that the car would suddenly jump into gear and run. Sometimes there were deadly consequences, when people were unlucky enough to be in a vehicle's path at the time of the jump. Many customers defined the situation as a quality problem, a fault in the design of the Audi 5000's transmission system. Audi maintained that there was no reliable evidence that the transmission was faulty. Instead, Audi blamed the incidents on bad drivers. No definitive evidence supported either story; it all depended on how one interpreted the events. Eventually the 5000 was recalled and an antilocking device installed. Audi still maintained there was no problem, but stakeholders, including potential car buyers, found the Audi customers to have the more believable and credible story (Versical, 1987). Unless there is a government action, such as a recall or a jury decision in a lawsuit, challenges based upon quality are resolved by stakeholders selecting the story they feel comes from the most credible source and acting accordingly.

Rumors represent another form of crisis in which believability is essential. A rumor occurs when an untruthful statement about an organization is circulated. Since 2004, Starbucks has been fighting a rumor that it does not support U.S. and British troops. Marine Sergeant Howard C. Wright was the original source of the rumor. He had sent e-mails to friends saying Starbucks did not support the war. Starbucks reached out him and explained the real situation. He then sent out e-mails correcting his mistake, but the rumor had already infected the Internet. In 2010, Starbucks issued an update to the rumor control, again noting that the rumor was false and noting how Starbucks works with the Red Cross and the USO to provide coffee for the troops. Starbucks had devoted considerable time and resources to fighting the rumor (Starbucks, 2010). Rumor experts recommend that organizations respond immediately to rumors by stating that the information is untrue and unjust (Gross, 1990). Once more, a premium is placed on the credibility and believability of the organization. Defusing a rumor requires that the organization be perceived as a credible channel of information—the stakeholders must believe that the organization is a source of accurate information. The organization must be more credible than the rumor.

The benefit of credibility is that it increases the believability of an organization's message. The more credible the organization, the more likely stakeholders are to believe and to accept the organization's definition of the crisis, to believe the organization's side of the story. A second characteristic of a favorable precrisis organization–stakeholder relationship would be stakeholders viewing the organization as credible.

An organization's reputation overlaps with credibility but is considered a separate construct. An organization's prior reputation can be likened to a bank account—an organizational bank that contains reputational capital. A favorable reputation builds up the account, while a crisis subtracts from the account. Under certain limited circumstances (Coombs & Holladay, 2006), a favorable reputation can act as a shield to protect an organization from harm. In most cases, however, a crisis will inflict reputational damage, the loss of reputational capital.

An organization with a favorable reputation can experience stakeholders ignoring bad news about the organization because they are unlikely to believe that a good organization did anything bad. Crises can be one of the forms of bad news that is deflected by a strong reputation. The disbelief gives the organization the benefit of the doubt during the initial phases of a crisis, which provides two advantages. First, it supplies a buffer against people assuming the worst. In a crisis, the worst is when stakeholders believe the organization is responsible for the crisis. A strong account suffers less from the withdrawals of a crisis. Second, a favorable precrisis reputation means that an organization has reputational capital to spend, unlike those that are unknown or disliked.

While most people are quick to believe the worst about organizations, a favorable reputation can lead stakeholders to believe the best. In turn, this means the stakeholders would not jump to negative conclusions about the crisis. This position would be reevaluated once the facts about the crisis begin to emerge. A favorable reputation may also afford protection from the negative speculation that crises often produce.

Negative speculation refers to the nonexpert opinions that often fill the information void created by a crisis. Organizations are wise to respond immediately to prevent this void from developing. However, negative speculation may come more quickly than the facts during a crisis (Carney & Jorden, 1993). The negative speculation feeds into people's willingness to assume the worst about organizations, particularly corporations. A favorable reputation counters the negative speculation and the willingness to believe the worst. A favorable reputation should lead stakeholders to discount the negative speculation and to believe the best about an organization until that belief is proved to be unfounded. The stakeholders are predisposed to wait to hear the organization's side of the story before drawing conclusions about the crisis. A strong, favorable precrisis organization–stakeholder relationship shields the organization from undue reputational harm and makes it easier for the organization to deliver its side of the story.

■ SOCIAL MEDIA CONSIDERATIONS

As we consider the crisis response, the channels used to deliver it become more complicated with the expanding social media channels. Crisis managers have historically used the news media, advertising (primarily newspapers), and Web sites to deliver the crisis response to stakeholders. News releases and press conferences attempt to infuse the organization's side of the crisis (crisis response) into the news coverage. The news media often ignore these influence efforts (Holladay, 2009). Advertising and Web sites allow crisis managers to directly state the crisis response. Newspapers have been a frequent channel for delivering apologies to stakeholders. This happened with Exxon during the *Valdez* crisis and with the CEO of Facebook during the privacy crisis of 2010. Web sites allow for posting of crisis responses either in news releases or as special messages. When Taco John's had an *E. coli* outbreak in 2006, the company placed its crisis response messages on its corporate Web site. There is an evolving expectation that Web sites will be a part of the crisis response delivery system (Caldiero, Taylor, & Ungureanu, 2010; Taylor & Kent, 2007). Combined, we can call the news media, advertising, and Web sites the traditional crisis communication channels.

The delivery channel decision is more complex today because there are more options as well as pressure from "experts" to use social media. It is important to remember that social media is a mix of channels, and some are more relevant than others depending on the crisis situation, including the nature of the crisis, the target stakeholders, and the crisis response message. As noted in Chapter 4, message mapping includes considering the most effective channels for distributing the crisis message. If the target stakeholders are unlikely to be utilizing social media, it is not a useful option. But if the crisis is transpiring in the social media, it has to be part of the mix. The strategic application of social media requires a coordination of the demands of the crisis situation and the possible contributions of the specific social media channel.

An important crisis aspect to consider when using social media is who is at risk. A crisis can place stakeholders and the organization at risk. However, crises can be divided between those that focus on the risk to stakeholders and those that focus on the risk to the organization. As noted earlier, stakeholder safety is the number one priority in a crisis. Natural disasters, product tampering, workplace violence, product harm, and accidents all create risks that can spread among stakeholders. In each crisis, there is specific instructing information that can help prevent injury to stakeholders. An organization needs to make stakeholders aware of the risk and the requisite protective actions. For instance, consumers need to know which peanut butter has salmonella and what they should do if they have a jar of it. Awareness of a crisis should trigger a search for crisis-related information by the stakeholders at risk. Refer back to the CPSC's use of social media for delivering instructing information as an illustration of this point. A perfect example is how Twitter has been used during natural disasters such as the San Diego wildfires and the H1N1 flu outbreak in 2009. The Centers for Disease Control saw its Twitter followers go from a few thousand to hundreds of thousands after the news media created awareness of the H1N1 risk.

Social media is audience driven. People have to visit sites or become followers to access the information. Today, social media is a natural part of the search when people require information such as how to protect themselves from a crisis risk. Microblogs, blogs, content communities, discussion boards, and social networking sites are logical places for instructing information (part of the crisis response) when the emphasis is on the risk to stakeholders. A word of warning is important here. Being part of social media can create an expectation for interaction. Crisis managers must ensure that they have the resources to deal with the additional requests for information that might flow in once stakeholders access the organization's crisis response. Social media can tax the crisis manager's ability to appear to be open and transparent if the crisis team cannot meet the information requests generated by social media.

Rumor and challenge crises are those that emphasize the risk to the organization. Neither of these crises presents a true risk to public safety. The organization is at risk from damage created by the rumor or the challenge to its practices. Social media makes it easier for rumors to spread and for stakeholders to challenge an organization. Note how in Chapter 3 the social media drove the rumor over the danger of Pampers. The American Family Association (2005) used social media in its efforts to have Ford Motor Company stop providing same-sex partner benefits and marketing in gay media—a challenge to Ford's practices. For both rumors and challenges, the stakeholders can initiate the crisis via social media. Crisis managers must be where the action is and respond in the social media where the crisis originated, extend the message to related social media, and use their Web site as a repository for additional information. Chapter 4 discussed when Greenpeace challenged Nestlé's sourcing of palm oil in a number of social media sources, including Facebook. Greenpeace argued that irresponsible palm oil production was destroying orangutan habitats. Ollie the orangutan created a Facebook page and asked Facebook users to make the page more popular than Nestlé's. Angry stakeholders hijacked Nestlé's Facebook page by posting criticism and condemnations of the company's palm oil sourcing. Experts commenting on the crisis management noted how Nestlé did not use its Facebook page as part of its response (Leonard, 2010). Conversely, Pampers did engage critics on its Facebook page, giving it yet another chance to combat the rumor. Crisis managers must embrace potential interactions with stakeholders as a chance to debunk the rumor and argue for their side of the challenge.

Crises in which the organization is at fault (organizational misdeeds) also create a unique demand. If the organization is at fault, some type of rebuilding is expected by stakeholders. The rebuilding is a type of atonement and can include a full apology, some form of compensation, or both. To stand a chance of being effective, the organization must make its atonement known to stakeholders. Hence, crisis managers should utilize all social media at their disposal. Wherever the organization had a presence prior to the crisis, the crisis response should appear. Content sites, such as YouTube, and discussion boards could be used even if there was no prior organizational presence. Content sites and discussion boards do not have the same need to cultivate followers and content that you find with microblogs, blogs, and social networking sites. Only the most motivated stakeholders will seek out the atonement crisis response because it is not related to their safety—it lacks an inherently attractive quality. But the chance to reach more people at a low cost should not be ignored. However, once again, the organization may have to cope with interaction expectations and be prepared for that potentiality.

■ FOLLOW-UP COMMUNICATION

With all the emphasis on initial response, it is easy to overlook the need for follow-up communication with stakeholders. Crisis communication should continue throughout the life cycle of the crisis. Crisis teams must stay in touch with stakeholders. While the initial response has a mass media emphasis, follow-up communication can be better targeted to individual stakeholders. Better targeting means using the channels best suited to reaching particular stakeholders and tailoring the message to fit their needs (Carney & Jorden, 1993; Clampitt, 1991; Fombrun & Shanley, 1990). For instance, major investors may learn about a crisis from the news media. Follow-up communication to investors would center on their primary concern, the financial implications of the crisis, and use either calls or specially printed updates from the investor relations department. The external stakeholder network from the Crisis Knowledge Map Directory is valuable at this point. As noted in Chapter 7, the external stakeholder network will have the necessary contact information and preferred channels for reaching the stakeholders.

In addition to answering new inquiries, follow-up communication involves delivering any promised information and updating stakeholders about new developments. As noted earlier, there are times when crisis managers do not have answers to stakeholder questions and would do best to promise to pass the information along as soon as they receive it (C. J. Stewart & Cash, 1997). It is essential that the crisis team fulfill these promises. The crisis team must report to stakeholders, even if only to say that the information was never found. Credibility and organizational reputation are built on matching words and deeds (Herbig, Milewicz, & Golden, 1994). The crisis managers' words include their promises, and their actions fulfill those promises. An organization loses credibility and damages the organization–stakeholder relationships when crisis managers fail to deliver on their information promises.

Updates inform stakeholders about the progress of the crisis management effort. Four pieces of information are crucial to updates. First, let stakeholders know how the recovery effort is progressing. Second, announce the cause of the crisis as soon as it is known, if the cause was not known at the time of the initial message. Third, inform stakeholders of any actions taken to prevent a repeat of the crisis, including when those changes have been implemented. Fourth, report to stakeholders any third-party support your organization is receiving. Third-party support means that outside groups are praising your crisis management efforts or agreeing with your assessment of the situation. Examples include noted crisis experts giving the crisis management effort a positive review in the news media or the government saying the organization's stated cause of the crisis is correct. Supplying these four kinds of information builds the credibility of the organization. Items 1, 2, and 3 reinforce a perception of control, while Item 4 provides added credibility with the endorsement of an outside expert. Social media is a natural channel for follow-up information. If stakeholders are following the crisis through social media, it is very easy for crisis managers to post updates. Social media is meant to facilitate interaction; hence, updating information is simple.

Three final points about follow-up communication must be made. First, the spokesperson and crisis team should continue to field and respond to inquiries throughout the crisis. The crisis team must track and answer all inquiries. This now includes those made through social media. Second, the spokesperson should continue to express compassion in the follow-up communications. Losing sight of the victims in later messages can call the initial concern into question. Was the organization simply posturing in the news media? The organizational compassion must be real and be reflected in the follow-up communication, which includes both words and actions (Bergman, 1994; T. H. Mitchell, 1986). If aid is promised to victims, make sure it appears. Third, employee assistance programs should continue monitoring and treating negative reactions to the traumatic event. Once more, tracking crisis information is critical. The crisis team should be recording what follow-up actions were promised on the Stakeholder Relations Worksheets. Again, credibility is based on the organization's words matching its actions.

University Application: Stakeholders

Fires are one of the primary risks faced by universities. When you have buildings, they can catch fire. Seton Hall was hit by a deadly dorm fire in the late 1990s, and my own campus had a classroom building fire during class time. In a crisis such as a building fire, who are the likely key stakeholders for your university? Does it matter if the fire is in a dorm or a classroom building? Why or why not? What options does the university have for contacting these stakeholders? What challenges would the university face in trying to communicate with these stakeholders?

■ CONCLUSION

The actions taken in the crisis response phase are informed by the crisis-related information and knowledge gathered during the crisis recognition phase. The crisis team seeks to contain the damage and to return to business as usual as soon as possible. Communication is essential to limiting the duration of the crisis because it is at the heart of the initial response, reputational management, informing stakeholders, and providing follow-up information. The initial response allows the crisis team to reestablish a sense of organizational control over events and to express compassion for victims. Taking early control of the crisis prevents rumors and speculation from needlessly intensifying the crisis damage. Moreover, the response must be quick and consistent while the organization remains open to communication with stakeholders.

Crisis communication is ideal for combating the reputational damage associated with a crisis. Crisis response strategies affect how stakeholders perceive the crisis and the organization in crisis. In addition, the crisis itself limits the type of strategies that can be used effectively. Crisis managers should select the strategies that fit best with their particular crisis situation. SCCT provides guidelines, not absolute rules, to help crisis managers select the most effective responses for protecting reputational assets in a given crisis situation. The Business Continuity Plan allows an organization to function during a crisis and to return to business as usual more quickly. Crisis managers must communicate to relevant stakeholders how the continuity plan affects their interaction with the organization. In addition to the initial response, crisis managers have a variety of follow-up information they must communicate to stakeholders, including delivery of previously promised information and updates regarding the progress of the crisis management efforts. The ongoing organization–stakeholder dialogue continues throughout the crisis management process.

Regular, two-way communication between the organization and stakeholders is the lifeblood of a favorable organizational–stakeholder relationship. The dialogue must be maintained during good times and bad. Crises are part of the bad times. Remembering the importance of communicating with stakeholders aids the crisis management team in its efforts to contain and recover from the crisis.

DISCUSSION QUESTIONS

1. What are the advantages and disadvantages of using full apologies during a crisis? Do you think partial apologies have any real value? Why or why not?

2. As a crisis manager, how can you prepare for using instructing and adjusting information prior to a crisis?

3. Why does attribution theory seem so fitting for crisis communication?

4. What other crisis types would you add to Table 8.2?

9

Postcrisis Concerns

Eventually, every crisis comes to an end. The immediate effects of the crisis are passed, and the organization returns to business as usual. However, crisis managers should not feel that their work is completed when the crisis ends. First, it is critical that crisis managers evaluate their efforts. Organizations learn to improve their crisis management through evaluation. Second, crises must still be monitored after they are resolved. Monitoring might involve cooperating in continuing investigations or supplying necessary updated information to stakeholders.

This chapter begins by examining the role of evaluation in crisis management learning. The evaluation efforts link back to earlier crisis management steps, thus reflecting the ongoing nature of crisis management. Evaluation is the key to improvement. One way to improve the crisis management process is by learning what the organization did right or wrong during a crisis. Evaluation yields insights that should be treated as crisis management lessons. Because lessons should be remembered, the idea of institutional or organizational memory is discussed after evaluation. The chapter ends by reviewing the follow-up activities a crisis manager may need to perform and how postcrisis actions naturally lead back to crisis preparation.

■ CRISIS EVALUATION

An actual crisis is a "tremendous opportunity for learning" (Pauchant & Mitroff, 1992, p. 158). Learning is accomplished through evaluation of the crisis management efforts in two distinct ways. First, how the organization dealt with the crisis, its crisis management performance, is evaluated, examining the efficacy of the crisis management plan (CMP) and its execution (Barton, 2001). The crisis team carefully examines all phases of its performance. Second, the crisis impact is evaluated, a review of the actual damage created by the crisis is conducted (Sen & Egelhoff, 1991). A natural link exists between the two forms of evaluation. The actual crisis damage should be less than the anticipated crisis damage if the crisis management efforts were effective. Thus, damage assessments provide a tangible indicator of crisis management success or failure.

Crisis Management Performance Evaluation

Crisis management performance is primarily a function of the quality of the CMP and the crisis team's ability to make it work. Failure could result from an ineffectual CMP, poor execution of the CMP, or both (Mitroff, Harrington, & Gai, 1996). An organization must understand the source of failure or success if it is to learn from either. What lessons are learned if the organization does not know what it did well or poorly? Moreover, there are certain structural features (e.g., technology, infrastructure) that can facilitate or inhibit crisis performance (Mitroff et al., 1996). All facets of the crisis management performance must be assessed to determine strengths and weaknesses.

Data Collection

Data collection is the first step in any evaluation process. Evaluation data comes from crisis records, stakeholder feedback, organizational performance measures, Internet comments, and media coverage. The various crisis records document vital information, such as the notification process, the collection and processing of information, the receiving and answering of stakeholder queries, the crisis-related messages sent by the organization, and significant decisions and actions taken by the crisis management team (CMT). The primary sources of crisis documentation are the Incident Report Sheets, the CMT Strategy Worksheets, the Stakeholder Contact Worksheets, and the Information Log Sheets. The crisis records should be reviewed to determine if there were any noticeable mistakes made by the CMT. For example, was important information not processed, were stakeholder queries ignored, or were inappropriate messages sent to stakeholders? Again, administrative help during the crisis is essential in completing the paperwork that is used in the postcrisis analysis.

All stakeholder groups involved in the crisis can be asked for feedback, including employees and external stakeholders. The feedback can be collected by structured surveys, interviews, or focus groups. Simple surveys seem to be the most effective method. They minimize the time demands placed on the stakeholders and ensure that the evaluators receive the information they want. Typical questions on such a survey include the person's role in the crisis, level of satisfaction with and ways to improve notification, comments on specific strengths or weaknesses in the crisis management performance, and suggestions for improving the CMP (Barton, 2001). Different evaluation forms are required for the crisis team members, employees, and external stakeholders because the three groups have different connections to the crisis management process. Obviously, it is more difficult to secure the cooperation of external stakeholders, but every effort must be made to gather data that will provide a holistic picture of the crisis management performance. Media coverage and Internet comments are two other types of stakeholder feedback. The CMT should collect these types of information about the crisis. The CMT may choose to hire an independent consulting firm to collect the crisis performance data.

Organizing and Analyzing the Crisis Management Performance Data

Once collected, the data must be organized for the analysis. A danger in evaluation is not performing a specific analysis. For crisis management, an overall "good" or "poor" performance evaluation would be too general. Specificity is the key to useful evaluation. Specify in detail what was done well and done poorly. The specifics tell organization evaluators what changes need to be made and what must be retained. Mitroff et al. (1996) provide a number of helpful suggestions for organizing and analyzing crisis evaluation data. They suggest using four major crisis variables: crisis type, crisis phases, systems, and stakeholders. These variables divide the evaluation data into small, discernible units. Crisis managers can target strengths and weaknesses more precisely when data are divided. The value of Mitroff and colleagues' approach becomes clearer when the application of the specific crisis variables is considered.

Organizations face many different types of crises. Crisis teams may not handle all crises equally well. Crisis managers should compare evaluations from different crisis types to ascertain if there are patterns of strengths and weaknesses that are crisis specific (Mitroff et al., 1996; Pearson & Mitroff, 1993). Categorizing evaluations by crisis type permits cross-comparisons, which is one form of analysis.

As discussed earlier, crises move through distinct phases. Crisis management has been organized around three phases, with each having subphases. Crisis teams may handle the phases and subphases with different degrees of success and failure. For instance, a team may be adept at finding information but have problems articulating the organizational crisis response. Dividing the crisis evaluation data by crisis phases and subphases can help identify if the crisis team or CMP (or both) is weak in a particular part of the cycle. The crisis team could work on the skills associated with that segment, and the CMP could be revised to improve preparation for that target. Only by dividing evaluation data according to phases and subphases can the analysis reveal these types of specific strengths and weaknesses.

Systems include technology, human factors, infrastructure, culture, and emotions and beliefs. Technical systems organize the company's work and would include specific tasks along with the tools and materials necessary to complete them. Evaluators might ask, "Was the CMT hampered by lack of technical system support for crisis management?" The human factor system is the integration of people and machinery. It examines the fit between people and technology. Evaluators might ask, "Were the crisis management problems a function of a poor match between people and technology?"

Infrastructure refers to the connection of the crisis management team to the functioning of the organization. A permanent CMT should exist and be integrated into the operation of the organization. Some organizations may choose to use software designed to organize and facilitate the flow of crisis communication. One such program is Public Information & Emergency Response (PIER). A human factors evaluation would examine the fit between PIER and the crisis team. Evaluators might ask, "Did the CMT fail because it is not considered a functioning part of the organization?"

The cultural system refers to the extent to which the organization is oriented toward crisis preparation. Evaluators might ask, "Were the problems a function of cultural constraints, such as suppressing bad news?" Last, the emotional and belief system represents the dominant coalition's mind-set about crisis management. Evaluators might ask, "Did the crisis management effort fail because the dominant coalition does not support crisis preparation or the crisis response?" The examination of system-specific concerns helps to determine if the crisis management performance might have been a function of structural factors rather than the CMP or the CMT (Mitroff et al., 1996).

The system variables reflect the ongoing nature of crisis management as well, since the evaluation of system variables is most appropriate during the preparation phase. An organization can and should identify system flaws before a crisis hits. However, sometimes the flaws are hidden and do not surface until an actual crisis occurs. For example, the dominant coalition may espouse support for crisis management until there is a crisis. Then the support may evaporate. Or the stress of the crisis management process may create unexpected problems in how people utilize technology.

Reactions from all stakeholders affected by the particular crisis are useful for a thorough evaluation. How did they feel about the crisis management performance? The only way to assess stakeholder reactions is to ask for them. A cardinal rule in evaluation is to not assume you know how people feel about a message or action. By considering each stakeholder separately, an organization can determine specific strengths and weaknesses. Evaluators can determine which actions were effective or ineffective for specific stakeholder groups. For example, investors might be happy with the crisis-related information given and how they received it, while the community may be disappointed with how they received their information. Specific stakeholder reactions also will indicate which parts of the stakeholder network are effective or ineffective during crisis management.

Regardless of how the data are divided, the key is to identify the specific strengths and weaknesses of the CMP, the performance of crisis team, and structural features of the organization. Evaluations that are too general serve little purpose if the goal is to improve crisis management performance. The CMP should be revised by building on the strengths and developing ways to correct the weaknesses.

Crisis team members must be evaluated for both individual-level and group-level factors. As noted in Chapter 5, certain knowledge, skills, and traits are helpful in a crisis team member. In addition, the crisis team must perform as a group. Thus, the group-level factors, such as group decision making, are relevant during evaluation. The crisis management evaluation data should yield assessments of how individual team members performed as well as how the team as a whole performed.

Impact Evaluation

The crisis management performance should help the organization by protecting it from damage in some way. Crisis management is designed to protect important organizational assets such as people, reputation, and financial concerns (Barton, 2001; Marcus & Goodman, 1991). The crisis management performance evaluation should include measures of damage factors that reflect success or failure in protecting these assets.

The damage factors include financial, reputational, human, secondary financial, Internet frames, media frames, and media coverage duration. The financial factors are fairly standard: earnings per share, stock prices, sales, and market share (Baucus & Baucus, 1997; Baucus & Near, 1991; Sen & Egelhoff, 1991).

The reputational factors involve perceptions of the organization. Three related elements are relevant to assessing crisis effects on reputation: (1) pre- and postcrisis reputation scores, (2) media and Internet coverage of the crisis, and (3) stakeholder feedback. Any organization that expends resources on managing its reputation should make the effort to track its reputation over time. The organization should assess its reputation on a regular basis by soliciting evaluations from stakeholders. Comparing pre- and postcrisis organizational reputations is the strongest indicator of the reputational impact of a crisis.

To reiterate, reputations are built from direct and indirect stakeholder experiences with the organization. During a crisis, stakeholders experience an organization through the media, the Internet, and its crisis management actions. The media portrayals of the organization and the crisis can be critical in shaping the perceptions of other stakeholders involved in the crisis (Fearn-Banks, 2001; Pearson & Clair, 1998). Stories of an uncaring organization in disarray erode a reputation and injure the stakeholder–organization relationship. The media's power intensifies when it is the primary channel for reaching stakeholders. Stories in the media become the central crisis experiences when stakeholders have no real contact with the organization and are dependent on the media for information. Experts believe stakeholder crisis evaluations will reflect the media depictions. Thus, if the media are critical of the organization, its reputation with stakeholders could suffer. Conversely, the reputation would be protected by favorable media portrayals (Nelkin, 1988). With the growing use of the Internet, especially social media, for crisis information, online coverage of a crisis is important for the same reasons. Most stakeholders, especially those who are not victims, are most likely to experience the crisis through some combination of the news media and the Internet.

Organizations should use standard publicity analysis techniques to evaluate crisis coverage in the media and online. Analysts can examine media and Internet reports for positive and negative statements about the organization. To preserve important details, the positive and negative statements should be grouped by subphase to indicate precisely where the crisis managers were perceived as doing something good or bad.

Social media provides one additional piece of evaluative information— responses from stakeholders. Stakeholders can post online how they felt about the organization's crisis management. Analysis of these comments can provide insights into the effectiveness of the crisis management effort. Three important insights are as follows: Did stakeholders accept or reject the crisis response strategies? What did stakeholders like or dislike about the crisis management effort? What else did stakeholders want the organization to do? Of course, the online comments are not necessarily a representative sample of stakeholders, so crisis managers must put this information in perspective. However, the stakeholders that do comment show they are involved and willing to take action, which makes them an important subset of stakeholders.

Media and Internet coverage is an imprecise substitute for actual measures of reputation. Stakeholders do not always absorb and parrot impressions from the news media or Internet. These sources are not all-powerful. Stakeholders may disagree with media reports, especially if the reports run counter to their perceptions of the organization.

Skilled crisis managers communicate to stakeholders through channels other than the news media and Internet, such as telephone, direct mail, or e-mail. A well-developed stakeholder network provides the foundation for more direct contact with stakeholders. Thus, assessing stakeholder satisfaction with the crisis management performance is critical. As noted previously, external feedback from stakeholders should be part of any crisis management performance evaluation. Negative feedback suggests that there will be reputational damage because stakeholders perceive the crisis as mishandled. Conversely, positive feedback indicates that the CMT's good work might help to protect the reputation. Stakeholder evaluations have limitations when used to evaluate reputations; they are an imprecise substitute for actual reputation measures. As with the media and Internet coverage, other factors are at work. Media analysis, Internet analysis, and stakeholder feedback provide crude reputational indices but are useful when direct measures of reputation are lacking.

Human factors focus on victims, including deaths, injuries, disruptions (e.g., evacuations, changes in daily routines caused by the crisis), and environmental damage. Injuries, deaths, and disruptions can be recorded for quantity and severity. Environmental damage is included with human factors because injuries and deaths are often associated with it, even though the victims are animals and plants in this case. Perhaps crisis management has no higher priority than to protect the human factors.

Secondary financial factors are a reminder of the crisis because they continue to drain financial resources. These include lawsuits (number and total value) and new regulations. A large number of lawsuits, or an expensive few, drain an organization's financial resources. Court costs are a burden on top of any financial settlements. The litigation costs help to explain why some organizations settle lawsuits out of court while professing innocence and stating that the settlement was necessary to end the costly litigation process. For example, MetPath, a leading medical testing laboratory, paid $35 million to settle fraud charges while maintaining that it had done nothing wrong. New regulations are actions the government takes in response to a crisis. For example, the government may enact regulations to prevent a repeat of a crisis. The U.S. government considered banning the use of capsules for over-the-counter medications after the Sudafed and second Tylenol tamperings. Compliance with new regulations can create a financial impact that lasts for years (Sen & Egelhoff, 1991).

Media frames refer to the success of placing the organization's side of the story in the media. The organization's side of the story involves accurate information about what happened in the crisis, the organization's response, and the organization's interpretation of the crisis. Analysts search for evidence markers of the organization's side of the story in the media reports. These include quotations from organizational spokespersons, media use of organizational sound bites, and accurate descriptions of the crisis event. Media frame success is measured in two ways. First is a comparison of the amount of organizational frame material versus counter-frame materials in the media coverage. For instance, who was quoted more by the media: the organization or its critics? Second is the accuracy of the crisis-related information appearing in the media. The higher the percentage of information the organization considers accurate, the more successful its media frame efforts. The same holds true for the frames that appear in Internet reports of the crisis.

The duration of the crisis's media coverage is the final evaluative point. Effective crisis management tries to move a crisis out of the media (Higbee, 1992). A crisis does this by becoming uninteresting and losing its newsworthiness. Effective crisis management seeks to inform stakeholders and bring closure to a crisis. Both actions reduce newsworthiness. The information vacuum created by a crisis makes it newsworthy. Once stakeholders have the facts, particularly the cause of the crisis, audience curiosity and interest fades. When actions such as repaired damage or a return to normal operations indicate that a crisis is over, the situation loses the news value of being unusual. Conversely, crisis management errors, such as instigating conflict, prolong media coverage by sustaining the newsworthiness of a crisis. Two cases illustrate the relationship between newsworthiness and media coverage.

In May 1985, E. F. Hutton officials pleaded guilty to 2,000 counts of wire and mail fraud and paid a $2 million fine. The story attracted mild media attention as people wondered what had happened at this high-profile investment firm. In September 1985, E. F. Hutton officials announced the results of former Attorney General Griffin Bell's investigation of the case. Bell had been hired by the company to find the cause of the crisis and to provide corrective measures. E. F. Hutton fired 14 executives criticized in the report and pledged to institute other reforms designed to prevent a repeat of the crisis (Koepp, 1985). The media quickly lost interest after the report was issued. Penalties had been paid, guilt admitted, the *why* question answered, and E. F. Hutton was working to prevent a repeat of the crisis. The crisis appeared resolved, stripping it of any newsworthiness.

In April 1996, the Equal Employment Opportunity Commission (EEOC) filed a major sexual harassment lawsuit against Mitsubishi Motor Manufacturing of America. The company denied the charges and began a series of attacks against the EEOC. The response was deemed hostile by many observers and was highlighted by a media event when about 2,900 Mitsubishi workers demonstrated at EEOC offices in Chicago. Technically, the protest was organized by workers. However, Mitsubishi played a major role in facilitating the demonstration by allowing time off and helping to arrange bus transportation to Chicago (Annen & McCormick, 1997). The verbal barbs aimed at the EEOC and the litigation continued through 1997, as did the negative media coverage. When Mitsubishi's consultant, former Labor Secretary Lynn Martin, released a report on improving the workplace, the media greeted the announcement with skepticism and the crisis remained alive. The Mitsubishi–EEOC conflict kept the story alive by making it newsworthy. Crisis managers should try to reduce, not increase, the newsworthiness of a crisis. A CMT has erred when its actions prolong media coverage of the crisis.

An assessment of the financial, reputational, human, secondary financial, media and Internet frame, and media duration factors enable you to measure the final impact of the crisis. But how does this help with the evaluation of crisis management performance? Alone, these factors do not evaluate crisis performance. They simply describe the impact of the crisis. What crisis managers must do is compare the outcome to (a) the projections made about what the impact would have been if no actions were taken to manage the crisis and (b) the desired objectives of the crisis management team. While speculation is involved in both cases, careful projections can be made. Similar procedures are used in evaluating issues management efforts (Jones & Chase, 1979).

Honesty is important. The CMT must not inflate the potential damage or low-ball their objectives if the exercise is to be meaningful. What the damage assessment provides is some objective verification that the effect of the crisis performance was positive, negative, or of no consequence to the organization.

Summary

All of the various crisis performance data and analysis should be condensed into a final report, complete with an executive summary and recommendations. Remember, the purposes are learning and improving crisis performance, not assigning blame. Once completed, the evaluation indicates (a) whether the CMT did what it should have done and did so effectively, (b) whether the CMP proved useful in anticipating and resolving situations created by the crisis, (c) if structural features facilitated or hindered the crisis management effort, and (d) the crisis damage. Combined, this evaluation identifies specific strengths and weaknesses of the CMT, the CMP, and the organization. Furthermore, the inclusion of damage analyses indicates whether a crisis management performance is deemed successful. Sometimes a crisis team can execute a CMP well but still face massive damage, or a team can perform a suspect plan poorly yet the organization suffers little damage. For example, Johnson & Johnson had no CMP when it successfully managed the 1982 Tylenol tampering. There are exceptions to all rules, but crisis managers should not count on luck. It is much wiser to prepare.

■ MEMORY AND LEARNING

As mentioned, analysis creates crisis lessons. But what use are crisis lessons if they cannot be recalled to help prevent a repeat of a mistake or to recreate a success? Remembering and recall are the domains of institutional or organizational memory (Pearson & Mitroff, 1993). Knowledge management favors the term *organizational memory* as the repository of organizational knowledge (Li, YeZhuang, & Ying, 2004). Like people, organizations can store information and knowledge for later use (Weick, 1979). A crisis should not be wasted, because "direct experience with a crisis, although painful, teaches more than even the best scenario ever could" (Newsom, VanSlyke Turk, & Kruckeberg, 1996, p. 544). Evaluation reveals the lessons that hard experience teaches the organization. And the crisis lessons must be remembered by becoming a part of institutional memory.

Effective use of institutional or organizational memory involves storage and retrieval (Li et al., 2004; Weick, 1979). First, there must be some means of recording and storing the crisis knowledge: the crisis documentation and the evaluation report, the crisis lessons. Storage options include hard copies and computer files. Either means requires redundancy and storage at multiple locations (Pauchant & Mitroff, 1992). Storage is more than recording knowledge; it also involves rating key crisis information for accuracy and comprehensiveness. Not all crisis information and knowledge are of the same quality, though. Some knowledge is more accurate—more fact than speculation—and more comprehensive—more complete and containing fewer potential errors (Garvin, 1996).

The crisis knowledge must be easy to retrieve for later use. Retrieval involves being able to search for and locate specific details (Weick, 1979). The intranet is a logical place to store crisis knowledge for easy retrieval. Intranet systems can use their own search mechanisms. Careful organization and input of the crisis knowledge will permit easy searches and retrieval during later crisis management efforts. Again, recording is not a simple process. The crisis knowledge must be carefully and accurately stored if it is to be useful. Each organization must develop its own system for organizing crisis knowledge into a format that is searchable and retrievable.

Organizational memory requires a word of warning—do not become a slave to memory (Weick, 1979). Crisis managers must be willing to disregard past actions and knowledge if they do not fit well with a current crisis. Blindly following past successes can lead to blunders when the past crisis is not wholly consistent with the current crisis. Organizational memory of crises can help to create an information acquisition bias. The memory of past crises is both a blessing and a curse. However, the skilled CMT should be able to overcome the blind spot of information acquisition bias.

But what good is a memory if it is never used? Crisis managers can carefully dissect the crisis management effort and skillfully record those lessons. If those lessons do not move from memory to action, the organization and the crisis teams have not learned. Organizational learning is a vast and complicated discipline. One short section in a book cannot do it justice but can lead crisis managers to learn more about the subject. Organizational learning seeks to understand how organizations adapt and change—how they learn. Of course, the term *organizational learning* itself is debated because isn't it really people in the organization that learn? But let's assume that organizations can learn. How might they learn from the evaluation of a crisis management effort? Ideally, the evaluation helps people in the organization understand what they are doing right and what they are doing wrong. The strengths are reinforced and weaknesses are corrected. Through correction comes adaptation and learning.

Argyris and Schön (1978) talk about two types of learning in organizations: single-loop and double-loop:

> When the error detected and corrected permits the organization to carry on its present policies or achieve its present objectives, then that error-and-correction process is *single-loop* learning. Single-loop learning is like a thermostat that learns when it is too hot or too cold and turns the heat on or off. The thermostat can perform this task because it can receive information (the temperature of the room) and take corrective action. *Double-loop* learning occurs when error is detected and corrected in ways that involve the modification of an organization's underlying norms, policies and objectives. (pp. 2–3)

We can apply these ideas to learning driven by crises. Some crises reveal simple factors that are easy to correct—single-loop learning. Other crises require a serious reconsideration of organizational principles and practices—double-loop learning. An industrial accident illustrates this point. An employee is unloading chemicals and unloads them into the wrong tank, resulting in a chemical reaction and explosion. Analysis of the crisis management effort finds that the employee was a new hire and had not been fully trained on chemical unloading procedures. All other employees are fully trained and would know not to mix the two chemicals. Training one employee is the solution—single-loop learning. But what if analysis reveals a general lack of safety training and enforcement of safety rules by management? The problem is systemic and requires a more complicated solution as the organization must wrestle with it safety culture—double-loop learning. The point is that organizational learning sounds easy but can be complex. Just because lessons are found and recorded does not mean they will be applied—there are no guarantees an organization will learn from a thorough evaluation of a crisis and crisis management effort.

■ POSTCRISIS ACTIONS

The responsibility of the crisis team continues until all crisis-related obligations are fulfilled. The postcrisis tasks can be divided into three groups: follow-up communication, cooperation with investigations, and

WHAT WOULD YOU DO?   BP AND TEXAS CITY: ACT 3

It is now three days since the initial blast at Texas City. The news media have been running stories about other accidents at the Texas City plant. One story announces that BP has the worst safety record in the petrochemical industry. A total of 15 people have been killed and over 100 injured. Twelve of the injured are still hospitalized. The U.S. Chemical Safety and Hazard Investigation Board (CSB) investigation team is on-site. The CSB is there to determine the cause of the blast. The CSB notes that key alarms were not working and that the startup was done even though important parts of the system were not working properly. Also, BP had not connected the damaged tower to a safety flare system. A recommendation to change the safety system had been made well before the accident, and BP management's own documents show that it were aware of the recommendation.

- What can you do to help craft an effective response to this crisis?

- What should BP be saying and doing now?

crisis tracking. Even though the organization has returned to normal operations and the immediate effects have dissipated, the cause of the crisis may still be under investigation by government officials. The crisis team must be sure to cooperate with any investigation. Cooperation builds goodwill with the government agencies involved and indicates to other stakeholders that the organization is open and honest. Openness leads to the topic of follow-up communication.

Follow-up communication is an extension of the crisis recovery phase. Crisis managers maintain positive organization–stakeholder relationships by keeping stakeholders informed about the crisis even when it is over and by continuing to answer new inquiries. Again, social media is ideal for follow-up information; the channels are designed for updating of information. Employee assistance efforts must continue as well, to help those overwhelmed by the trauma of the crisis. Crisis managers should update the stakeholders on the progress and results of ongoing investigations and the actions being taken to prevent a repeat of the crisis. In regard to preventing future crises, crisis managers might tell stakeholders when the changes have been completed and how well the changes are working. The changes actually become part of the crisis prevention subphase, since the actions are designed to prevent future crises.

Special consideration should be given to memorials, which celebrate or honor the memory of people or events. Crises have the potential to trigger memorializing, especially when there is loss of life. The September 11 attacks and the Oklahoma City bombing resulted in memorializing. Memorials are important because they help people mourn and cope with grief and they provide an opportunity to recognize rescuers (Foot, Warnick, & Schneider, 2005). Organizations and/or stakeholders may feel the need to create memorials. A memorial can be viewed as a follow-up to the recognition of those injured or lost immediately after a crisis occurs. Shortly after an accident killed six employees in Kinston, North Carolina, West Pharmaceuticals held a memorial service, and a year later it dedicated two memorial plaques in the lobby of its new Kinston facility.

Memorials can be off-line, such as the plaques in Kinston, or online. Following the explosion and sinking of the Deepwater Horizon, Transocean created a condolence Web site. The site recognized the 11 employees who died and gave people an opportunity to post messages and share memories, photographs, and videos of those who perished. September 11 saw the creation of the Cantor Families Memorial Web site for employees of Cantor Fitzgerald and the Association of Flight Attendants creating an "In Memoriam" page for those they had lost (Foot et al., 2005). The Cantor Families Memorial has individual tribute pages for the departed employees, arranged in alphabetical order. Each page has a set format, but people are permitted to write their own tributes. Foot et al. (2005) note that the Web memorial is "a remarkable example of individual memorializing on a corporately produced site" (p. 82). Here is the statement that appears on the home page for the Cantor Families Memorial site:

> On the morning of September 11th, we lost more than a team. We lost family. We mourn the losses of our siblings, our best friends, and our partners. We cannot imagine work or life without them nor their many unique qualities and characteristics. They have enriched our lives immeasurably, and in us, their spirits shall live on.
>
> This Web site was created for the Cantor family of companies and all employees of eSpeed, Inc., Cantor Fitzgerald, L.P., and TradeSpark, L.P., to commemorate all those lost in the World Trade Center tragedy. It is dedicated to preserving and celebrating the memory of our families, our friends, and our colleagues. Please join with us now in paying tribute to those who have so deeply touched—and continue to touch—our lives. (*In Loving Memory*, n.d.)

Online memorials permit more of a personal touch—ordinary people can leave personal comments (Hess, 2007). Leaving comments about grief and loss help people complete the healing process (Carlson & Hocking, 1988; Siegl & Foot, 2004). Crisis managers may want to encourage or facilitate the creation of online memorials and even offline memorials if people within the organization feel it will help in the recovery process. The examples from Cantor Fitzgerald and Transocean show there are different ways to facilitate the development of online memorials. The key is that stakeholders affected by the crisis have a place to go that helps with the grieving process. Crisis managers also should scan the Internet for spontaneous online memorials. Photo-sharing sites are a logical place for online memorials to emerge, but stakeholders might create memorial Web sites as well. Crisis managers could then provide links to these memorial sites to other stakeholders in order to help build a community for healing.

Any crisis must be monitored when it is over, even if no changes are initiated. Crisis tracking monitors the factors that produced the crisis to see whether another threat may arise. Crisis tracking feeds back into signal detection and crisis preparation. Simply put, the postcrisis phase ends with crisis managers moving back to the actions involved in the precrisis phase of crisis management; the process is ongoing.

WHAT WOULD YOU DO? | **DIAMOND PET FOODS AND TOXIC DOG FOOD: ACT 2**

You are still actively recalling your product when a second problem arises. Some smaller news outlets are reporting that Diamond Pet Foods knew there was aflatoxin in the corn but used it anyway. The stories imply that your company knowingly put dogs at risk. There is no evidence to support this story, though it could be a result of Diamond Pet Foods management saying they did see high levels of aflatoxin being found in 2005 corn shipments. However, all shipments were tested per company regulations, and problematic shipments were rejected.

- Does your company need to address this new concern?

- Why or why not?

- If you decide that action is necessary, how will you address this new concern?

■ CONCLUSION

Even when a crisis is perceived to be over, the efforts of the crisis management process remain in motion. The crisis management performance must be evaluated. Careful evaluation is essential to improved performance. The downside is that a thorough evaluation is time-consuming and somewhat painful. Still, the rewards more than justify the expenditure of resources. Evaluation and crisis documentation should become part of the functional institutional or organizational memory. A well-organized recording of crisis knowledge will allow the knowledge to be used effectively during future crisis management efforts. Last, the crisis team must help any continuing investigations, maintain the flow of follow-up information to stakeholders, and continue to track the crisis. In so doing, the crisis team has a natural segue back to the precrisis phase of crisis management, showing that crisis management can be an ongoing process.

DISCUSSION QUESTIONS

1. How often do you feel key stakeholders should be updated with post-crisis information?

2. How can crisis logs help to make postcrisis updates more effective?

3. What is the danger of having an organizational crisis memory?

4. What are some of the barriers you would face when conducting a post-crisis evaluation? How might you overcome those barriers?

Epilogue

Lessons and Challenges for Crisis Communication

n other writings I have argued that all the various crisis communication activities employed in crisis management can be divided into two categories: (1) managing information and (2) managing meaning. The information void created by a crisis demands the collection and analysis of information. Without processing information, crisis teams could never make the decisions required to drive action. Preparation and prevention require careful information processing as well. Managing meaning involves efforts to influence how stakeholders, both internal and external, perceive threats, the crisis, the crisis response, and the organization involved in the crisis. Managing meaning is critical because it can determine whether action is taken on a threat or crisis and stakeholders' affective and behavioral reactions following a crisis (Coombs & Holladay, 2005; Jin & Cameron, 2007; Jin & Pang, 2010).

The three stages of crisis management and the two categories of crisis communication can be combined for the crisis communication array (Coombs, in press), which is illustrated in Figure E.1. The visual helps crisis managers "see" the various applications of crisis communication throughout the crisis management process. In this chapter, the crisis communication array serves as the organizing framework for summarizing what we really know about crisis communication. Understanding the crisis communication knowledge base is a crucial element in articulating a reliable set of recommendations about crisis communication. Unfortunately, the practice of crisis communication runs ahead of theory. That means we see practices emerging that are in use but have yet to be researched. It is important to consider these emerging trends, as they lack evidence but are still important challenges for crisis managers.

Figure E.1   Crisis Communication Array

Crisis Phase	Managing Information	Managing Meaning
Precrisis/Prevention and Preparation		
Crisis Response		
Postcrisis/Learning		

Source: Adapted from "Crisis Communication: A Developing Field" (p. 479), by W. T. Coombs, in R. L. Heath (Ed.) *The SAGE Handbook of Public Relations* (Thousand Oaks, CA: SAGE). Copyright © 2010, SAGE Publications, Inc.

■ EVIDENCE-BASED CRISIS COMMUNICATION

Both medicine and management have witnessed a growing evidence-based movement. An evidence-based approach means that physicians or managers use data for decisions, not simply speculation or accepted wisdom (Rousseau, 2005). I have argued that crisis communication would benefit from an evidence-based approach (Coombs, 2007, 2010). Crisis communication is a relatively young discipline born of a need to address very real problems. Typical of applied fields, it began as collections of "war stories" as crisis managers described what they had done to combat a crisis. Slowly a body of accepted wisdom began to emerge. Even more slowly, researchers began to test some of the accepted wisdom and develop theories to explain why certain actions should or should not be taken in a crisis. For instance, the accepted wisdom said to avoid saying "no comment" and to get the organization's message out fast. Later research demonstrated that when stakeholders hear, "No comment," they assume the organization is guilty and management is trying to hide something from them. Additional research found that organizations suffer less reputational damage when they are the first to report that a crisis exists, what the researchers termed *stealing thunder*. In both cases the research provided evidence to support the accepted wisdom.

We now have a growing body of crisis communication theory that seeks to guide crisis management efforts. Table E.1 lists some of the key theories and researchers tied to each approach. Moreover, some researchers are using experimental methods to test theories, thereby creating actual evidence for evidence-based crisis communication. The move to experimental methods is important because crisis communication research has been dominated by case studies. While case studies can be insightful, their results are more speculation than evidence. The crisis case studies utilize qualitative research methods, resulting in the speculative nature of their findings (Stacks, 2002).

Table E.1   Key Crisis Theories and Researchers

Crisis Communication Theories	Theorists
Corporate Apologia	Hearit
Image Restoration Theory/Image Repair Discourse	Benoit
Focusing Event	Fishman, Birkland
Discourse of Renewal	Seeger, Ulmer, Sellnow
Situational Crisis Communication Theory	Coombs, Holladay
Contingency Theory (Integrated Crisis Mapping)	Cameron, Jin, Pang

■ CRISIS COMMUNICATION LESSONS, RECOMMENDATIONS, AND TRENDS

This section summarizes the findings that have emerged from the growing body of crisis communication research. I resist using the term *best practices* because that often implies a limited, prescriptive framework. Crisis communication is very dynamic and difficult to reduce to a reliable set of actions to be taken in any crisis. Rather, this section is a collection of lessons that crisis managers can draw upon when preparing for or managing a crisis. The lessons are arranged using the six areas identified in the crisis communication array. In addition, I have included recommendations and trends. Recommendations are common advice given to crisis managers that have yet to be tested. Recommendations are logical and reflect common sense. Trends are emerging practices that lack theory and research but are factors that demand attention. Trends reflect how theory is behind practiced in crisis communication.

Precrisis Managing Information

Crisis teams are more effective when they train.

Crisis teams must train with new technology or they will not use the technology during a crisis.

Recommendation: Update the crisis management plan at least annually.

Recommendation: When possible, create a message prior to the crisis to save time.

Recommendation: Prepare dark Web sites and some social media for use during a crisis.

Precrisis Managing Meaning

- Trend: Social media is increasingly important to crisis scanning and monitoring.
- Trend: Paracrises are increasing in frequency, demanding public crisis prevention.

Crisis Response Managing Information

Ineffective instructing information reduces the effectiveness of the crisis response and threatens public safety.

Web sites and social media can be valuable communication channels during a crisis.

- Trend: Technology is increasing the ability of crisis teams to share information even when they are not in the same location.
- Trend: Sharing information internationally is becoming a greater concern with the rise of international crises.

Crisis Response Managing Meaning

When organizations are the first to report about a crisis, the damage to the reputation is reduced.

"No comment" will be interpreted negatively by stakeholders.

Adjusting information reduces the reputational threat from a crisis.

Apology and compensation are equally effective at protecting reputations.

Crisis responsibility is positively correlated with reputational damage and anger.

Crisis responsibility is negatively correlated with purchase intention.

Increased anger results in a greater likelihood of negative word of mouth.

A negative prior reputation increases the reputational threat from a crisis.

A history of prior crisis increases the reputational threat from a crisis.

Appearing pleasant on camera increases credibility and decreases perceived deceptiveness.

Recommendation: Avoid speculating during a crisis.

Recommendation: Create a message map to add clarity and speed to the crisis response.

Recommendation: Use search engine protocols to your advantage in online crisis messages.

Recommendation: Use mass notification systems to save time and lives and to provide some legal advantages.

Recommendation: Provide counseling to employees and other stakeholders when needed.

Recommendation: Keep all employees informed about the crisis management effort.

- Trend: The challenge of managing meaning is greater across national boundaries with more international crises.

Postcrisis Managing Information

Recommendation: Deliver any information promised to stakeholders during the crisis response.

- Trend: Social media is increasingly used to provide follow-up information.
- Trend: Social media provides a chance to interact with stakeholders after a crisis.

Postcrisis Managing Meaning

Social media can be used to evaluate stakeholder reaction to a crisis and the organization's crisis response.

Recommendation: Analyze the crisis management effort, and try to facilitate organizational learning.

- Trend: Online memorials are likely to appear after crises.

■ TRENDS AS CHALLENGES

While trends have yet to generate the research necessary to create evidence, crisis managers must be aware of the challenges they create and that will shape the future of crisis communication. The trends identified in the lessons section fall into three categories: social media, international crises, and technology.

Social Media

Stakeholders are actively creating and sharing content online through messages and images. Crisis managers must learn to harness the power of social media by integrating it into efforts to scan for and monitor crisis threats. One consequence is that some crisis threats need to be managed in public. These paracrises will appear very similar to crises but are really efforts to address a crisis threat. Paracrises are most closely associated with challenges, rumors, and product harm crises. They blur the lines separating precrisis and crisis response. Social media has already proved its value to crisis response. Still, we lack insights into its exact value in providing instructing information and how best to utilize the interactive nature of social media during a crisis. Crisis managers need to understand how social media and traditional Web sites can be used to create online memorials following a crisis. The challenge is how to effectively coordinate the organization's follow-up communication with these spontaneous memorials.

International Crises

The future of business is increased internationalization. Increasingly, goods and services are produced and/or distributed in more than one country. The transnational companies behind these goods and services are located in a home country, where the base of operation is, and host countries, where other assets are. Moreover, most supply chains are now transnational. International crises arise as transnational organizations must manage a crisis in two or more countries. There are two types of international crises: host and global. A host occurs in one or more host countries. Global crises appear in the home country and one or most host countries. Both types require companies to manage crises outside of their own country and comfort zone. Crisis managers will be less familiar with how to manage a crisis and communicate in the host countries than in the home country. Crisis managers must resist ethnocentric tendencies as they cope with stakeholders in different cultures, unfamiliar media systems and online usage patterns, and different legal concerns (Coombs, 2008).

Carrefour is a French department store chain similar to Walmart and Tesco. In 2008, French protestors repeatedly attacked the Olympic torch as it when through France. The torch was extinguished a few times and the route had to be altered. The French protestors were unhappy that the 2008 Olympics were in Beijing when China was abusing human rights, especially in Tibet. The attacks were viewed as an insult by many Chinese citizens, and Carrefour, as a symbol of France, came under fire. The Internet was swimming with calls to boycott Carrefour to go along with the many off-line protests against Carrefour. The company was in a global crisis. The crisis was in China (host country) but also had ramifications for the home country, as the

French human rights stakeholders were not pleased with Carrefour's efforts to support the 2008 Olympics. The situation did not stabilize for Carrefour until the Chinese government requested that people not punish Carrefour for protestors with no connection to the company.

Technology

New technology is driving Internet changes as new communication channels continue to appear. Crisis managers must attempt to understand how each new channel might affect the practice. Another concern is understanding how to integrate technology into crisis team operations. Mass notification software is not static, and crisis managers must assess how any changes might help in crisis communication. Technology can be used to keep crisis team members in contact when they are in different locations and provide software that can help to manage the information processing required during a crisis. Crisis Commander is an example of a set of software solutions designed to aid crisis information sharing and processing. It provides emergency notification, allows crisis teams members to stay in contact with one another, offers a way to access plans and other needed information, and provides logs for recording information (Crisis Commander, 2008).

■ CONCLUSION

Crisis communication is a dynamic field. Research and practice are constantly adding new ideas that can be valuable to crisis managers. Throughout this book, I have synthesized existing crisis management ideas with some new ideas to produce a communication-based framework for approaching crisis management. The framework is intended to be a tool for integrating the diverse writings and ideas about crisis management into a manageable guide. The crisis management process has been divided into three stages as a way to organize and synthesize the various insights. The three-stage model emphasizes the ongoing nature of the crisis management process and communication demands.

Crisis management never ends. At any given time, the crisis manager is simply working on different parts of the process. I believe the integrative power of this book offers unique insights into crisis management. I hope it has informed your views on the crisis management process.

DISCUSSION QUESTIONS

1. What types of crises do you feel would be the most difficult to manage? What makes them so difficult to manage?

2. Do you feel that not using new communication technologies in crisis communication will actually hurt a crisis response or simply make an organization look like it is behind the times? What is the true value of new communication technology to crisis communication?

3. If you could make five recommendations to an organization about crisis communication, what would they be? What is the value of each of your recommendations?

4. What makes managing international crises so difficult?

5. What special communicative challenges are created by international crises?

6. What recommendations would you make to crisis managers about using social media before, during, and after a crisis?

Appendix

Possible Case Studies

Company	Year	Event	Location
Disney	1997–2005	Boycott by American Family Association	
Union Carbide Corporation	1998	Nitrogen leak and asphyxiation	Hahnville, LA
Morton International	1998	Explosion and fire	Paterson, NJ
Sonat Exploration	1998	Vessel failure	Pitkin, LA
Tosco Corporation	1999	Oil refinery fire	Martinez, CA
Concept Sciences	1999	Hydroxylamine explosion	
eBay	2000	Computer hacking	
Amazon.com	2000	Computer hacking	
Buy.com	2000	Computer hacking	
NuWood	2001	Workplace violence	Goshen, IN
Wendy's	2001	Challenged by PETA for not meeting animal welfare guidelines	
Bethlehem Steel	2001	Facility fire	Chesterton, IN
BP Amoco	2001	Hot plastic accident	Augusta, GA
Motiva Enterprises	2001	Refinery explosion and fire	Delaware City, DE

(Continued)

(Continued)

Company	Year	Event	Location
Georgia-Pacific	2002	Hydrogen sulfide gas leak	Pennington, AL
Third Coast Industries	2002	Facility fire	Brazoria County, TX
DPC Enterprises	2002	Chlorine transfer hose rupture and release	Festus, MO
Kaltech Industries	2002	Facility explosion	New York, NY
Tyco International	2002	Executives stealing money	
Enron	2002	Illegally hiding debt from investors	
Adelphia	2002	Illegally hiding debt from investors	
WorldCom	2002	Illegally hiding debt from investors	
HealthSouth	2002	Illegally hiding debt from investors	
Air Midwest	2003	Flight 5481 crash due to improper maintenance	Charlotte, NC
Lockheed Martin	2003	Workplace violence	Meridian, MS
Chi-Chi's	2003	Hepatitis outbreak	Pittsburgh, PA
First Chemical	2002	Explosion of distillation tower	Pascagoula, MS
BLSR Operating	2003	Vapor cloud fire	Rosharon, TX
D. D. Williamson	2003	Vessel failure	Louisville, KY
Technic	2003	Facility explosion	Cranston, RI
Isotec	2003	Explosion of distillation tower	Miami Township, OH
West Pharmaceutical Services	2003	Facility explosion and fire	Kinston, NC

Company	Year	Event	Location
CTA Acoustics	2003	Facility explosion and fire	Corbin, KY
Honeywell	2003	Chlorine gas release	Baton Rouge, LA
Hayes Lemmerz	2003	Series of explosions at facility	Huntington, IN
DPC Enterprises	2003	Chlorine gas leak	Glendale, AZ
Merck	2004	Heart attacks and strokes from VIOXX	
McDonald's	2004	CEO Jim Cantalupo dies of heart attack	
Giant Industries	2004	Gasoline component released and exploded	Gallup, NM
MFG Chemical	2004	Toxic allyl alcohol vapor release	Dalton, GA
Formosa Plastics	2004	Polyvinyl chloride explosion	Illiopolis, IL
Qwest Communications International	2005	Illegally hiding debt from investors	
San Francisco 49ers	2005	Improper team media training video	
Acetylene Service Company	2005	Gas explosion	Perth Amboy, NJ
Marcus Oil	2005	Storage tank failure	Houston, TX
BP	2005	Series of explosions at facility	Texas City, TX
Ford Motor Company	2005, 2006	Boycott by American Family Association	
Synthron	2006	Facility explosion	Morganton, NC
Cadbury	2006	Food poisoning from chocolate	
Dell, Apple, and Toshiba	2006	Defective laptop batteries	

(Continued)

(Continued)

Company	Year	Event	Location
HP	2006	Unethical means to obtain phone records	
Reebok	2006	Lead in child's bracelet	
Earthbound Farms and Dole	2006	*E. coli* in spinach	
Princess Cruises	2006	Fire on board a ship	
Princess Cruises	2006	Steering malfunction	
Taco Bell	2006	*E. coli* in green onions	
JetBlue	2007	Passengers stuck on planes	
Menu Foods	2007	Melamine in pet food recall	
Harry & David	2007	Undeclared nut allergen	
Campbell Soup	2007	Plastic in soup	
Fisher-Price	2007	Entrapment hazard in child's swing	
Polaris Industries	2007	Bearing failure in all-terrain vehicles	
Lowe's	2007	Fire hazard in halogen lights	
Bassettbaby	2008	Entrapment hazard in a crib	
Walmart	2008	Lead poison hazard in charms	
Arctic Cat	2008	Inability to control speed	
Nestlé	2008	Aluminum in strawberry powder	
Matterhorn Group	2008	Plastic in novelty pops	
Bayer CropScience	2008	Facility explosion	Charleston, WV
AstraZeneca	2009	Marketing of Seroquel	
Dole Foods	2009	Lawsuit about *Bananas* film	
Ketchum	2009	Insulted client with tweet	

Company	Year	Event	Location
KFC	2009	Failure to have enough chicken for giveaway	
Peanut Corporations of America	2009	Peanut butter paste recall	
Ryanair	2009	Dispute over BBC interview	
Toyota	2009	Recall over sticking accelerator pedal	
Amazon.com	2009	Deleting books by George Orwell	
Red Bull	2009	Traces of cocaine found in product	
Maclaren	2009	Stroller recall due to finger hazard	
Kellogg	2009	Closed Eggo factory due to contamination	Atlanta, GA
Burger King	2009	Use of Mexican flag in Spanish-language ad	
Apple	2009	Exploding iPhones in Europe	
BP	2010	Deepwater Horizon explosion and oil spill	Gulf of Mexico
Activision	2010	Fired key executives	
Tesoro	2010	Refinery fire	Anacortes, WA
POM Wonderful	2010	Controversial ads	
Johnson & Johnson	2010	Product recall for smell and contamination	
Royal Caribbean	2010	Quick return to Haiti	
Nestlé	2010	Palm oil conflict with Greenpeace	
H&M	2010	Destroying good clothing rather than donating it	
Pampers	2010	Rumors about products harming babies	
HP	2010	Laptop battery fire hazard	

(Continued)

Company	Year	Event	Location
Hoover	2010	Vacuum recalled for shock hazard	
Kleen Energy	2010	Facility explosion	Middletown, CT
DuPont	2010	Toxic release of phosogene	Belle, WV
Air New Zealand	2010	"Cougar" promotion and video	

References

About.com. (2002). *Febreze toxic to pets?* Retrieved October 7, 2010, from http:// urbanlegends.about .com/library/blfebrez.htm

Abrams, A. L. (n.d.). *Legal strategies: Crisis management and accident investigation.* Retrieved October 5, 2010, from http://www.asse.org/ practicespecialties/riskmanage ment/docs/Abrams%20Paper.pdf

Agle, B. R., Mitchell, R. K., & Sonnenfeld, J. A. (1999). Who matters to CEOs? An investigation of stakeholder attributes and salience, corporate performance, and CEO values. *Academy of Management Journal, 42,* 507–525.

Ahluwalia, R., Burnkrant, R. E., & Unnava, H. R. (2000). Consumer response to negative publicity: The moderating role of commitment. *Journal of Marketing Research, 27,* 203–214.

Ajzen, I. (2002). Perceived behavioral control, self-efficacy, locus of control, and the theory of planned behavior. *Journal of Applied Social Psychology, 32,* 665–683.

Allen, M. W., & Caillouet, R. H. (1994). Legitimation endeavors: Impression management strategies used by an organization in crisis. *Communication Monographs, 61,* 44–62.

Alsop, R. J. (2004). *The 18 immutable laws of corporate reputation: Creating, protecting, and repairing your most valuable asset.* New York: Free Press.

American Family Association. (2005). *Ford supports homosexual polygamy.* Retrieved October 17, 2010, from http://media.afa.net/newdesign/ ReleaseDetail.asp?id=3464

American Management Association. (2003). *Crisis management and security issues 2004 survey.* Available from http://www.amanet.org/ training/articles/2004-Crisis-Managements-and-Security-Issues-16.aspx

Ammerman, D. (1995). What's a nice company like yours doing in a story like this? In L. Barton (Ed.), *New avenues in risk and crisis management* (Vol. 3, pp. 3–8). Las Vegas: University of Nevada Las Vegas, Small Business Development Center.

Annen, P., & McCormick, J. (1997, November 24). More than a tuneup: Tough going in a fight against sexual harassment. *Newsweek,* pp. 50–52.

Argyris, C., & Schön, D. (1978). *Organizational learning: A theory of action perspective,* Reading, MA: Addison-Wesley.

Arpan, L. M., & Pompper, D. (2003). Stormy weather: Testing "stealing thunder" as a crisis communication strategy to improve communication flow between organizations and journalists. *Public Relations Review, 29,* 291–308.

Arpan, L. M., & Roskos-Ewoldsen, D. R. (2005). Stealing thunder: An analysis of the effects of proactive disclosure of crisis information. *Public Relations Review, 31,* 425–433.

Augustine, N. R. (1995). Managing the crisis you tried to prevent. *Harvard Business Review, 73*(6), 147–158.

Baker, M. (n.d.). *Odwalla and the E. coli outbreak.* Retrieved October 7, 2010, from http://www.mallen baker.net/csr/CSRfiles/crisis05 .html.

Balik, S. (1995). Media training: Boot camp for communicators. *Communication World, 12,* 22–25.

Barbaro, M., & Gillis, J. (2005, September 6). Wal-Mart at forefront of hurricane relief. *Washington Post.* Retrieved October 10, 2010, from http://www.washingtonpost .com/wp-dyn/content/article/ 2005/09/05/AR2005090501598 .html

Barge, J. K. (1994). *Leadership: Communication skills for organizations and groups.* New York: St. Martin's.

Baron, R. A. (1983). *Behavior in organizations: Understanding and managing the human side of work.* Boston: Allyn & Bacon.

Barry, R. A. (1984, March). Crisis communications: What to do when the roof falls in. *Business Marketing, 69,* 96–100.

Barton, L. (1995, August). *Your crisis management plan.* Paper presented at the meeting of New Avenues in Crisis Management, Las Vegas, NV.

Barton, L. (2001). *Crisis in organizations II* (2nd ed.). Cincinnati, OH: College Divisions South-Western.

Baskin, O., & Aronoff, C. (1988). *Public relations: The profession and the practice* (2nd ed.). Dubuque, IA: William C. Brown.

Baucus, M. S., & Baucus, D. A. (1997). Paying the piper: An empirical examination of longer-term financial consequences of illegal corporate behavior. *Academy of Management Journal, 40*(1), 129–151.

Baucus, M. S., & Near, J. P. (1991). Can illegal corporate behavior be predicted? An event history analysis. *Academy of Management Journal, 34*(1), 9–36.

Benoit, W. L. (1995). *Accounts, excuses, and apologies: A theory of image restoration.* Albany: State University of New York Press.

Benoit, W. L. (1997). Image repair discourse and crisis communication. *Public Relations Review, 23*(2), 177–180.

Benson, J. A. (1988). Crisis revisited: An analysis of strategies used by Tylenol in the second tampering episode. *Central States Speech Journal, 39,* 49–66.

Berg, D. M., & Robb, S. (1992). Crisis management and the "paradigm case." In E. L. Toth & R. L. Heath (Eds.), *Rhetorical and critical approaches to public relations* (pp. 93–110). Hillsdale, NJ: Lawrence Erlbaum.

Bergman, E. (1994). Crisis? What crisis? *Communication World, 11*(4), 9–13.

Bhattacharya, C. B., & Sen, S. (2003). Consumer-company identification: A framework for understanding consumers' relationships with companies. *Journal of Marketing, 67*(4), 76–88.

Billings, R. S., Milburn, T. W., & Schaalman, M. L. (1980). A model of crisis perception: A theoretical and empirical analysis. *Administrative Science Quarterly, 25,* 300–316.

Birch, J. (1994). New factors in crisis planning and response. *Public Relations Quarterly, 39,* 31–34.

Blackshaw, P., & Nazzaro, M. (2004). *Consumer-generated media (CGM) 101.* Retrieved October 7, 2010, from http://www.brandchannel .com/images/Papers/222_CGM.pdf#search='intelliseek%20consumer%20generated%20media%20101

Blythe, B. T., & Stivariou, T. B. (2003). *Negligent failure to plan: The next liability frontier?* Retrieved October 5, 2010, from http://ehstoday.com/safety/ehs_ imp_36448/index.html

Boffey, P. M. (1986, February 19). Shuttle head says he was not told of cold readings. *New York Times,* p. A1.

Botan. C., & Taylor, M. (2004). Public relations: The state of the field. *Journal of Communications, 54,* 645–661.

Bradford, J. L., & Garrett, D. E. (1995). The effectiveness of corporate communicative responses to accusations of unethical behavior. *Journal of Business Ethics, 14,* 875–892.

Brewer, L., Chandler, R. C., & Ferrell, O. C. (2006). *Managing risks for corporate integrity: How to survive an ethical misconduct disaster.* Mason, OH: Thomson.

Brummett, B. (1980). Towards a theory of silence as a political strategy. *Quarterly Journal of Speech, 66,* 289–303.

Bryson, J. M. (2004). What to do when stakeholders matter: Stakeholder identification analysis techniques. *Public Management Review, 6,* 21–53.

Burgoon, J. K., Birk, T., & Pfau, M. (1990). Nonverbal behaviors, persuasion and credibility. *Human Communication Research, 17,* 140–169.

Business Roundtable. (2002). *Business Roundtable's post-9/11 crisis communication toolkit: Best practices for crisis planning, prevention and continuous improvement.* Retrieved October 10, 2010, from http://www.docstoc.com/docs/411987/Business-Roundtables-Post-9-1-Crisis-Communications-Toolkit

Caldiero, C., Taylor, M., & Ungureanu, L. (2010). Organizational and media use of technology during fraud crises. In W. T. Coombs & S. J. Holladay (Eds.), *The handbook of crisis communication* (pp. 396–409). Malden, MA: Wiley-Blackwell.

Canadian Imperial Bank of Commerce. (n.d.). *Stakeholder engagement.* Retrieved October 21, 2010, from https://www.cibc.com/ca/inside-cibc/environment/stakeholder-engagement.html

Carlson, A. C., & Hocking, J. E. (1988). Strategies of redemption at the Vietnam Veterans Memorial. *Western Journal of Communication, 52,* 203–215.

Carney, A., & Jorden, A. (1993). Prepare for business-related crises. *Public Relations Journal, 49,* 34–35.

Carroll, C. E., & McCombs, M. E. (2003). Agenda-setting effects of business news on the public's images and opinions about major corporations. *Corporate Reputation Review, 6,* 36–46.

Caruba, A. (1994). Crisis PR: Most are unprepared. *Occupational Hazards, 56*(9), 85.

Center, A. H., & Jackson, P. (1995). *Public relations practices: Managerial case studies and problems* (5th ed.). Englewood Cliffs, NJ: Prentice Hall.

The changing landscape of liability: A director's guide to trends in corporate environmental, social and economic liability. (2004). Available from http://www.sustainability .com/library/the-changing-land scape-of-liability

Clampitt, P. G. (1991). *Communicating for managerial effectiveness.* Newbury Park, CA: Sage.

Clarkson, M. B. E. (1991). Defining, evaluating, and managing corporate social performance: A stakeholder management model. In J. E. Post (Ed.), *Research in corporate social performance and policy* (pp. 331–358). Greenwich, CT: JAI.

Clarkson, M. B. E. (1995). A stakeholder framework for analyzing and evaluating corporate social performance. *Academy of Management Review, 20,* 92–117.

Coates, J. F., Coates, V. T., Jarratt, J., & Heinz, L. (1986). *Issues management: How you can plan, organize, and manage for the future.* Mt. Airy, MD: Lomond.

Cohen, J. R. (2002). Legislating apology: The pros and cons. *University of Cincinnati Law Review, 70,* 819–895.

Conway, T., Ward, M., Lewis, G., & Bernhardt, A. (2007). Internet crisis potential: The importance of a strategic approach to marketing communications. *Journal of Marketing Communications, 13,* 213–228.

Coombs, W. T. (1995). Choosing the right words: The development of guidelines for the selection of the "appropriate" crisis response strategies. *Management Communication Quarterly, 8,* 447–476.

Coombs, W. T. (1998). The Internet as potential equalizer: New leverage for confronting social irresponsibility. *Public Relations Review, 24,* 289–304.

Coombs, W. T. (2002). Assessing online issue threats: Issue contagions and their effect on issue prioritization. *Journal of Public Affairs, 2,* 215–229.

Coombs, W. T. (2004a). Impact of past crises on current crisis communications: Insights from situational crisis communication theory. *Journal of Business Communication, 41,* 265–289.

Coombs, W. T. (2004b). A theoretical frame for post-crisis communication: Situational crisis communication theory. In M. J. Martinko (Ed.), *Attribution theory in the organizational sciences: Theoretical and empirical contributions* (pp. 275–296). Greenwich, CT: Information Age.

Coombs, W. T. (2005). The terrorist threat: Shifts in crisis management thinking and planning post-9/11. In D. O'Hair, R. Heath, & G. Ledlow (Eds.), *Communication, communities, and terrorism, Volume III: Communication and the media* (pp. 211–225). Mahwah, NJ: Lawrence Erlbaum.

Coombs, W. T. (2006a). *Code red in the boardroom: Crisis management as organizational DNA*. Westport, CT: Praeger.

Coombs, W. T. (2006b). The protective powers of crisis response strategies: Managing reputational assets during a crisis. *Journal of Promotion Management, 12,* 241–259.

Coombs, W. T. (2007). Attribution theory as a guide for post-crisis communication research. *Public Relations Review, 33,* 135–139.

Coombs, W. T. (2008). The future of crisis communication from an international perspective. In T. Nolting & A. Tieben (Eds.), *Krisenmanagement in der mediengesellschaft (arbeitstitel) potenziale und perspektiven in der krisenkommunikation* [Crisis management in media society: Potentials and perspectives] (pp. 275–287). Wiesbaden, Germany: VS-Verlag.

Coombs, W. T. (2010). Pursuing evidence-based crisis communication. In W. T. Coombs & S. J. Holladay (Eds.), *Handbook of crisis communication* (pp. 719–725). Malden, MA: Blackwell.

Coombs, W. T. (in press). Crisis communication: A developing field. In R. L. Heath (Ed.), *Handbook of public relations* (2nd ed.). Thousand Oaks, CA: Sage.

Coombs, W. T., & Chandler, R. C. (1996). Crisis teams: Revisiting their selection and training. In L. Barton (Ed.), *New avenues in risk and crisis management* (Vol. 5, pp. 7–15). Las Vegas: University of Nevada Las Vegas, Small Business Development Center.

Coombs, W. T., & Holladay, S. J. (1996). Communication and attributions in a crisis: An experimental study of crisis communication. *Journal of Public Relations Research, 8,* 279–295.

Coombs, W. T., & Holladay, S. J. (2001). An extended examination of the crisis situation: A fusion of the relational management and symbolic approaches. *Journal of Public Relations Research, 13,* 321–340.

Coombs, W. T., & Holladay, S. J. (2002). Helping crisis managers protect reputational assets: Initial tests of the situational crisis communication theory. *Management Communication Quarterly, 16,* 165–186.

Coombs, W. T., & Holladay, S. J. (2004). Reasoned action in crisis communication: An attribution theory-based approach to crisis management. In D. P. Millar & R. L. Heath (Eds.), *Responding to crisis: A rhetorical approach to crisis communication* (pp. 95–115). Mahwah, NJ: Lawrence Erlbaum.

Coombs, W. T., & Holladay, S. J. (2005). Exploratory study of stakeholder emotions: Affect and crisis. In N. M. Ashkanasy, W. J. Zerbe, & C. E. J. Hartel (Eds.), *Research on emotion in organizations: Volume 1: The effect of affect in organizational settings* (pp. 271–288). New York: Elsevier.

Coombs, W. T. & Holladay, S. J. (2006). Halo or reputational capital: Reputation and crisis management. *Journal of Communication Management, 10,* 123–137.

Coombs, W. T., & Holladay, S. J. (2010). *PR strategy and application: Managing influence*. Malden, MA: Wiley-Blackwell.

Coombs, W. T., & Schmidt, L. (2000). An empirical analysis of image restoration: Texaco's racism crisis. *Journal of Public Relations Research, 12*(2), 163–178.

Cooper, R. (1997, Summer). A historical look at the PepsiCo/Burma boycott. *The Boycott Quarterly,* 12–15.

"Corporate conscience award" presented to Chiquita by Social Accountability International. (2003, October 8). Retrieved October 5, 2010, from http://phx.corporate-ir.net/phoenix.zhtml?c=119836&p=irol-newsArticle&ID= 456528&highlight=

Corporate Leadership Council. (2003). *Crisis management strategies.* Retrieved September 12, 2006, from http://www.executiveboard.com/EXBD/Images/PDF/Crisis%20Management%20Strategies.pdf#search='corporate%201eadership%20council%20crisis%20management

Covello, V., Minamyer, S., & Clayton, K. (2007). *Effective risk and crisis communication during water security emergencies: Summary report of EPA sponsored message mapping workshop.* Cincinnati, OH: U.S. Environmental Protection Agency. Retrieved October 13, 2020, from http://www.epa.gov/nhsrc/pubs/600r07027.pdf

Crable, R. E., & Vibbert, S. L. (1985). Managing issues and influencing public policy. *Public Relations Review, 11,* 3–16.

Creating the best crisis comms teams—One crisis at a time. (2003, January 27). *PR News.* Available from http://www.prnewsonline.com/news/6266.html

Crisis Commander. (2008). *About crisis commander.* Retrieved October 14, 2010, from http://www.crisiscommander.com/

Dagnoli, J., & Colford, S. W. (1991, March 18). Brief slump expected for Sudafed. *Advertising Age,* p. 53.

Daniels, T. D., Spiker, B. K., & Papa, M. J. (1997). *Perspectives on organizational communication* (4th ed.). Dubuque, IA: William C. Brown & Benchmark.

Darling, J. R. (1994). Crisis management in international business: Keys to effective decision making. *Leadership & Organizational Development Journal Annual, 15*(8), 3–8.

Davies, G., Chun, R., da Silva, R. V., & Roper, S. (2003). *Corporate reputation and competitiveness.* New York: Routledge.

Dawar, N., & Pillutla, M. M. (2000). Impact of product-harm crises on brand equity: The moderating role of consumer expectations. *Journal of Marketing Research, 27,* 215–226.

de Turck, M. A., & Miller, G. R. (1985). Deception and arousal: Isolating the behavioral correlates of deception. *Human Communication Research, 12,* 181–201.

Dean, D. H. (2004). Consumer reaction to negative publicity: Effects of corporate reputation, response, and responsibility for a crisis event. *Journal of Business Communication, 41,* 192–211.

Denbow, C. J., & Culbertson, H. M. (1985). Linking beliefs and diagnosing image. *Public Relations Review, 11,* 29–37.

Dilenschneider, R. L. (2000). *The corporate communications bible: Everything you need to know to become a public relations expert.* Beverly Hills, CA: New Millennium.

Dilenschneider, R. L., & Hyde, R. C. (1985). Crisis communications: Planning for the unplanned. *Business Horizons, 28,* 35–38.

Dionisopolous, G. N., & Vibbert, S. L. (1988). CBS vs. Mobil Oil: Charges of creative bookkeeping. In H. R. Ryan (Ed.), *Oratorical encounters: Selected studies and sources of 20th century political accusation and apologies* (pp. 214–252). Westport, CT: Greenwood.

dna13. (2010). *Speed of conversations.* Retrieved October 6, 2010, from http://www.dna13.com/solutions/key-challenges/align

Dobbin, B. (2006, April 12). *Bausch & Lomb: Source of infection unknown.* Retrieved October 5, 2010, from http://www.breitbart.com/article.php?id=D8GUGTBG3&show_article=1

Does Airborne really stave off colds? (2006). Retrieved October 6, 2010, from http://abcnews.go.com/GMA/Health/story?id=1664514

Donaldson, T., & Preston, L. E. (1995). The stakeholder theory of the corporation: Concepts, evidence, and implications. *Academy of Management Review, 20,* 65–91.

Donath, B. (1984, September). Why you need a crisis PR plan. *Business Marketing, 69,* 4.

Dornheim, M. A. (1996). Recovered FMC memory puts new spin on Cali accident. *Aviation Week & Space Technology, 145*(11), 58–62.

Dowling, G. (2002). *Creating corporate reputations: Identity, image, and performance.* New York: Oxford University Press.

Dozens evacuate after chemical leak. (2009, October 27). Retrieved October 21, 2010, from http://

www.click2houston.com/news/21441833/detail.html

Dozier, D. M. (1992). The organizational roles of communications and public relations practitioners. In J. E. Grunig (Ed.), *Excellence in public relations and communication management* (pp. 327–356). Hillsdale, NJ: Lawrence Erlbaum.

Duffy, B., & Beddingfield, K. T. (1996, August 5). The sound of silence: More evidence from TWA Flight 800 suggests there was a bomb aboard. *U.S. News & World Report,* pp. 28–31.

Dunham, W. (2010, April 2). *Obama previews rhetoric for midterm elections.* Retrieved June 8, 2010, from http://www.reuters.com/article/idUSTRE63109B20100402

Dutton, J. E. (1986). The processing of crisis and non-crisis strategic issues. *Journal of Management Studies, 23,* 501–517.

Dutton, J. E., & Ashford, S. J. (1993). Selling issues to top management. *Academy of Management Review, 18,* 397–428.

Dutton, J. E., & Duncan, R. B. (1987). The creation of momentum for change through the process of strategic issue diagnosis. *Strategic Management Journal, 8,* 279–295.

Dutton, J. E., & Jackson, S. E. (1987). Categorizing strategic issues: Links to organizational action. *Academy of Management Review, 12,* 76–90.

Dutton, J. E., & Ottensmeyer, E. (1987). Strategic issue management systems: Forms, functions, and context. *Academy of Management Review, 12,* 355–365.

Egelhoff, W. G., & Sen, F. (1992). An information-processing model of crisis management. *Management*

Communication Quarterly, 5, 443–484.

Endsley, M. R. (1995). Toward a theory of situation awareness in dynamic systems. *Human Factors, 37,* 32–64.

Entine, J. (1998). *Intoxicated by success: How to protect your company from inevitable corporate screwups.* Retrieved October 7, 2010, from http://www.jonentine.com/ethical_edge/corp_screwups.htm

Entine, J. (1999). *The Odwalla affair: Reassessing corporate social responsibility.* Retrieved October 7, 2010, from http://www.jonentine.com/articles/odwalla.htm

Ewing, R. P. (1979). The uses of futurist techniques in issues management. *Public Relations Quarterly, 24*(4), 15–18.

Fahey, A., & Dagnoli, J. (1990, June 18). PM ready to deal with outdoor ad foes. *Advertising Age,* pp. 1, 31.

Fairhurst, G. T., & Sarr, R. A. (1996). *The art of framing: Managing the language of leadership.* San Francisco: Jossey-Bass.

Fearn-Banks, K. (2001). *Crisis communications: A casebook approach* (2nd ed.). Mahwah, NJ: Lawrence Erlbaum.

Feeley, T. H., & de Turck, M. A. (1995). Global cue usage in behavioral lie detection. *Communication Quarterly, 43,* 420–430.

Finet, D. (1994). Sociopolitical consequences of organizational expression. *Journal of Communication, 44*(4), 114–131.

Fink, S. (1986). *Crisis management: Planning for the inevitable.* New York: AMACOM.

Fink, S., Beak, J., & Taddeo, K. (1971). Organizational crisis and change. *Journal of Applied Behavioral Science, 7,* 15–37.

Fitzpatrick, K. R. (1995). Ten guidelines for reducing legal risks in crisis management. *Public Relations Quarterly, 40*(2), 33–38.

Fitzpatrick, K. R., & Rubin, M. S. (1995). Public relations vs. legal strategies in organizational crisis decisions. *Public Relations Review, 21*(1), 21–33.

Flin, R. (2006, June). *Naturalistic decision making and crisis management.* Paper presented at ISCRAM-TIEMS, Summer School, Tilburg, Netherlands.

Folkes, V. S., Koletsky, S., & Graham, J. L. (1987). A field study of causal inferences and consumer reaction: The view from the airport. *Journal of Consumer Research, 13,* 534–539.

Fombrun, C. J. (2005). Building corporate reputation through CSR initiatives: Evolving standards. *Corporate Reputation Review, 8,* 7–11.

Fombrun, C., & Shanley, M. (1990). What's in a name? Reputation building and corporate strategy. *Academy of Management Journal, 33,* 233–258.

Fombrun, C. J., & van Riel, C. B. M. (2004). *Fame and fortune: How successful companies build winning reputations.* New York: Prentice Hall.

Foot, K., Warnick, B., & Schneider, S. M. (2005). Web-based memorializing after September 11: Toward a conceptual framework. *Journal of Computer-Mediated Communication, 11,* 72–96.

Foundation for Critical Thinking. (2009). *Glossary of critical thinking terms.* Retrieved October 8, 2010, from http://www.criticalthinking.org/articles/ glossary.cfm

Frank, J. N. (1994). Plan ahead for effective crisis management, expert advises. *Beverage Industry, 85*(4), 22.

Friedman, M. (2002). *Everyday crisis management: How to think like an emergency physician.* Naperville, IL: First Decision Press.

Fuchs-Burnett, T. (2002, May/July). Mass public corporate apology. *Dispute Resolution Journal, 57,* 26–32.

Garvin, A. P. (1996). *The art of being well informed.* Garden City Park, NY: Avery.

Geraghty, K., & Desouza, K. C. (2005). Optimizing knowledge networks. Retrieved October 7, 2010, from http://www.eknowtion.com/show_article.php?id=10

Gilman, A. (2004, September 27). Creating a message map for risk communication. *PR News.* Available from http://web.lexis-nexis.com/universe

Goldhaber, G. M. (1990). *Organizational communication* (5th ed.). Dubuque, IA: William C. Brown.

Goldstein, I. L. (1993). *Training in organizations: Needs assessment, development and evaluation* (3rd ed.). Monterey, CA: Brooks/Cole.

Gonzalez-Herrero, A., & Pratt, C. B. (1995). How to manage a crisis before—or whenever—it hits. *Public Relations Quarterly, 40*(1), 25–29.

Gonzalez-Herrero, A., & Pratt, C. B. (1996). An integrated symmetrical model of crisis communications management. *Journal of Public Relations Research, 8*(2), 79–106.

Gower, K. K. (2006). Truth and transparency. In K. Fitzpatrick & C. Bronstein (Eds.), *Ethics in public relations: Responsible advocacy* (pp. 89–106). Thousand Oaks, CA: Sage.

Gray, P. (1996, August 5). The search for sabotage. *Time,* pp. 28–32.

Greenpeace. (2010). *Nestlé killer: Ask Nestlé to give rainforests a break.* Retrieved October 7, 2010, from http://www.greenpeace.org/international/campaigns/climate-change/kitkat/

Gross, A. E. (1990, October 11). How Popeye's and Reebok confronted product rumors. *Adweek's Marketing Week,* pp. 27, 30.

Grunig, J. E. (1992). Communication, public relations, and effective organizations: An overview of the book. In J. E. Grunig (Ed.), *Excellence in public relations and communication management* (pp. 1–30). Hillsdale, NJ: Lawrence Erlbaum.

Grunig, J. E., & Repper, F. C. (1992). Strategic management, publics, and issues. In J. E. Grunig (Ed.), *Excellence in public relations and communication management* (pp. 117–158). Hillsdale, NJ: Lawrence Erlbaum.

Guth, D. W. (1995). Organizational crisis experience and public relations roles. *Public Relations Review, 21*(2), 123–136.

Hall, P. (2006, January 16). *The PR sherp: PR experts address no comment and net mischief.* Available from http://www.prnewsonline.com/news/6190.html

Halonen-Rollins, M., & Halinen-Kaila, A. (2005). *Customer knowledge management competence: Towards a theoretical framework.* Retrieved October 7, 2010, from http://www.computer.org/portal/web/csdl/doi/10.1109/HICSS.2005.180

Hanging in the Febreze. (2005). Retrieved October 7, 2010, from http://www.snopes.com/critters/crusader/febreze.asp

Härtel, C., McColl-Kennedy, J. R., & McDonald, L. (1998). Incorporating attribution theory and the theory of reasoned action within an affective events theory framework to produce a contingency predictive model of consumer reactions to organizational mishaps. *Advances in Consumer Research, 25,* 428–432.

Hays, C. L. (2003, August 14). Wal-Mart opens wallet in effort to fix its image. *The New York Times.* Retrieved October 7, 2010, from http://sfgate.com/cgi-bin/artile.cgi?f=/c/a/2003/08/14/BU185832.DTL

Headley, L. O. (2005). *Failure to protect employees from terrorism may lead to liability.* Available from http://www.law.com/jsp/tx/PubArticleFriendlyTX.jsp? id=1136455510408

Hearit, K. M. (1994). Apologies and public relations crises at Chrysler, Toshiba, and Volvo. *Public Relations Review, 20*(2), 113–125.

Hearit, K. M. (1996). The use of counterattack in apologetic public relations crises: The case of General Motors vs. Dateline NBC. *Public Relations Review, 22,* 233–248.

Hearit, K. M. (2001). Corporate apologia: When an organization speaks in defense of itself. In R. L. Heath (Ed.), *Handbook of public relations* (pp. 501–511). Thousand Oaks, CA: Sage.

Hearit, K. M. (2006). *Crisis management by apology: Corporate response to allegations of wrongdoing.* Mahwah, NJ: Lawrence Erlbaum.

Heath, R. L. (1988). Organizational tactics for effective issues management.

In R. L. Heath (Ed.), *Strategic issues management* (pp. 99–121). San Francisco: Jossey-Bass.

Heath, R. L. (1990). Corporate issues management: Theoretical underpinnings and research foundations. In J. E. Grunig & L. A. Grunig (Eds.), *Public relations research annual* (Vol. 2, pp. 29–66). Hillsdale, NJ: Lawrence Erlbaum.

Heath, R. L. (1994). *Management of corporate communication: From interpersonal contacts to external affairs.* Hillsdale, NJ: Lawrence Erlbaum.

Heath, R. L. (1997). *Strategic issues management: Organizations and public policy challenges.* Thousand Oaks, CA: Sage.

Heath, R. L. (1998). New communication technologies: An issues management point of view. *Public Relations Review, 24,* 273–288.

Heath, R. L. (2005). Issues management. In R. L. Heath (Ed.), *Encyclopedia of public relations* (Vol. 1, pp. 460–463). Thousand Oaks, CA: Sage.

Heath, R. L., Lee, J., & Ni, L. (2009). Crisis and risk approaches to emergency management planning and communication: The role of similarity and sensitivity. *Journal of Public Relations Research, 21,* 123–141.

Heath, R. L., & Nelson, R. A. (1986). *Issues management: Corporate public policy making in an information society.* Beverly Hills, CA: Sage.

Heath, R. L., & Palenchar, K. J. (2000). Community relations and risk communication: A longitudinal study of the impact of emergency response messages. *Journal of Public Relations Research, 12,* 131–161.

Heinberg, P. (1963). Relationships of content and delivery to general effectiveness. *Speech Monographs, 30,* 105–107.

Herbig, P., Milewicz, J., & Golden, J. (1994). A model of reputation building and destruction. *Journal of Business Research, 31,* 23–31.

Hess, A. (2007). In digital remembrance Vernacular memory and the rhetorical construction of web memorials. *Media, Culture & Society, 29,* 812–830.

Hewlett-Packard Development Company. (2010). *Stakeholder engagement.* Retrieved October 21, 2010, from http://www.hp.com/hpinfo/globalcitizenship/commitment/stakeholders.html

Hibbard, J. (1997). Shell oil shifts safety data to intranet. *Computerworld, 31*(21), 20–21.

Higbee, A. G. (1992, October). Shortening the crisis lifecycle: Seven rules to live by. *Occupational Hazards, 54,* 137–138.

Hiltz, S. R. (2006, June). *Partially distributed virtual teams: A tutorial, hands-on experience, and discussion of their use in emergency response.* Paper presented at ISCRAM-TIEMS Summer School, Tilburg, Netherlands.

Hirokawa, R. Y. (1985). Discussion procedures and decision-making performance: A test of a functional perspective. *Human Communication Research, 12,* 203–224.

Hirokawa, R. Y. (1988). Group communication and decision making performance: A continued test of the functional perspective. *Human Communication Research, 14,* 487–515.

Hirokawa, R.Y., & Rost, K. (1992). Effective group decision making in organizations. *Management Communication Quarterly, 5,* 267–288.

Hobbs, J. D. (1995). Treachery by any other name: A case study of the Toshiba public relations crisis. *Management Communication Quarterly, 8,* 323–346.

Holladay, S. J. (2009). Crisis communication strategies in the media coverage of chemical accidents. *Journal of Public Relations Research, 21,* 208–215.

Holladay, S. J., & Coombs, W. T. (1994). Speaking of visions and visions being spoken: An exploration of the effects of content and delivery on perceptions of leader charisma. *Management Communication Quarterly, 8*(2), 165–189.

Holtz, S. (1999). *Public relations on the net: Winning strategies to inform and influence the media, the investment community, the government, the public, and more!* New York: AMACOM.

Holtz, S. (2007, September 18). Dark blogs: A bad idea for crisis communication [Web log]. Retrieved October 6, 2010, from http://blog.holtz.com/index.php/dark_blogs_a_bad_idea_for_crisis_communication/

Hopper, D. I. (2002). *Hacking up, disclosure down, FBI survey says.* Retrieved October 12, 2010, from http://seclists.org/isn/2002/Apr/0042.html

Ice, R. (1991). Corporate publics and rhetorical strategies: The case of Union Carbide's Bhopal crisis. *Management Communication Quarterly, 4,* 341–362.

In a crisis. (1993). *Public Relations Journal, 49*(9), 10–11.

In loving memory: Cantor families memorial. (n.d.). Retrieved October 14, 2010, from http://www.cantor families.com/cantor/jsp/index.jsp

Irvine, R. B., & Millar, D. P. (1996). Debunking the stereotypes of crisis management: The nature of business crises in the 1990's. In L. Barton (Ed.), *New avenues in risk and crisis management* (Vol. 5, pp. 51–63). Las Vegas: University of Nevada Las Vegas, Small Business Development Center.

Jin, Y., & Cameron, G. T. (2007). The effects of threat type and duration on public relations practitioner's cognitive, affective, and conative responses to crisis situations. *Journal of Public Relations Research, 19,* 255–281.

Jin, Y., & Pang, A. (2010). Future directions of crisis communication research: Emotions in crisis—The next frontier. In W. T. Coombs & S. J. Holladay (Eds.), *Handbook of crisis communication* (pp. 677–682). Malden, MA: Blackwell.

Jones, B. L., & Chase, W. H. (1979). Managing public policy issues. *Public Relations Review, 5*(2), 3–23.

Kamer, L. (1996). When the crisis is orchestrated: Corporate campaigns and their origins. In L. Barton (Ed.), *New avenues in risk and crisis management* (Vol. 5, pp. 64–72). Las Vegas: University of Nevada Las Vegas, Small Business Development Center.

Katz, A. R. (1987). 10 steps to complete crisis planning. *Public Relations Journal, 43,* 46–47.

Kaufmann, J. B., Kesner, I. F., & Hazen, T. L. (1994, July/August).

The myth of full disclosure: A look at organizational communications during crises. *Business Horizons, 37,* 29–39.

Kellerman, B. (2006, April). When should a leader apologize and when not? *Harvard Business Review,* pp. 73–81.

Kelly, K. (1990, September 24). Dayton Hudson finds there's no graceful way to flip-flop. *BusinessWeek,* p. 50.

Kempner, M. W. (1995). Reputation management: How to handle the media during a crisis. *Risk Management, 42*(3), 43–47.

Kiley, D. (1991, March 11). Sudafed deaths spark a backlash against capsules. *Adweek's Marketing Week,* p. 6.

"Killer Coke" or innocent abroad? (2006, January 23). *BusinessWeek,* pp. 46–48.

Kilmann, R. H., & Thomas, K. W. (1975). Interpersonal conflict-handling behaviors as reflection of Jungian personality dimensions. *Psychological Reports, 37,* 971–980.

Klein, J., & Dawar, N. (2004). Corporate social responsibility and consumers' attributions and brand evaluations in a product-harm crisis. *International Journal of Marketing, 21,* 203–217.

Kleindorfer, P. R., Freeman, H., Lowe, R. A. (2000). *Accident epidemiology and the U.S. chemical industry: Preliminary results from RMPInfo.* Retrieved October 13, 2010, from http://opim.wharton.upenn.edu/risk/downloads/00-1-15.pdf

Koepp, S. (1985, September 16). Placing the blame at E. F. Hutton. *Time,* p. 54.

Kolfschoten, G. L., & Appelman, J. H. (2006, June). *Collaborative engineering in crisis situations.* Paper presented at ISCRAM-TIEMS Summer School, Tilburg, Netherlands.

Kolfschoten, G. L., Briggs, R. O., de Vreede, G.J., Jacobs, P. H. M., & Appelman, J. H. (2006). A conceptual foundation of the thinkLet concept for collaboration engineering. *International Journal of Human-Computer Studies, 64,* 611–621.

Komaki, J., Heinzmann, A. T., & Lawson, L. (1980). Effects of training and feedback: Component analysis of a behavioral safety program. *Journal of Applied Psychology, 65,* 261–270.

Kouzes, J. M., & Posner, B. Z. (1993*). Credibility: How leaders gain and lose it, why people demand it.* San Francisco: Jossey-Bass.

Kreps, G. L. (1990). *Organizational communication: Theory and practice* (2nd ed.). New York: Longman.

Lackluster online PR no aid in crisis response. (2002). Available from http://www.prnewsonline.com/news/5957.html

Laczniak, R. N., DeCarlo, T. E., & Ramaswami, S. H. (2001). Consumers' responses to negative word-of-mouth communication: An attribution theory perspective. *Journal of Consumer Psychology, 11,* 57–73.

Larson, C. U. (1989). *Persuasion: Reception and responsibility* (5th ed.). Belmont, CA: Wadsworth.

Lauzen, M. M. (1995). Toward a model of environmental scanning. *Journal of Public Relations Research, 7*(3), 187–204.

Lawmakers blast Enron's "culture of corporate corruption." (2002). Retrieved October 7, 2010, from http:// archives.cnn.com/2002/LAW/02/03/enron/

Leon, M. (1983). Tylenol fights back. *Public Relations Journal, 11,* 10–14.

Leonard, A. (2010, March 19). *Nestlé's brave Facebook flop.* Retrieved October 7, 2010, from http://www.salon.com/news/social_media/index.html? story=/tech/htww/2010/03/19/nestle_s_brave_facebook_flop

Lerbinger, O. (1997). *The crisis manager: Facing risk and responsibility.* Mahwah, NJ: Lawrence Erlbaum.

Levick, R. (2005, August 17). *In staging responses to crises, complacency plays a big role.* Available from http://www.prnewsonline.com/news/7220.html

Levitt, A. M. (1997). *Disaster planning and recovery: A guide for facility professionals.* New York: John Wiley & Sons.

Li, A., YeZhuang, T., & Ying, Q. Z. (2004). *An empirical study on the impact of organizational memory on organizational performance in manufacturing companies.* Available from http://www.computer.org/portal/web/csdl/abs/proceedings/hicss/2004/2056/08/2056toc.htm

Littlejohn, R. F. (1983). *Crisis management: A team approach.* New York: American Management Association.

Loewendick, B. A. (1993, November). Laying your crisis on the table. *Training & Development,* pp. 15–17.

Lukaszewski, J. E. (1987). Anatomy of a crisis response. *Public Relations Journal, 43,* 45–47.

Mackinnon, P. (1996). When silence isn't golden. *Financial Executive, 12*(4), 45–48.

Magiera, M. (1993, June 21). Pepsi weathers tampering hoaxes: It's textbook case of how to come through a PR crisis. *Advertising Age*, p. 1.

Marcus, A. A., & Goodman, R. S. (1991). Victims and shareholders: The dilemmas of presenting corporate policy during a crisis. *Academy of Management Journal, 34*, 281–305.

Martine, M. (2007, August 23). How to start a business blog, part 10: Crisis management plan [Web log]. Retrieved October 6, 2010, from http://remarkablogger.com/2007/08/23/crisis-blog-planning/

Maynard, R. (1993, December). Handling a crisis effectively. *Nation's Business*, pp. 54–55.

McCroskey, J. C. (1997). *An introduction to rhetorical communication* (7th ed.). Boston: Allyn & Bacon.

McGinley, L. (1997). *Of mice and men: How Ex-Lax, trusted for nearly a century became a cancer risk*. Retrieved October 6, 2010, from http://www.junkscience.com/news/exlax.html

McGraw, D. (1996, January 8). Human error and a human tragedy: The aftermath of the American Airlines crash. *U.S. News & World Report*, p. 38.

McKeen, J. D., Zack, M. H., & Singh, S. (2006). *Knowledge management and organizational performance: An exploratory study*. Retrieved October 7, 2010, from http://www.computer.org/portal/web/csdl/doi/10.1109/HICSS.2006.242

Mecham, M. (1986, February 19). Shuttle probe gets testy: Who knew about the cold and when? *USA Today*, p. 1A.

Meserve, J. (1999). *One company still dealing with Melissa*. Retrieved October 7, 2010, from http://www.networkworld.com/news/1999/0401melissa.html

Milas, G. H. (1996). Guidelines for organizing TQM teams. *IIE Solutions, 28*(2), 36–39.

Mintz, P., & Di Meglio, F. (2006, April 17). Bausch & Lomb: Crisis management 101. *BusinessWeek*. Retrieved October 5, 2010, from http://www.businessweek.com/investor/conent/apr2006/pi20060417_741558.htm

Mitchell, R. K., Agle, R. A., & Wood, D. J. (1997). Toward a theory of stakeholder identification and salience: Defining the principle of who and what really counts. *Academy of Management Review, 22*, 853–886.

Mitchell, T. H. (1986). Coping with a corporate crisis. *Canadian Business Review, 13*, 17–20.

Mitroff, I. I. (1994). Crisis management and environmentalism: A natural fit. *California Management Review, 36*(2), 101–113.

Mitroff, I. I., Harrington, K., & Gai, E. (1996). Thinking about the unthinkable. *Across the Board, 33*(8), 44–48.

Mitroff, I. I., & McWinney, W. (1987). Disaster by design and how to avoid it. *Training, 24*, 33–34, 37–38.

Mohr, B. (1994, March). The Pepsi challenge: Managing a crisis. *Prepared Foods*, pp. 13–14.

Moore, R. H. (1979). Research by the conference board sheds light on problems of semantics, issue identification and classification—and some likely issues for the '80s. *Public Relations Journal, 35*, 43–46.

Mukherjee, D., Nissen, S. E., & Topol, E. J. (2001). Risk of cardiovascular events associated with selective cox-2 inhibitors. *Journal of the American Medical Association, 286,* 954–959.

Myers, K. N. (1993). *Total contingency planning for disasters: Managing risk, minimizing loss, ensuring business continuity.* New York: John Wiley & Sons.

National Research Council. (1996). *Computing and communications in the extreme: Research for crisis management and application.* Washington, DC: National Academy Press.

Nelkin, D. (1988). Risk reporting and the management of industrial crises. *Journal of Management Studies, 25,* 341–351.

Nestlé open forum on deforestation, Malaysia. (n.d.). Retrieved October 7, 2010 from http://www.nestle .com/InvestorRelations/Events/ AllEvents/Nestle_ open_forum_ on_deforestation_Malaysia.htm

New survey finds crisis training is primarily learned on the job. (2006, March 20). Available from http://www .prnewsonline.com/news/8190 .html

Newsom, D., VanSlyke Turk, J., & Kruckeberg, D. (1996). *This is PR: The realities of public relations* (6th ed.). Belmont, CA: Wadsworth.

Nicholas, R. (1995, November 23). Know comment. *Marketing,* pp. 41–43.

Norton, R. W. (1983). *Communicator style: Theory, applications, and measures.* Beverly Hills, CA: Sage.

O'Connor, M. F. (1985). Methodology for corporate crisis decision-making. In S. J. Andriole (Ed.), *Corporate crisis management* (pp. 239–258). Princeton, NJ: Petrocelli.

O'Hair, D., Friedrich, G. W., Wiemann, J. M., & Wiemann, M. O. (1995). *Competent communication.* New York: St. Martin's.

Olaniran, B. A., & Williams, D. E. (2001). Anticipatory model of crisis management: A vigilant response to technological crises. In R. L. Heath (Ed.), *Handbook of public relations* (pp. 487–500). Thousand Oaks, CA: Sage.

Oneupweb. (2007). *Principles of crisis management in a viral age: Integrating the tools and lessons of Search 2.0 into a comprehensive crisis response.* Retrieved October 6, 2010, from http://internetetopinion .files.wordpress.com/2008/01/ crisis_management.pdf

O'Reilly, T. (2005). What is Web 2.0? Retrieved June 8, 2010, from http://oreilly.com/web2/archive/ what-is-web-20.html

Outzen, R. (2010). BP's shocking memo. Retrieved October 7, 2010, from http://www.thedailybeast .com/blogs-and-stories/2010-05- 25/shocking-bp-memo-and-the- oil-spill-in-the-gulf/full/

Owyang, J. (2007). *Defining the term: "Online community."* Retrieved October 21, 2010, from http:// www.web-strategist.com/blog/ 2007/12/28/defining-the-term- community/

Palenchar, M. J. (2005). Risk communication. In R. L. Heath (Ed.), *Encyclopedia of public relations* (Vol. 2, pp. 752–755). Thousand Oaks, CA: Sage.

Palenchar, M. J., & Heath, R. L. (2007). Strategic risk communication: Adding value to society. *Public Relations Review, 33,* 120–129.

Pampers calls rumors completely false. (2010). Retrieved October 6, 2010, from http://www.prnewswire .com/news-releases/pampers- calls-rumors-completely-false- 92997194.html

Patel, A., & Reinsch, L. (2003). Companies can apologize: Corporate apologies and legal liability. *Business Communication Quarterly, 66,* 17–26.

Paton, D., & Flin, R. (1999). Disaster stress: An emergency management perspective. *Disaster Prevention and Management, 8,* 261–267.

Pauchant, T. C., & Mitroff, I. I. (1992). *Transforming the crisis-prone organization: Preventing individual, organizational, and environmental tragedies.* San Francisco: Jossey-Bass.

Paul, R., & Nosich, G. M. (n.d.). *A model for the national assessment of higher order thinking.* Retrieved October 21, 2010, from http://test.critical thinking.org/print-page.cfm?page ID=591

Pearson, C. M., & Clair, J. A. (1998). Reframing crisis management. *Academy of Management Review, 23*(1), 59–76.

Pearson, C. M., & Mitroff, I. I. (1993). From crisis prone to crisis prepared: A framework for crisis management. *The Executive, 7*(1), 48–59.

Perry, D. C., Taylor, M., Doerfel, M. L. (2003). Internet-based communication in crisis management. *Management Communication Quarterly, 17,* 206–232.

PhRMA. (2005). *PhRMA guiding principles: Direct to consumer advertisements about prescription medicines.* Retrieved October 6, 2010, from http://www.phrma .org/files/attachments/DTC Guidingprinciples.pdf

Pines, W. L. (1985). How to handle a PR crisis: Five dos and five don'ts. *Public Relations Quarterly, 30*(2), 16–19.

Podolack, A. (2002, September 1). Crisis management teams. *Risk Management.* Retrieved October 21, 2010, from http://www.rmmag .com/Magazine/PrintTemplate .cfm?AID=1630

Procter & Gamble files lawsuit against Vi-Jon Laboratories. (2006, February 15). Retrieved October 6, 2010, from http://news.thomasnet.com/ company story/477793

P&G reaches settlement agreement with Vi-Jon Laboratories. (2006, April 18). Retrieved October 6, 2010, from http://www.thefreelibrary.com/ P%26G+Reaches+Settlement+ Agreement+With+Vi-Jon+Labo ratories.-a0144606904

Putnam, L. L., & Poole, M. S. (1987). Conflict and negotiation. In F. M. Jablin, L. L. Putnam, K. H. Roberts, & L. W. Porter (Eds.), *Handbook of organizational communication: An interdisciplinary perspective* (pp. 549–599). Newbury Park, CA: Sage.

Putnam, T. (1993). Boycotts are busting out all over. *Business and Society Review, 85,* 47–51.

Rancer, A. S., Baukus, R. A., & Infante, D. A. (1985). Relations between argumentativeness and belief structures about arguing. *Communication Education, 34,* 37–47.

Ray, S. J. (1999). *Strategic communication in crisis management: Lessons from the airline industry.* Westport, CT: Quorum.

Redding, W. C. (1972). *Communication within the organization.* Lafayette, IN: Purdue Research Foundation.

Reeves, M. (1996). Weaving a web at the office: Intranets are all the rage in networking technology. *Black Enterprise, 27*(4), 39–41.

Regester, M. (1989). *Crisis management: How to turn a crisis into an opportunity.* London: Hutchinson.

Richardson, B. (1994). Socio-technical disasters: Profile and prevalence. *Disaster Prevention and Management, 3*(4), 41–69.

Richmond, V. P., & McCroskey, J. C. (1997). *Communication: Apprehension, avoidance, and effectiveness* (5th ed.). Boston: Allyn & Bacon.

Rojas, B. (2006, March/April). Wal-Mart: Beyond business. *Continuity Insights,* pp. 10–13.

Rousseau, D. M. (2005). Is there such a thing as "evidence-based management"? *Academy of Management Review, 31,* 256–269.

Rowley, T. J. (1997). Moving beyond dyadic ties: A network theory of stakeholder influence. *Academy of Management Review, 22,* 887–910.

Rupp, D. (1996). Tech versus touch. *HR Focus, 73*(11), 16–18.

Ryan, C. (1991). *Prime time activism: Media strategies for grassroots organizing.* Boston: South End Press.

Ryan, C. (1998). *Three killed in explosion at chemical plant outside Reno.* Retrieved September 13, 2006, from http://www.lasvegassun.com/news/1998/jan/07/three-killed-in-explosion-at-chemical-plant-outsid/

Safko, L., & Brake, D. K. (2009). *The social media bible: Tactics, tools and strategies for business success.* Hoboken, NJ: John Wiley & Sons.

Sanger, D. E. (1986, February 28). Communications channels at NASA: Warnings that faded along the way. *New York Times,* p. A13.

Savage, G. T., Nix, T. W., Whitehead, C. J., & Blair, J. D. (1991). Strategies for assessing and managing organizational stakeholders. *The Executive, 5*(2), 61–75.

Schuler, A. J. (2002). *Does corporate culture matter? The case of Enron.* Retrieved October 7, 2010, from http://www.schulersolutions.com/enron_s_corporate_culture.html

Seeger, M. W., Sellnow, T. L., & Ulmer, R. R. (2003). *Communication and organizational crisis.* Westport, CT: Praeger.

Seeger, M., & Ulmer, R. R. (2001). Virtuous responses to organizational crisis: Aaron Feuerstein and Milt Cole. *Journal of Business Ethics, 31,* 369–376.

Seitel, F. P. (1983). 10 myths of handling bad news. *Bank Marketing, 15,* 12–14.

Sellnow, T. L., Seeger, M. W., & Ulmer, R. R. (2002). Chaos theory, informational needs, and natural disasters. *Journal of Applied Communication Research, 30,* 269–292.

Sellnow, T. L., Ulmer, R. R., & Snider, M. (1998). The compatibility of corrective action in organizational crisis communication. *Communication Quarterly, 46,* 60–74.

Sen, F., & Egelhoff, W. G. (1991). Six years and counting: Leaning from crisis management at Bhopal. *Public Relations Review, 17*(1), 69–83.

Several missing in Nevada explosion. (1998). *CNN Interactive.* Retrieved October 13, 2010, from http://www.cnn.com/US/9801/07/reno.explosion/index.html?iref=allsearch

Sewell, D. (1997, August 12). Small businesses feeling the pain. *Houston Chronicle.*

Sewell, D. (2010). *P&G hosts bloggers in defense of Pampers Dry Max.* Retrieved October 21, 2010, from http://abcnews.go.com/Business/wireStory?id=10704040

Shrivastava, P., & Mitroff, I. I. (1987, Spring). Strategic management of corporate crises. *Columbia Journal of World Business, 22,* 5–11.

Siegl, E., & Foot, K. A. (2004). Expression in the post-September 11th Web sphere. *Electronic Journal of Communication, 14*(1–2). Retrieved October 14, 2010, from http://www.cios.org/EJCPUBLIC/014/1/01414.html

Smallwood, C. (1995). Risk and organizational behavior: Toward a theoretical framework. In L. Barton (Ed.), *New avenues in risk and crisis management* (Vol. 4, pp. 139–148). Las Vegas: University of Nevada Las Vegas, Small Business Development Center.

Smith, C. A. P., & Hayne, S. C. (1997). Decision making under time pressure: An investigation of decision speed and decision quality of computer-supported groups. *Management Communication Quarterly, 11*(1), 97–126.

Smith, E. B. (1998, January 13). The Zilog mystery: What made so many workers so sick? *USA Today,* pp. B1, B3.

Snyder, A. (1991, April 8). Do boycotts work? *Adweek's Marketing Week,* pp. 16–18.

Snyder, L. (1983). An anniversary review and critique: The Tylenol crisis. *Public Relations Review, 9,* 24–34.

Sonnenfeld, S. (1994). Media policy—What media policy? *Harvard Business Review, 72*(4), 18–19.

Soper, R. H. (1995, August). *Crisis management strategy plan formulation and implementation.* Paper presented at the meeting of New Avenues in Crisis Management, Las Vegas, NV.

Stacks, D. W. (2002). *Primer of public relations research.* New York: Guilford.

Starbucks. (2010). *Starbucks support of the troops/military.* Retrieved October 13, 2010, from http://news.starbucks.com/article_display.cfm?article_id=198

Stephenson, B., & Blackshaw, P. (2006). *Power shift: How the Internet gives consumers the upper hand—and what proactive automakers can do about it.* New York: Nielsen BuzzMetrics. Retrieved October 6, 2010, from http://www.nielsen-online.com/downloads/us/buzz/nbzm_wp_Automotive.pdf

Stewart, C. J., & Cash, W. B., Jr. (1997). *Interviewing: Principles and practices* (8th ed.). Dubuque, IA: William C. Brown.

Stewart, T. D. (2002). *Principles of research in communication.* Boston: Allyn & Bacon.

Stohl, C., & Coombs, W. T. (1988). Cooperation or cooptation: An analysis of quality circle training manuals. *Management Communication Quarterly, 2,* 63–89.

Stohl, C., & Redding, W. C. (1987). Messages and message exchange processes. In F. M. Jabling, L. L. Putnam, K. H. Roberts, & L. W. Porter (Eds.), *Handbook of organizational communication: An interdisciplinary perspective* (pp. 451–502). Newbury Park, CA: Sage.

Strauss, G. (1998, January 13). Embezzlement growth is "dramatic." *USA Today,* pp. 1A, 2A.

Sturges, D. L. (1994). Communicating through crisis: A strategy for organizational survival. *Management Communication Quarterly, 7,* 297–316.

Sullivan, M. (1990). Measuring image spillover in umbrella-branded products. *Journal of Business, 63,* 309–329.

Tan, A. S. (1985). *Mass communication theories and research.* New York: John Wiley & Sons.

Taylor, M., & Kent, M. L. (2007). A taxonomy of crisis response on the Internet. *Public Relations Review, 33*(2), 140–146.

Taylor, M., & Perry, D. C. (2005). Diffusion of traditional and new media tactics in crisis communication. *Public Relations Review, 31*(2), 209–217.

Techtronic Floor Care Technology. (2010). *Important notice regarding Hoover windtunnel T-series rewind bagless upright vacuums distributed prior to November 23, 2009.* Retrieved October 13, 2010, from http://www.hoover.com/customerservice/tseriesrewindrecall.aspx

Tesser, A., & Rosen, S. (1975). The reluctance to transmit bad news. In L. Berkowitz (Ed.), *Advances in experimental social psychology* (Vol. 8, pp. 193–232). New York: Academic Press.

Thomas, E. J. (1999, Summer). Odwalla. *Public Relations Quarterly.* Retrieved October 10, 2010, from http://findarticles.com/p/articles/mi_qa5515/is_199907/ai_n21442792/

Thompson, C. (2008, February 1). Is the tipping point toast? *Fast Company.* Retrieved October 21, 2010, from http://www.fastcompany.com/magazine/122/is-the-tipping-point-toast.html?page=0%2C5

Trahan, J. V., III. (1993). Media relations in the eye of the storm. *Public Relations Quarterly, 38*(2), 31–33.

Trotto, S. (2006, June 2). *Study finds companies snooping on employee e-mail.* Retrieved October 7, 2010, from http://mobilitytoday.com/news/006557/email_snooping

Tsouderos, T. (2008, November 18). Company caves to moms' Motrin ad backlash. *Chicago Tribune.* Retrieved October 21, 2010, from http://articles.chicagotribune.com/2008-11-18/news/0811170682_1_moms-bloggers-sling

Tsui, J. (1993). Tolerance for ambiguity, uncertainty audit qualification and bankers' perceptions. *Psychological Reports, 72,* 915–919.

Twardy, S. A. (1994). Attorneys and public relations professionals must work hand-in-hand when responding to an environmental investigation. *Public Relations Quarterly, 39*(2), 15–16.

Tyler, L. (1997). Liability means never being able to say you're sorry: Corporate guilt, legal constraints, and defensiveness in corporate communication. *Management Communication Quarterly, 11*(1), 51–73.

Ulmer, R. R. (2001). Effective crisis management through established stakeholder relationships. *Management Communication Quarterly, 14,* 590–615.

Ulmer, R. R., & Sellnow, T. L. (2002). Crisis management and discourse of renewal: Understanding the potential for positive outcomes in crisis. *Public Relations Review, 28,* 361–365.

Ulmer, R. R., Sellnow, T. L., & Seeger, M. W. (2006). *Effective crisis communication: Moving from crisis to opportunity.* Thousand Oaks, CA: Sage.

Versical, D. (1987, May). An anatomy: Dealers, critics review Audi's crises management. *Automotive News,* p. 1.

Voit, L. (2008). *Participation, openness, conversation, community, connectedness . . . Yes that's what social media is all about!* Retrieved June 8, 2010, from http://www.isnare.com/?aid=595202&ca=Marketing

Wacka, F. (2005). *Crisis blogs—Plan them well.* Retrieved October 10, 2010, from http://www.webpronewscanada.com/2005/0223.html

Wagstaff, J. (2006). Kryptonite' task and the real cluetrain lesson [Web log]. Retrieved October 6, 2010, from http://loosewire.typepad.com/blog/2004/11/kryptonites_tas.html

Walsh, B. (1995). Beware of the crisis lovers. *Forbes, 155*(12), A17–A18.

Wang, W. T., & Belardo, S. (2005). *Strategic integration: A knowledge management approach to crisis management.* Retrieved October 7, 2010, from http://www.computer.org/portal/web/csdl/doi/10.1109/HICSS.2005.559

Ware, B. L., & Linkugel, W. A. (1973). They spoke in defense of themselves: On the generic criticism of apologia. *Quarterly Journal of Speech, 59,* 273–283.

Watson, R. (1996, September 2). Next, a "Eureka" piece. *Newsweek,* pp. 48–50.

Watts, D. J., & Peretti, J. (2007, May). Viral marketing for the real world. *Harvard Business Review.* Retrieved October 21, 2010, from http://hbr.org/2007/05/viral-marketing-for-the-real-world/ar/1

Wehr, L. (2007, April 19). *JetBlue & Taco Bell: Lessons in crisis marketing.* Retrieved October 6, 2010, from http://www.imediaconnection.com/content/14452.asp

Weick, K. E. (1979). *The social psychology of organizing* (2nd ed.). Reading, MA: Addison-Wesley.

Weick, K. E. (1988). Enacted sensemaking in crisis situations. *Journal of Management Studies, 25,* 305–317.

Weick, K. E. (1993). The collapse of sensemaking in organizations: The Mann Gulch disaster. *Administrative Science Quarterly, 38,* 628–652.

Weiner, B. 1986. *An attributional theory of motivation and emotion.* New York: Springer Verlag.

Weinstein, S. (1993). The hoax that failed. *Progressive Grocer, 72*(8), 17.

The well-provisioned war room and why you need one. (2005, October 26). Available from http://www.prnewsonline.com/mediarelations/The-Well-Provisioned-War-Room-And-Why-You-Need-One_7473.html

Williams, D. E., & Olaniran, B. A. (1994). Exxon's decision-making flaws: The hypervigilant response to the *Valdez* grounding. *Public Relations Review, 20*(1), 5–18.

Wilsenbilt, J. Z. (1989, Spring). Crisis management planning among U.S. corporations: Empirical evidence and a proposed framework. *SAM Advanced Management Journal,* 31–41.

Wilson, S., & Patterson, B. (1987, November). When the news hits the fan. *Business Marketing, 72,* 92–94.

Wood, D. J. (1991). Corporate social performance revisited. *Academy of Management Review, 16,* 691–718.

Zinn, L., & Regan, M. B. (1993, July 5). The right moves baby. *Business Week,* p. 31.

Index

About the Author

W. Timothy Coombs, PhD, Purdue University, is a full professor in the Nicholson School of Communication at the University of Central Florida. He is the 2002 recipient of the Jackson, Jackson & Wagner Behavioral Science Prize from the Public Relations Society of America for his crisis research, which led to the development and testing of the Situational Crisis Communication Theory (SCCT). SCCT provides recommendations about how crisis managers should respond to crises by evaluating key elements of the crisis situation. Dr. Coombs has published widely in the areas of crisis management and preparedness, including a number of journal articles and book chapters. His research includes the award-winning book *Ongoing Crisis Communication* as well as *Code Red in the Boardroom: Crisis Management as Organizational DNA*. He is coauthor of a number of books, including *It's Not Just PR* and *Public Relations Strategy and Application: Managing Influence* with Sherry Holladay and *Today's Public Relations* with Robert Heath. He has edited *The Handbook of Business Security* Volumes 1 and 2 and coedited *The Handbook of Crisis Communication* with Sherry Holladay. He was part of the Darden School of Management's Batten Institute "Defining Leadership: A Forum to Discuss Crisis Leadership Competency" and has a chapter in the related publication, *Executive Briefing on Crisis Leadership*. Dr. Coombs has lectured on the subject of crisis management at various venues in the United States, Denmark, Norway, Sweden, Belgium, the United Kingdom, Hong Kong, and Australia. He has also consulted with companies in the petrochemical and health care industries on crisis-related topics.

SAGE Research Methods Online

The essential tool for researchers

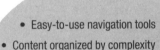